W9-ANG-035

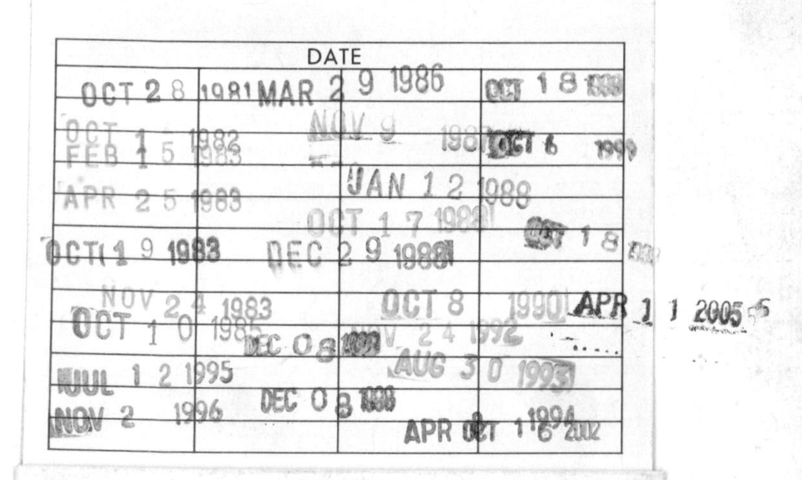

HUNTING THE WHITETAIL DEER

AN OUTDOOR LIFE BOOK

HUNTING THE WHITETAIL DEER

Russell Tinsley

OUTDOOR LIFE • FUNK & WAGNALLS
New York

Published by Book Division, Times Mirror Magazines, Inc.

Library of Congress Catalog Card Number: 65-14986
Funk & Wagnalls Hardcover Edition: ISBN 0-308-10326-2
Paperback Edition: ISBN 0-308-10327-0

First Edition, 1965
Five Printings

Second Edition, Revised and Updated, 1977

Manufactured in the United States of America

To My Father,
who taught me most of what I know about deer hunting, and

To My Mother,
who inspired me to put it down on paper

Contents

Preface

THE WHITETAIL DEER is a unique animal. It has proved compatible with civilization and actually has flourished and expanded its range while some other wildlife has fallen on troubled times.

"Many international big-game hunters class big whitetail bucks among the world's greatest trophies," observes my friend Bruce Brady, field editor for *Outdoor Life* magazine. "They do so not because of the size of the antlers those bucks carry, which are actually small when compared with the racks of many other antlered species. They do so out of respect for the whitetail's intelligence."

Some people have described the whitetail as the smartest critter on four feet—a cunning, crafty animal. A sagacious quarry.

You must learn to respect the deer's formidable defense system if you are to outwit it. Perhaps the greatest mistake the typical hunter makes is that he does not respect his quarry. He is playing the game on the animal's terms, in its bailiwick. The odds are against the hunter.

Yet deer hunting is more than simply a man-deer confrontation. John Madson in his booklet *The White-tailed Deer* perhaps describes it best: "Deer hunting is not truly a contest between man and deer. It's a competition between man and nature. You aren't really competing with the deer, but with snowy forest, cold feet, a growling belly, and your own discouragement and willingness to quit. Overcome these and you've won an important contest with yourself. You may also be awarded the first prize—one of the most splendid big-game animals in the world."

Russell Tinsley

1

The Abundant Whitetail

NO MATTER where you live in the United States, there is probably good whitetail deer hunting within a short drive of your home. The whitetail is literally everywhere, not only in the United States (where it exists or has been found in all the contiguous states) but also in most of northern Mexico and southern Canada. It is quite adaptable and can survive under almost all conditions and circumstances. That's why it is, by far, our most abundant and most popular big-game animal.

While much of our wildlife has dwindled before the march of civilization, the whitetail deer has thrived and multiplied. Today there are more whitetails roaming the land than ever before, and it isn't unusual to sight them within the limits of some of our largest cities, even on the outskirts of New York City. There are so many deer, in fact, that overpopulations have become a serious problem in many areas.

In a scientific study, E. T. Atwood discovered more than 500 plants which the whitetail in the United States eats for forage. This is one reason why the whitetail has remained a dominant figure on our wildlife scene. Another reason is good protection by law. Still another is the animal's ability to take advantage of almost any kind of terrain, from the flat, almost bare prairies to the heavily timbered hills.

I recall a time years back when I was quail hunting in a long-abandoned field in southern Alabama, near the town of Stockton, just above Mobile. The grass was about knee high, a solid carpet of it. My companion and I were slipping along, watching two ranging bird dogs half-hidden in the foliage ahead, when suddenly the dogs went on point. Half raising my shotgun, I advanced cautiously, expecting any moment the familiar whir of a quail rising into the air. But lo and behold, a whitetail deer suddenly jumped into sight and bounded away through the grass with those familiar long, graceful leaps.

I discovered a bed of matted grass where the deer had been lying before we spooked it into the open. The field was surrounded by dense pine timber, and why the deer had chosen the tall grass for its midday bed, I don't know. But you'll often find deer in places where you least expect to see them.

Contrast this incident with one which happened to me some time later. I was squirrel hunting in southern Missouri, below Joplin in the foothills of the Ozark Mountains. While pussyfooting through the heavily timbered woods, I eased around a cluster of sycamore saplings and surprised two feeding deer. I could almost have reached out and touched them. I don't know which was the more startled, me or the deer.

These were the two extremes of terrain—open, overgrown field and dense, timbered woods—and whitetail deer can be found in just about every kind of imaginable cover between the two. In states such as Maine, Oregon, Michigan, and Pennsylvania, you'll find whitetails roaming hills and mountains covered with hardwood trees; in the Everglades of Florida they inhabit a terrain that is virtually all water, and conservation officers must use airboats to make periodic checks on them; in the plantation country of Concordia Parish in Louisiana, they'll be seen in the table-flat country under huge oak trees draped with Spanish moss; and in the Mexican state of Sonora, across the border from Arizona, they roam an arid, cactus-covered desert.

This, then, is the whitetail deer, a very adaptable animal which can learn to live and reproduce in almost any environment, from the cold, wet climate of the mountains to the dry, stifling heat of the desert.

Basically, however, the whitetail is a fairly predictable animal, as wild creatures go. It prefers woody terrain, stealing out of the timber late in the evening to feed on into the night, returning to the cover the following morning to bed down during the daylight hours. It usually spends its lifetime in a pretty limited area, less than a square mile. Around abandoned apple orchards in Washington and Oregon, you'll find whitetails coming out of the surrounding woods into the orchards early and late in the day. The same is true in Texas, where as the sun sinks toward the western horizon, deer steal out of the woods to feed, particularly in the lush green oat fields. Dr. William B. Davis, writing in a Texas Parks and Wildlife Department bulletin titled "The Mammals of Texas," points out that it has been found by experiment that deer are most easily observed in the hour just before dark.

The whitetail deer found throughout the United States, in Canada, and in Mexico is one and the same animal, even though the whitetail in Georgia may vary greatly in size from its counterpart in Maine, and a whitetail in northern Missouri will be larger on the average than one found in southern Missouri. Size ranges from the occasional 200-pound-plus specimens found in Missouri, Wisconsin, Michigan, and Maine to the diminutive and rare Key deer, weighing less than 70 pounds, which are restricted to a few islands lying off the coast of southern Florida.

Our most abundant big-game animal, the whitetail is equally at home on the flat, bare prairies of the Southwest, the heavily wooded terrain of the Northeast, or the swamplands of the Everglades.

Some years ago, I had occasion to hunt whitetail deer in the neighboring states of New Mexico and Texas within a time span of two weeks. In the Lincoln National Forest of New Mexico, I bagged a forkhorn which field-dressed 118 pounds; a week later I killed a forkhorn near the small community of Mason in central Texas which field-dressed a mere 58 pounds. Yet the antler size of the two animals was almost identical. There was that much variance in weight even though the two animals belonged basically to the same subspecies.

In all, there are nine or ten organized subspecies, depending on which authority you believe. *The Hunter's Encyclopedia* lists ten different subspecies: the Virginia deer, Eastern whitetail deer, Northern Virginia deer, Key deer, Coues deer, Louisiana deer, Plains whitetail, Northwestern whitetail, Florida whitetail, and Texas whitetail. The most abundant is the typical Eastern whitetail deer, found from Virginia up through Pennsylvania and New York to Maine.

But despite the different subspecies grouped within the entire whitetail family, the deer looks practically the same no matter where you meet it. The Maine deer hunter would immediately recognize the Florida whitetail as the same animal he hunts in Maine. The only noticeable differences would be in size and color. The antlers of the whitetail, unlike those of the mule deer, have all the points growing off two main beams. The tail has the familiar white underside, which has come to be called the "white flag" because a scared whitetail has a habit of tossing the tail straight up and waving the white back and forth as it runs. Nearly all whitetails have the same general coloring, brownish in fall and winter, reddish in summer.

The antlers of whitetails also will vary in size in different parts of the country. Biologists say the mineral content of the soil where deer range is the determining factor as far as antler size is concerned. For instance, in southern Texas, a brushy region from which many record heads have come, the general size of the antlers will be much larger than those on deer in neighboring Louisiana and Arkansas. A deer with four points on either antler will be called an eight-pointer in the East, but in the West, hunters know it as a three-pointer (only the points on one antler are counted, disregarding the brow point). An average mature whitetail deer has from six to ten points, generally eight—six main points, three on either beam, and two brow points, one growing out of each beam just above the head.

The whitetail is a very cunning and sly animal, a real challenge to hunters. Many nimrods claim it is our most elusive big-game animal. It is a master of the disappearing act, slipping out of the thickest cover without a give-away sound. Yet it also can run swiftly when spooked into the open.

Many hunters can walk into a section of woods heavily populated with deer, roam around for several days, and come out believing that there hasn't been one of the critters within miles. I once knew a man who spent two days hunting on Manitoulin Island, which lies in the northern part of Lake Huron and boasts a considerable population of whitetails, and never saw a deer. He said only the betraying tracks revealed that deer were there at all. A whitetail won't dash into the open, showing itself, unless it absolutely must. It would much rather catfoot away quietly, slipping around until it is well out of hearing before it bolts for freedom.

I had the opportunity to watch such a drama many years ago in south-central New Mexico, near the village of Piñon. I was sitting on a butte-like hill overlooking a wide, shallow draw, hunkered down on an outcropping of rock while my two hunting companions stalked through the piñons and brush, moving slowly, watching and listening.

Suddenly I glimpsed movement out in front of Clarence Brown. I lifted my binocular and looked. A large whitetail buck was slipping ahead of him, far enough ahead so that he was shielded from the hunter by a wall of brush. The buck didn't hurry. He stayed just far enough ahead to escape detection.

There was no chance for a shot without endangering Clarence, so I merely watched curiously. The buck moved along ahead of the hunter for perhaps 100 feet before cutting off at an angle, ghosting through the brush. He circled around, got behind the hunter, ducked into another clump of brush, and practically vanished. His dark coat blended perfectly with his habitat. Only occasionally could I catch a fleeting glimpse of movement as he made good his retreat. There wasn't a chance for a shot.

This is typical of the whitetail. It has an uncanny sense of knowing which route to take, away from danger. Seldom will one, frightened, run straight to or away from the hunter. Instead, it cuts away, using every bit of available cover to handicap its pursuer during its escape.

Once, while hunting in this same area of New Mexico, I sighted a large herd of deer moving along the opposite side of a wide and shallow canyon. I studied the deer through my binocular. One was an exceptionally large buck, a real trophy.

Despite the various subspecies distributed throughout the country, the whitetail is basically the same animal no matter where you find him. The antlers are characterized by two main beams, each with a number of points—from six to ten in mature bucks. The tail is white on the underside, and the coloring is brownish in fall and winter, reddish in summer.

I watched the deer as they walked along the rim, silhouetted by the morning sun. Perhaps 100 yards farther along they dropped off into the canyon, quartering across at a tangent. I mentally laid out a course they would follow and backtracked until I was hidden by trees, then ran, bent double, as fast as I could without making undue commotion to a point of brush which would give me vantage overlooking the deer's route, within 100 yards of where they would likely pass.

Just as I slipped into the wedge of brush, one of the tail-end deer in the procession caught the unnatural movement. The doe snorted, alarmed. It would seem logical that a noise from behind would have pushed the deer ahead, along the same route they were following. But instead, they flared off in all directions like a flushed covey of quail and bolted into the brushy innards of the canyon. The dozen or more whitetails disappeared as quickly and completely as if they'd been passed over by a magician's wand.

The whitetail deer's basic line of defense is its sensitive smelling apparatus and sonarlike hearing. It also possesses extremely sharp eyesight, but it depends primarily on smelling and hearing to protect it against its enemies. A domestic cow can walk through the woods right up on a deer without the wild animal becoming alarmed; but let a hunter try the same thing, and the deer will readily notice the difference in the footsteps.

But despite this omnipresent cunning bred into the whitetail, the animal can be quickly tamed when handled correctly. I've seen many that made gentle pets, particularly those raised in captivity from fawns. And mature deer can become fairly tame, even if they have no contact with civilization until they become adults.

I witnessed a rare sight a few years back on the Dolores Ranch, about 20 miles outside the city of Laredo on the Texas-Mexico border. The ranch, with only a small natural deer population of its own, had been liberally stocked with deer from the sprawling King Ranch. These deer, adapted to the abundant foodstuffs found on the King Ranch, of race-horse fame, were hard pressed to survive on the cactus-covered, almost grassless countryside near Laredo. From the time the adult deer were released, ranch hands supplemented their natural diet with cattle feed. Every evening a cowboy would go to a site near a stock pond, rattling a bucket and scattering the feed. Almost immediately, deer would start materializing out of the brush, several dozen of them. There was everything from young does and spike bucks to old bucks with bragging-sized racks of antlers. The deer would crowd around the ranch hand, feeding, oblivious to any onlookers who came to gaze upon the spectacle. It was almost like feeding a herd of domestic cattle.

The mating season of the deer, or "rut" as it is more commonly called, occurs in the fall, triggered by cold weather and shorter days. Usually the first abrupt drop in temperature, close to freezing, will start the mating. During this time, closely watch any gathering of does, since a buck is almost sure to be nearby. The neck of the buck will swell considerably and his

The mating season occurs in the fall at the onset of cold weather. Bucks fight among themselves for the does, often trailing their prospective mate for miles.

Fawns are born in the spring and remain under the mother's care until early fall when they lose their telltale spots and take on the brownish hue of adult deer.

A whitetail buck with velvet still on his antlers. Antler growth begins in April or May; as the rut approaches the velvet is shed; and the antlers drop off in late December or January. This cycle is repeated every year in healthy bucks.

glands will give off a strong odor. Bucks will fight among themselves for the affection of a lady friend, squaring off to clash their antlers together, pawing the ground and snorting. On rare occasions the antlers will become hopelessly locked together and the deer will perish of starvation.

After a gestation of about seven months, the doe will drop either one or two fawns. Sexual maturity in a doe usually isn't reached until she is 18 months of age, or the second fall after birth. Her first offspring is apt to be a single fawn, but after that it is quite common for her to bear twins. The young will lie low, depending for safety on their natural camouflage, while the mother ranges several hundred feet in either direction to feed. But as soon as they are able to move about, she will take them with her. Normally, they are weaned in early fall when they also lose their telltale spots and take on the more familiar brownish hue.

The buck sheds his antlers every year. Timing of this antler growth cycle is what biologists call photoperiodism. Somehow the deer detects changes in light intensity, or length of days, and these changes affect the pineal gland at the base of the brain. Among the documentation of this "biological clock" were studies done at Brown and Texas A&I universities. At Brown

University, bucks were kept indoors and the normal annual lighting pattern was reversed, prompting the deer to grow antlers in the winter and shed them in the summer. It also was found that constant light or constant darkness had an insignificant effect on the antler cycle, but if the bucks were put on a schedule of 12 hours of light and 12 hours of darkness, the control of the antler cycle was turned off and the bucks kept their hardened antlers and stayed in rut year round.

At Texas A&I University, Dr. Paul Mazur removed the pineal gland from one of young twin whitetailed bucks. The pineal gland is about the size of a pea and produces a hormone called melatonin. Both bucks grew antlers as yearlings, but only the normal one shed them in January. In early summer when the normal buck began growing new antlers, his brother still had his winter coat and antlers, his endocrine system being unable to respond to changes in day length.

When the antlers drop off, only two reddish stubs even with the head hair remain. But once these stubs begin to grow into antlers, the change is dramatic. Antlers are the fastest-growing bone known. When the rut nears and the sexual glands begin to activate, the antlers become hardened and the buck rubs the mosslike substance called velvet off against sapling trees. The scraped trees are called deer rubs.

When a deer's sexual glands are damaged, as by castration when jumping over a fence or by being pierced by thorns, the deer never loses the velvet covering, the antlers never become solid, and the antlers take on all kinds of weird shapes. These deer with the velvet antlers are known as stags. And for some inexplicable reason, a few deer seem to be born without any male organs, even though they have all the other visible features of bucks, even the antlers. But in this case the antlers never develop properly and the bucks never lose their velvet. In some rare instances even does grow antlers. I once saw a doe bagged near Canoe Creek in northeast Pennsylvania which carried a nice eight-point rack of antlers.

Contrary to popular belief, the age of a deer cannot be accurately determined by the size of his antlers. A grandpa buck, in his declining years, may sport no larger a headset than an 18-month-old deer. A properly developed second-year deer should have at least forked antlers, perhaps even six or eight points. Small hardened spikes protruding through the skin indicate the deer isn't healthy or isn't properly developed. This family-tree characteristic can be bred into other deer. Large antlers are the result partly of heredity, partly of nutrition.

A whitetail buck can develop quickly. For example, Allen Courtney bagged a deer in Missouri's Clark County, not far from his hometown of Kahoka. The buck carried a huge 12-point rack and field-dressed 203 pounds, yet Dunbar Robb of the Missouri Department of Conservation examined the buck and found him to be only 3½ years old.

A hunter with no formal training can estimate the age of whitetails to about two years of age by examining the teeth. The fawn will acquire its middle pair of permanent incisors at about nine months, while the remainder of the incisors and the premolars will be milk teeth, tiny in size. By 18 months of age, the milk teeth will be replaced by permanent teeth. At least two of the molars are fully developed, while the third will shortly emerge. By two years, the permanent teeth are acquired. From then on, only a qualified wildlife biologist can accurately gauge a deer's age by noting the wear on teeth. At about five years old, the ridges of a deer's teeth no longer are sharp, having been worn until they rise only slightly above the dentine.

The dramatic upsurge of whitetail deer populations within the past few decades can be attributed to several factors. Good conservation measures and sound protective legislation are two of them. Another is the practice of cleaning out underbrush and allowing young trees to grow, providing more browse. In places today it is common practice to trap deer and transplant them to areas of limited or no population. Usually, baited wooden traps are used, but on the swampy Delta Wildlife Refuge in southern Louisiana, the deer are captured through the use of helicopters and airboats, of all things. After being moved to suitable habitat, the deer usually thrive and multiply.

One of the first moves to conserve our deer was the inauguration of deer seasons. Before the turn of the century, the deer was mostly unprotected. But about 1900 the first game laws were passed. In Pennsylvania, for example, there were only about 200 deer killed in 1907. By 1923 this number

At the end of the growing cycle, just before the rut, the buck removes the velvet by rubbing his antlers against saplings.

had risen to 6,452 legal bucks. In 1940 more than 30,000 were killed. Today, Pennsylvania ranks as one of our leading deer-producing states with a harvest of more than 100,000 yearly.

Many state wildlife departments have found a hard core of obdurate hunters who refuse to accept the idea of killing antlerless deer, but studies have proved conclusively that an overpopulation is a curse that won't magically go away. As a Louisiana Wildlife and Fisheries Commission report noted, "When deer are allowed to increase in numbers to the point when the herd exceeds the carrying capacity of the range, visible changes take place. The range shows signs of deterioration. Additionally, over a period of time, deer bagged showed a lowered average weight. Lack of sufficient browse also results in deer herds becoming susceptible to disease and this usually results in a substantial die-off."

At the carefully regulated, fenced-in George Wildlife Reserve of the University of Michigan, more than 40 years of research has revealed that the controlled harvesting of bucks, does, and fawns is necessary to keep deer populations at the numbers which can be nourished properly on any given amount of land. The university's Wildlife Management Department attempts to maintain a population of 40 deer per square mile on the reserve, which is just under 2 square miles in size. Census counts determine how many surplus animals need to be removed in any given year. Over a 31-year time span, a total of 1,250 deer were harvested, 44 percent antlered deer, 56 percent antlerless. Yet the result was a stable and healthy herd of 80 adequately nourished animals.

Various management methods are used in the states where a cull-the-herd process is needed. Some states have special "doe days." Others allow the taking of antlerless deer by special permit. Many have either-sex seasons.

This, then, is the story of whitetail deer, the No. 1 wildlife success story of the past century, our No. 1 big-game hunting animal, the pride and joy of hunters everywhere.

WHAT WILL IT WEIGH?

Dressed weight in pounds	Live weight in pounds	Dressed weight in pounds	Live weight in pounds
40	55	130	165
50	65	140	180
60	80	150	190
70	90	160	205
80	105	170	215
90	115	180	230
100	130	190	240
110	140	200	255
120	155	210	265

2

Deer Cartridges, Guns, and Sights

THERE IS NO "best" deer gun, one that will adequately cover all needs and circumstances. Choice of weapon for hunting whitetail deer is an individual and personal thing, based on each hunter's particular needs. A nimrod after deer in the Pocono Mountains of northeastern Pennsylvania wouldn't want or need the same type of rifle used by a hunter after whitetails in the Devil's Nest area of Nebraska's Knox County. The former is heavy timber where shots normally will be at extremely close range; the latter is more open country, with rolling hills, where longer shots are probable.

There are several considerations to keep in mind when shopping for a deer weapon: type of terrain where you'll be hunting, whether or not you're a beginning or experienced hunter, state laws, how good a shot you are, whether it will be a deer gun exclusively or will be utilized for many different types of game.

When speaking of the deer gun, we are referring basically to calibers. The choice of an action is more a personal preference (see next chapter). Whether you pick a bolt-action, slide-action, lever-action, or semi-automatic isn't really important. What is important is that you select the kind of action that suits you best, learn to use it, and stick with it.

The most popular deer load of all is the time-honored .30/30. In the hands of a fairly competent shooter, this cartridge is more than adequate for whitetail deer. I've killed many deer with the .30/30, most of them one-shot kills. In fact, my first deer gun was a .30/30, and of the first five bucks I bagged, four were killed with the .30/30. The one big advantage of the .30/30 is that it is so commonplace that you can find ammunition for your rifle no matter where you may be. This is one cartridge that all sporting-goods stores stock.

The .30/30 has enjoyed phenomenal popularity even though it isn't what you'd call a long-range cartridge. It performs best at ranges of up to 150 yards. The reason for its continued popularity, of course, is that most whitetails, in fact more than 80 percent, are bagged at a range of less than 100 yards. The very nature of the whitetails' habitat, in most cases, calls for short-range shooting and a bullet that won't be deflected off target. Authority John Wootters recommends sharp-nosed, high velocity bullets here, while others recommend heavy brush busters.

Naturally there's room for choice. Each hunter has to evaluate his own situation and needs and get a gun that will do the job for him. This means a complete outfit—rifle, cartridge, and sight. And don't forget to have your state laws in mind when picking a deer cartridge. A few states prohibit anything smaller than .25 caliber for deer.

Just about any big-game rifle can be used for deer hunting. The .30/06 and .270, two long-time favorites, are both popular, although the deer hunter really doesn't require a cartridge this powerful. But it is always better to be overpowered rather than underpowered. This way a shot that may be off its mark a few inches can still deliver a fatal punch, preventing needless crippling and waste of game.

If you are shopping for an all-purpose cartridge, one for whitetails plus other big-game hunting, the venerable .30/06 would be difficult to fault. It is loaded in a variety of bullet weights—110, 125, 150, 180, and 220 grains. And like ammunition for the .30/30, the ammunition for the .30/06 is available virtually everyplace. But the .30/06 is primarily a cartridge for bolt-action rifles, which presents another problem. If you find a rifle style and action you like, you must of course use the cartridge this weapon is chambered for. But buying an adequate cartridge for whitetail hunting is not that precise anyway. There isn't, for example, much difference between the .30/06 and the .308, though arguing the merits of one over the other makes for interesting coffee breaks. The .308 can be purchased in bullet weights of 110, 125, 150, 180, and 200 grains. The muzzle velocity of the .30/06 in 180 grains is 2,700 feet per second, while the same bullet weight in .308 is 2,610 fps; the two perform nearly the same.

It is difficult to pinpoint the *minimum* deer load. Anything smaller than the .250 Savage should be ruled out. For the experienced hunter and expert shot, the .250 Savage might be sufficient, but the less experienced may need something drastically more potent, like the .30/06 and .308. The average hunter, an adequate hunter and adequate shot but nothing extraordinary, can get by with something like the .30/30 and .243.

The trend nowadays is to high velocity. More and more cartridges are showing up on the market that are "souped up." This added velocity has several advantages. For one, it makes for flatter bullet trajectory and consequently better bullet placement, especially at longer ranges when hunting in more open country like that found in the northern Mexican state of Sonora, across from Arizona. For another, the high-velocity bullets kill better, since a bullet kills partly by shock. Some have argued that a high-velocity bullet is easily sidetracked by brush, and that a slower and bigger bullet, like the .35 Remington, will plow its way right through. But any bullet will be somewhat deflected by brush.

Yet velocity alone is not enough. You also need penetration and knock-down power from the bullet. A fast-moving light bullet causes considerably more damage on the surface, where it enters, but it doesn't do much inside to disrupt the animal's vital life-sustaining organs. Even where legal, cartridges such as the .222, .223, .22/250, and .26/06 are not, in my opinion, acceptable deer loads, even in the hands of the experienced. This evaluation is based purely on personal observation. I have seen too many deer wounded with light, high-velocity cartridges. And while on the subject I think the .30 Carbine should be outlawed in the deer woods. Slow-moving (1,980 fps) and light (110 grains), this bullet is a deer crippler and not much else.

My votes for the best all-around whitetail cartridges are the .243 and 6 mm. The 100-grain bullet of the .243 Winchester leaves the muzzle at a velocity of 3,070 feet per second, while that of the 6mm Remington, same 100-grain size, is 3,190. Both bullets have sufficient sectional density for good killing power. Sectional density is the ratio of bullet length to diameter. Length in a bullet is always desirable for better results. The added length means better accuracy, more sustained velocity, and more striking force. Of two bullets, one of .25 caliber and another of .30 caliber, which weigh the same, the .25-caliber will give the better performance simply because of the smaller bore diameter, which means the .25 bullet must necessarily be longer. For instance, a 100-grain bullet in the .243 would be more desirable than a comparable 100-grain bullet in the .30/06.

The rifles in the variety of actions chambered for the .243 and 6mm are lightweight, making for fast handling, a definite asset in most whitetail deer hunting. These cartridges are fairly dependable in light brush, yet also are good at the extreme ranges, 200 yards and up.

However, in heavier brush you may want to select a stubbier bullet with more weight, to bore through cover. The shooter will be sacrificing velocity, but it isn't really needed for close-range brush shooting. Most hunters seen around the Catskill Mountains of New York will be using weapons chambered for the .30/30 and .35 Remington. The Ruger Carbine, chambered for the .44 Magnum cartridge, was designed specifically for close-range brush shooting. The cartridge, like the .35 Remington, is designed to plow through the brush rather than ricochet.

One main gripe against the bigger calibers, such as the .30/06 and .308, is that they destroy too much meat. The truth is, though, that any bullet is going to destroy meat when it hits an animal in a vital area. The .30/06 naturally will destroy more tissue than the .30/30, but there is the advantage of having more killing power when the bullet placement isn't where it is supposed to be. A whitetail hit in the flank with a .30/06 bullet isn't going far; however, one struck in the same general vicinity with a .30/30 may escape to die a slow lingering death in the woods.

What this all boils down to is that each hunter must buy a deer gun to suit his individual needs. This will be his "best" gun for deer hunting. Generally, the most popular whitetail deer calibers are those in the .250 Savage to .30/06 and .308 range, with the .30/30, 6mm, and .243 being the mean.

A good basic rule to follow is to go to the heavier bullets, like the .35 Remington, .30/06, .308, and .44 Magnum for dense brush shooting, and the flatter-trajectory cartridges like the .243 and 6mm for hunting in more sparsely timbered areas where cover is lighter and shots are often longer.

Most deer hunters buy and use commercial ammunition, primarily because of its convenience, but also because they figure if some reputable firm like Winchester makes it, the stuff is plenty good, which it is.

But there is something to be said for rolling your own. The obvious reasons are that handloading is a pleasant hobby and is a money saver. With rifle ammo, you eliminate repeated purchase of the most expensive component, the brass case, which can be reused. Put another way, you might not actually realize a savings, since the reloader tends to shoot more, but you get more for your money.

Yet, according to my friend John Wootters, author of *A Complete Guide to Practical Handloading*, no matter which cartridge is your choice for your style of deer hunting, it can be made more effective by handloading your ammunition.

According to Wootters, "In general, a medium-weight bullet is correct in calibers .264 and up, while the heaviest available slugs should be used in smaller bores, but even more important is that the chosen bullet be capable of good expansion and good penetration on whitetails at the velocities and ranges at which they're usually shot. In Michigan this might be 35 yards, while in southern Texas it could be 200 yards. There is simply no way that the same bullet can be exactly right for both jobs."

Wootters adds, "Some testing is necessary for each handloader to decide on the best bullet for his own type of hunting, but I've had good results with the Noslers, Hornadys, the Mag-Tips and the Grand Slam bullets from Speer, the Winchester soft points, and the Bitter-roots."

Handloading really is not that difficult, but it does demand common-sense judgment, for there are other things involved than just making a rifle go bang. Safety, of course, is always the first consideration. And then there is absolute mechanical reliability. You don't want to blow the chance of a lifetime because your rifle malfunctioned due to faulty ammo. As Wootters explains, handloaded cartridges used for deer hunting must feed, fire, extract, and eject perfectly. Almost perfectly is not good enough.

Get a comprehensive how-to book, such as the one by Wootters, and learn all about handloading and master it before you brew ammunition for deer hunting.

Is the extra effort really worth it? Wootters emphatically thinks so: "Reloaded ammo is usually better for your specific purposes than factory loads; almost always more accurate in your particular rifle; often more powerful and flatter-shooting; and offering that all-important, hand-tailored bullet performance," he says. "It also is just as uniform and safe, if the reloader has his wits about him while he works. Most of all, reloading is a pleasure in itself, and most of us find a little extra measure of satisfaction in taking a fine trophy buck with a cartridge which we ourselves planned and assembled."

For hunting in heavy brush and dense timber, a shotgun frequently is the logical choice (all but five of the 48 states which have deer seasons allow the use of shotguns, but only 23 permit the use of buckshot). In some states, such as Delaware, Ohio, Indiana, Illinois, Iowa, Massachusetts, and New Jersey, law dictates that only shotguns can be used for deer hunting. The shotgun is also popular in some other states, as in St. Martin's Parish, in the Louisiana Cajun country, where deer are hunted with dogs, and shots usually are at close range with the deer running. The shotgun is one of the deadliest of all weapons at close range, delivering a powerful wallop.

The shotgun armed with solid-slug shotshells also is very good in thick-growth shooting. For more than two decades, the shotgun with slugs along with bow-and-arrow have been the only legal weapons on annual controlled hunts at the 10,000-acre government arsenal at Ravenna, Ohio. Jack Streeter, long-time supervisor of the public-lottery hunt, feels that the shotgun-slug combination is the deadliest he has ever seen used inside 70 yards. Rifled slugs are deadly to 75 yards and can give riflelike precision with 3-inch groups from a gun equipped with a slug barrel and proper sights.

Nowadays the use of buckshot is pretty much restricted to parts of the swampy South where deer are run with dogs and shots are at fast-moving targets at extremely close range. No. 0 shot is effective to maybe 40 yards, with 00 good for perhaps 10 yards farther. Ideally, buckshot should be used inside 35 yards for quick, humane kills.

You can use your regular bird gun, if it will do the job. Some are fairly accurate, others are erratic. And the choke isn't as critical as you might suspect. Generally the most open-choked improved cylinder shoots slugs with the best accuracy (grouping), but don't take my word as gospel. In some guns you'll get superior results with modified or open choke. Give your bird gun a try with slugs and find out how it performs.

But the conventional shotgun does have drawbacks. Its 26- or 28-inch barrel is a bit awkward to handle in the woods. You'll need to install a rifle-type sight, even if nothing more than a Slug Site, an inexpensive device with an adhesive base which sticks firmly on the shotgun barrel and later can be removed. This sight is a strip of blued steel, turned up at either end, notched at the rear and with a bead in front, to give a 7½-inch sight radius.

Much better is a shotgun designed specifically for slug shooting. Several different models are available. They have adjustable open sights and short 20-, 22-, or 24-inch barrels for fast handling. Typical are the Browning B/

2000 "Buck Special," Ithaca Model 51 "Deerslayer," Remington 1100 "Deer Gun" (autoloaders), Ithaca Model 37 "Deerslayer," Remington 870 "Brushmaster," and Mossberg 500 "Slugster" (slide actions). These are not individual models but only modifications of basic production shotguns. On those with interchangeable barrels, all you need do is invest in the special slug barrel and clamp it into place. Open sights are standard, but some guns are tapped to take peep sights. The Ithaca Model 51, among others, has a grooved sight base for scope mounting. Frankly, I prefer a slide-action gun because I just don't have that much confidence that an autoloader will function flawlessly. These autoloaders have tended to jam and malfunction in the most critical of situations. Also with the autoloader there is the temptation to rapidly jerk off a second or third shot at a running deer without aiming properly.

No. 0 and 00 buck are available only in 12 gauge, since they don't pattern well in the smaller gauges. There will be nine pellets of 00 shot in a conventional 12-gauge shell and 12 No. 0 pellets. Magnum loads will contain 12 of No. 00 in the 2¾-inch shell and 15 in the 3-inch Magnum. Any full-choke 12-gauge gun is satisfactory for deer hunting if it will pattern half of its shots within a 30-inch circle at 50 yards. When shooting buckshot, aim at the deer's head and neck. A body-shot deer is apt to run for miles.

Rifled slugs come in .410, 20, 16, and 12 gauge, but only the last two pack enough wallop for deer hunting. In muzzle velocity and energy, the slugs compare favorably with the heavier rifle bullets used in brush shooting, although they can't match the accuracy. A rifled shotgun slug (404 grains, .729 caliber) leaves the muzzle with a velocity of 1,600 feet per second in 12 gauge and with 2,400 foot-pounds of energy. It holds up well, too, for 50 yards, still having 1,370 fps of energy in retained velocity.

Most all production rifles come from the factory equipped with standard open sights. This type of sight is the fastest of all to use and it is extremely popular with brush shooters. But open sights come in many designs and shapes, most of them bad. The shallow V's and U's, ones that the sighter can see through and get down in, are the best. The tendency with the open sight is for the hunter to overshoot, because he isn't getting down in the sight properly. The worst open sights are the buckhorn types, with the

For best results with peep sights, unscrew the small sight disc, shown here, and throw it away. Then sight through the larger screw hole remaining. Peep sights have micrometer adjustments for windage and elevation.

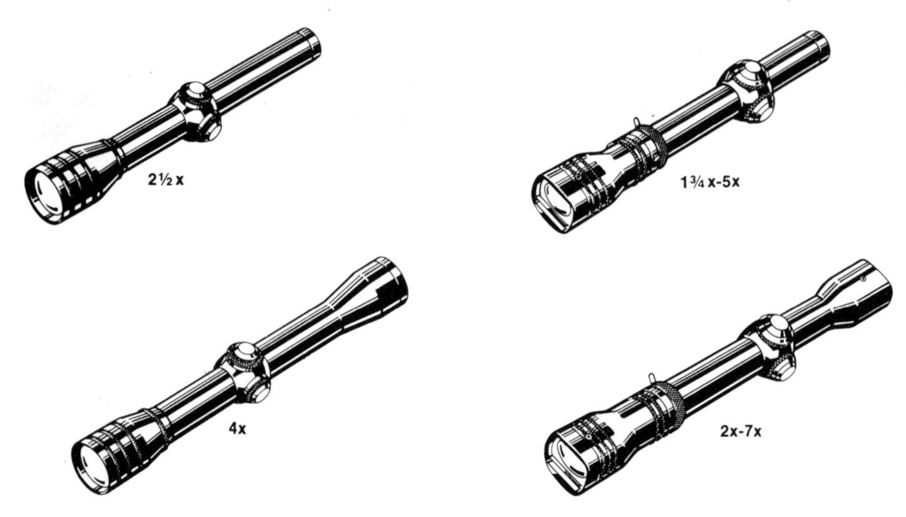

Scope sights are available in fixed and variable powers. Deer hunters use 4× in most situations; a 2½× is better for snap shooting in dense cover. Scope sights can be mounted on rifles and shotguns. Lever-action rifles must be side ejecting to allow mounting.

wrap-around tops that look good but serve no purpose except to cut out light and keep the hunter from sighting properly.

The open sight also has a range limitation. Up to 100 yards it is fairly adequate, but at ranges of 200 yards and more, it is practically worthless.

The person who buys an expensive big-game rifle should be willing to lay out some more cash to get a good sight. After all, a rifle can't hit its mark unless the bullet is guided accurately. The peep sight is better, economical, and almost as fast as open sights. First thing to do with a peep is to unscrew the disc with the small aperture and throw it away. Only the large screw hole remains; aim through this. Just because you can command a wide view of countryside through the larger opening doesn't mean it won't be accurate. On the contrary. It will be just as accurate as the small aperture, and at the same time it will be quicker and easier to use. For a front sight, pick an even post in a color that can be distinguished under most conditions. Red is exceptionally good. Ivory is acceptable.

The peep is extremely accurate up to 100 yards and beyond. In the brush, the experienced shooter can pull down on a running deer almost as fast with the peep as he can with open sights. The big drawback to the peep is that it is often placed too close to the eye for absolutely safe use on a recoiling big-game rifle. There's always the outside chance the sight may get jammed back into the eye.

The best all-purpose sight, as far as I'm concerned, is the telescope. It is a lifesaver for the person with failing eyesight. It also makes for more precise bullet placement and, in some instances, takes the place of a binocular for proper game identification. The scope is a fairly good sight even for brush shooting and running shots when the hunter gets used to it.

The 4×, or four-power, scope probably is the best all-round sight for deer

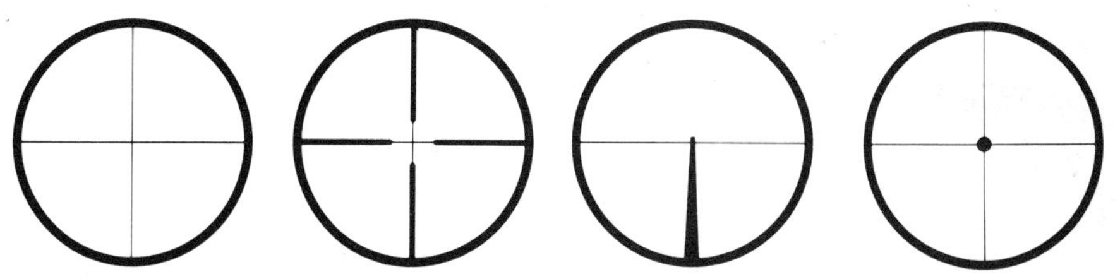

Four of the most common types of reticules (from left): crosshairs, dual X, post and crosshair, and dot. Crosshairs are less helpful than the others when the hunter has to get off a fast shot.

hunting. It is exceptionally adaptable to longer shooting and passable as a brush sight. But it isn't fast enough to use in real dense cover. My friend Tom Hayes, a long-time deer hunter with experience in many states, had a versatile outfit which included a 4× scope and a quick-detachable peep sight. The peep is carried in his cartridge belt. If the sudden need arises, he can quickly dismount the scope, ram the peep into place, and be ready for close, fast shooting.

For close-range and snap shooting, the 2½× scope is much superior to the 4×. The lower-power sight has more light-gathering capabilities, a wider field of view, and a greater latitude of eye relief—all advantages when hunting in heavy cover.

Despite what you may have heard to the contrary, a scope is extremely fast for picking up running game, particularly in medium to sparse cover. It just takes a little getting used to. The one big advantage of it is that the shooter has to line up only two objects, the crosshairs of the scope and the target. Everything appears in the same plane. On the alternatives, the open and peep sights, he must align the back and front sights as well as the target. And of these two, the peep is quicker because the front sight is just placed on the target as it is centered in the aperture.

But the scope does have some disadvantages. First, the field of view is limited, and the more power, the less field the sight provides. But the wide-angle feature of some scopes makes them somewhat more effective at close range in getting a running deer into your sight picture. These are sold

A side mount such as this permits the use of scope or iron sights.

under such trade names as Weaver "V-W," Williams "Wide Guide," and Redfield "Low Profile." Williams advertises that its 4× "Wide Guide" has a 35-foot-plus field at 100 yards compared to the normal field of approximately 28 feet. With open or peep sights, the shooter, accustomed to getting on the animal with both eyes open, can immediately pick up his target. The scope takes just a little longer. And in heavy cover the so-called "picket effect" might distract the aim. This effect is caused by the deer running through trees with cover between the animal and shooter. The trees flash across the scope and it is almost like trying to aim through a picket fence.

Actually, the choice of a sight will vary with the terrain. Under most circumstances, I recommend the scope. In heavy brush, where shots will be real close and often running, I think the peep is best. It is a matter of weighing the advantages of a particular sight against the disadvantages. The main drawbacks to the scope are that on a deer standing close, the shooter may see nothing but hair, making it difficult to pinpoint the bullet accurately; and on close, running deer it takes a split-second longer to pick the animal up and get on it. But I can count on my fingers the number of running deer I have killed; yet it would require all my fingers and toes, plus some, to count those I have missed. Hitting a fleeing deer requires real skill. A scant few of us have the ability to put the bullet in a vital area. All too often we simply shoot at the entire deer. This is inviting crippled game. For this reason I recommend the scope sight. It is far better not even to get a shot at a deer when you're not sure of putting the bullet in a killing spot than to "throw lead" and hope the bullet somehow finds its mark. The hallmark of the topflight deer hunter is to ambush the quarry without first being detected, to work for shots within the realm of his ability, and to try to make that first shot count every time. It seems foolhardy to me to select a particular sight just because the shooter *might* get a chance at a running deer. Take the positive approach, I say, and use the sight that will perform best under the most circumstances. Play the odds. And the best all-purpose sight, I repeat, is the scope.

If you might be hunting in heavy cover, however, and need a fast sight for close shooting and will take the time to learn how to use it for optimum results, then consider the peep-scope combination. With practice, the shooter can remove the scope and substitute the peep in mere seconds. Thus in more open country he can employ the scope; the peep is the choice for heavy cover. The scope also is handicapped in rain or mist, and this is another obvious advantage of having an auxiliary sight like the detachable peep in reserve. Otherwise, cradle the scope under your waterproof jacket until you're prepared to shoot.

So the hunter after whitetail deer should evaluate the terrain he will be hunting and pick a scope that best suits his particular needs. As already explained, the 4× sight is appropriate for open terrain; the lower-powered 2½× is better for heavy cover. Fixed-power scopes are less expensive and will satisfy almost everyone's needs, but for a few dollars more you can buy a variable scope. By a simple twist of a dial you can increase or decrease the power. Weaver markets a V4.5 (1½-4½×) which is superb for hunting whitetails. This is true also for Leupold's VARI-X II 1-4×. And most of the other major scope manufacturers offer similar models. If you'd like a bit more power, you might consider a 2-7× or a 3-9×. Just keep in mind that the wider range of power and the more power, the bulkier the sight. A 3-9×, for instance, is much larger than a 1-4×.

But simply picking the needed power is only part of the job. Just as important is the reticule. While common crosshairs are the No. 1 seller, crosshairs are difficult to pick up when snap-shooting in heavy cover. Perhaps the post reticule is best. This gives the illusion of shooting with open sights, and the post shows up readily.

The post for short-range shooting, like that in typical whitetail-deer country, should be large enough to stand out boldly, something with a flat top with a slope of about 4 to 6 minutes of angle. The horizontal crosshair is optional, although I prefer to have it.

Another good reticule for fast shooting is the dot. But again, the dot should be large and bold so that the shooter can readily pick it up when he's trying to get off a fast shot, about a 3- or 4-minute dot. The main drawback to either the post or dot is that it tends to cover up the target at long ranges, but since most whitetails are shot at ranges of less than 80 yards, this isn't a serious handicap unless you plan on using your rifle for several purposes, from long-range varmint shooting to deer hunting. In this case it might be wise to have interchangeable scopes, one of high power for varmint shooting and a low-power job for deer. Trying to make one fixed-power scope serve several widely diversified tasks is only defeating your basic purpose.

For an all-purpose scope I would suggest a variable with crosshairs. In fact, many hunters prefer crosshairs to either a post or dot. The standard crosshairs are the same width, all the way up and down. A very popular crosshair is coarse on the outside, tapering to a very fine line at the cross. Go to a sporting-goods store and look through scopes with the various reticules and compare them to see which you like best. Again let me stress that the hunting terrain should have a major influence on your decision. The requirements are different for thick woods and open country.

Modern rifles are tapped to accept scope sights, but on certain hammer-cocking-style lever-action rifles, such as the Marlin 336 and Winchester 94, it is necessary to attach a hammer extension to the existing thumb spur if you install a scope.

A scope even can be mounted on one of the shotguns made specifically for slug shooting. Here you might want to Weaver 1.5× fixed-power or a Leupold 1-4× variable turned to its lowest setting. Because of the short ranges involved in slug shooting, the less magnification the better. Weaver also markets an unusual sight called "Qwik-Point," which is something of a hybrid between a peep sight and the scope with no magnification. The Qwik-Point has a blaze-orange dot in the center, and the gunner simply puts this dot on the mark and pulls the trigger. While a few shotguns are ready-made to accept scopes, rather than mount a scope yourself, you should take it to a reliable gunsmith for a proper job.

But the scope is more than just a device for lining up on a deer. In early morning and late afternoon, two prime times for seeing deer, and also on dark overcast days when the light is bad, a quality scope has light-gathering power. A shooter often can place a bullet pretty accurately with a scope when there is not enough light even to see open sights, much less aim with them.

I remember a time when my dad, O. D. Tinsley, and I discovered just how valuable a scope can be under such adverse conditions. We were heading back to where we'd parked our auto one dark, overcast November day, after hunting through the day without seeing a legal buck. The premature dark was quickly settling over the countryside and we were hurrying.

We were walking briskly down a game trail, not paying any particular attention to anything around us, when suddenly a commotion in a nearby clump of oak saplings brought us to an abrupt halt. We squinted our eyes and looked intently, trying to make out in the fading light what had caused the ruckus.

About then a nice buck ran out of the trees, trotted up to the side of a hill, and paused about 80 yards away. "Take him," Dad instructed softly.

I raised my .30/30 with open sights and tried to pull down on the buck. But the sights blurred and I couldn't make shape out of shadow.

"I can't, I can't," I whispered hoarsely. "Too dark to see."

Dad quickly raised his .300 Savage with the 4× Weaver scope, steadied the weapon, and squeezed the trigger. At the muzzle blast, the six-pointer (Eastern count) dropped heavily. The slug had entered just where Dad was aiming, right beyond the shoulders.

Without the aid of a scope we'd never have gotten that buck.

The scope sight also has the ability almost to "see" through the brush. This penetrating trait is a definite asset to the whitetail deer hunter.

I am a firm believer in getting one sight, such as a scope, and becoming intimately familiar with it, rather than switching from one type to another. The modern scope is dependable and rugged (especially the quality brands), and there is little likelihood that you will damage one or that conditions will dictate an auxiliary sight. But there might come a time, such as during a rain, when the scope becomes more of a bother than an asset. It is difficult to keep a scope dry and do much serious hunting.

You can remove one sight and substitute another—take off a scope and snap on a peep sight. But there are also swing-away scope mounts. One example is the Pachmayr Lo-Swing. A built-in latch holds the scope in rigid shooting position, yet it can be flipped aside so that you can use the factory-mounted open sights. Another possibility is a see-through mount or an off-set scope. Williams "Sight-Thru" looks like one ring perched atop another. Here the top ring holds the scope and the open sights are clearly visible through the bottom ring, giving you a choice. Williams also makes a side mount; by using different rings, you can position the scope over or to the side of the open iron sights. Your best bet for getting a "combination" is to consult with a gunsmith. Many sporting-goods stores do not carry specialty mounts, and few salesmen know how to install them.

If I had to have only one sight I would undoubtedly pick the scope. Anything else would be an auxiliary sight, nothing more. I'm convinced that the advantages of the scope far outweigh the disadvantages, and that the scope definitely scores higher on all things you look for in a sight than either the peep or open sights. A scope sight makes a good shooter an even better shot, and it assures more clean kills and less cripples.

SHOTGUN BALLISTICS

Rifled Slugs

Gauge	Shell Length	Slug Weight ounces	Velocity muzzle	Velocity 50 yds.	Velocity 100 yds.	Energy foot pounds muzzle	Energy foot pounds 50 yds.	Energy foot pounds 100 yds.
410	2½ inches	⅕	1,830	1,335	1,025	650	345	205
28	2¾	½	1,600	1,175	950	1,245	670	440
20	2½	⅝	1,600	1,175	950	1,555	840	550
16	2¾	⅞	1,600	1,175	950	2,175	1,175	765
12	2¾	1	1,600	1,175	950	2,485	1,350	875

Drop in Inches

Gauge	25 yds.	50 yds.	100 yds.
410	.4	1.6	8.2
28	.5	2.1	10.4
20	.5	2.1	10.4
16	.5	2.1	10.4
12	.5	2.1	10.4

Pellets

Gauge	Shell Length	Number of Pellets	Velocity muzzle	Velocity 20 yds.	Velocity 50 yds.	Energy foot pounds muzzle	Energy foot pounds 20 yds.	Energy foot pounds 50 yds.
12	2¾″	12 of No. 0	1,300	1,120	960	140	100	70
12	3″	15 of No. 00	1,250	1,085	940	185	140	105
12	2¾″	12 of No. 00	1,325	1,135	970	210	155	110
12	2¾″	9 of No. 00	1,325	1,135	970	210	155	110

Drop in Inches

Gauge	Shell Length	Number of Pellets	20 yds.	50 yds.
12	2¾″	12 of No. 0	.5	3.3
12	3″	15 of No. 00	.5	3.5
12	2¾″	12 of No. 00	.4	3.2
12	2¾″	9 of No. 00	.4	3.2

(All tabulations made for full choke, 30 inch barrel)

BALLISTICS OF MOST POPULAR DEER CARTRIDGES

Cartridge	Bullet wgt. grains	Bullet type	Velocity ft. per sec. muzzle	Velocity ft. per sec. 100 yds.	Energy foot pounds muzzle	Energy foot pounds 100 yds.	Mid-range trajectory 100 yds.	Mid-range trajectory 200	Mid-range trajectory 300
6mm Remington	100	Exp.	3,190	2,920	2,260	1,890	0.5	2.1	6.5
.243 Winchester	100	S.P.	3,070	2,790	2,090	1,730	0.5	2.2	5.5
.250 Savage	100	S.P.	2,820	2,460	1,760	1,340	0.6	2.9	7.4
.257 Roberts	100	Exp.	2,900	2,540	1,870	1,430	0.6	2.9	7.4
.257 Roberts	117	S.P.	2,650	2,280	1,820	1,350	0.7	3.4	8.8
.270 Winchester	100	S.P.	3,580	3,160	2,840	2,210	0.4	1.7	4.5
.270 Winchester	130	Exp.	3,440	2,850	2,840	2,340	0.5	2.1	5.3
.270 Winchester	150	S.P.	2,800	2,400	2,610	1,920	0.7	3.0	7.8
7mm Mauser (7×57)	175	S.P.	2,490	2,470	2,410	1,830	0.8	3.7	9.5
.280 Remington	150	Exp.	2,810	2,580	2,630	2,220	0.6	2.6	6.5
.30/30 Winchester	150	Exp.	2,410	2,020	1,930	1,360	0.9	4.2	11.0
.30/30 Winchester	170	S.P. & Exp.	2,220	1,890	1,860	1,350	1.2	4.6	12.5
.30 Remington	170	S.P. & Exp.	2,220	1,890	1,860	1,350	1.2	4.6	12.5
.30/40 Krag	180	S.P. & Exp.	2,470	2,420	2,440	1,790	0.8	3.8	9.9
.30/40 Krag	220	Exp.	2,200	1,990	2,360	1,930	1.0	4.4	11.0
.30/06 Springfield	110	S.P.	3,420	2,880	2,850	2,020	0.4	2.1	5.6
.30/06 Springfield	150	Exp.	2,970	2,670	2,930	2,370	0.6	2.4	6.1
.30/06 Springfield	180	Exp.	2,700	2,470	2,910	2,440	0.7	2.9	7.0
.30/06 Springfield	220	S.P.	2,410	2,120	2,830	2,190	0.8	3.9	9.8
.300 Savage	150	S.P.	2,670	2,350	2,370	1,840	0.7	3.2	8.0
.300 Savage	180	Exp.	2,370	2,160	2,240	1,860	0.9	3.7	9.2
.303 Savage	190	S.P.	1,980	1,680	1,650	1,190	1.3	6.2	15.5
.300 H&H Magnum	180	Exp.	2,920	2,670	3,400	2,850	0.6	2.4	5.8
.300 H&H Magnum	220	Exp.	2,620	2,370	3,350	2,740	0.7	3.1	7.7
.303 British	215	S.P.	1,280	1,900	2,270	1,720	1.1	4.9	12.5
.32 Winchester Sp.	165	O.P.E.	2,280	1,920	1,900	1,350	1.0	4.7	12.5
.32 Winchester Sp.	170	S.P.	2,280	1,870	1,960	1,320	1.0	4.8	13.0
.32 Remington	170	S.P. & Exp.	2,220	1,890	1,860	1,350	1.0	4.9	13.0
.35 Remington	200	Exp.	2,210	1,830	2,170	1,490	1.1	5.2	14.0
.300 Winchester Mag.	150	S.P. & Exp.	3,400	3,050	3,850	3,100	0.4	1.9	4.8
.300 Winchester Mag.	180	S.P. & Exp.	3,070	2,850	3,770	3,250	0.5	2.1	5.3
.264 Win. Magnum	100	S.P.	3,700	3,260	3,040	2,360	0.4	1.6	4.2
.264 Win. Magnum	140	S.P.	3,200	2,940	3,180	2,690	0.5	2.1	4.9
.44 Magnum	240	S.P.	1,750	1,360	1,630	985	1.6	8.4	—
.444 Marlin	240	S.P.	2,400	1,845	3,070	1,815	1.0	5.4	16.5

Exp.—Expanding S.P.—Soft Point O.P.E.—Open Point Expanding

3

Choosing a Deer Rifle

THE MODEL 94 Winchester carbine set the standard for today's deer rifle. It was the type of gun which appealed to the deer hunter, being light of weight for carrying and short for fast handling in the brush where most whitetails are hunted.

The Model 94 was originally introduced in 1894 and chambered for .32/40 and .38/55 black-powder cartridges. But it reached its peak of success when it was chambered for the popular .30/30 cartridge.

The first repeating rifles were heavy and cumbersome. They were not primarily hunting weapons; their foremost use was for protection. The hunting of deer for food dates back to Plymouth Rock; any rifle was potentially a hunting weapon. But the emphasis on light weight and fast handling evolved well after the first repeating actions were perfected.

The first repeating rifle was the Volcanic, put into production in the mid-nineteenth century. It had a lever action and was the forerunner of the famous Winchester lever-action guns which revolutionized the concept of a deer-hunting weapon.

The revolutionary lever-feed action of the Volcanic rifle was designed by B. Tyler Henry, and the gun was mass-produced by what is now the Smith & Wesson Company. The Volcanic was followed by the Henry lever-action repeaters, and in 1866 the first rifle carrying the Winchester brand name was introduced—the Winchester '66, chambered for the .44-caliber rimfire cartridge. This particular rifle in different versions was in production for 25 years.

Winchester really came into its own, however, with the introduction of the Winchester '73—"The Gun that Won the West." This was a modification of the Winchester '66 and was chambered for the .44/40, first center-fire cartridge developed by Winchester. The cartridge had a .44-caliber bullet powered by a 40-grain powder charge.

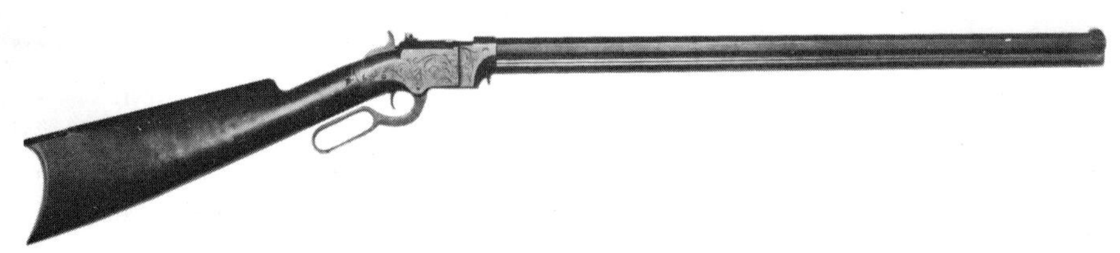

The first repeating rifle was the Volcanic, designed by B. Tyler Henry and put into production in the mid-1800s. Its lever-action mechanism was the forerunner of the famous Winchester '66 and '73.

Marlin introduced a lever-action repeater in 1881 for the .45/70 cartridge and also the .40/50/260 and the .45/85/285. The Marlin Firearms Company earlier had brought out a single-shot level gun in 1861 chambered for .32 long rimfire and centerfire cartridges.

Savage put its initial lever-action gun into production in 1895. It was made for Savage by the Marlin Firearms Company, and was chambered for the .303 cartridge. Savage's famous Model 99 was introduced in 1899, also chambered for the .303, and this has been a favorite deer-hunting weapon ever since. In 1912 the Model 99 was chambered for the .22 Savage Hi-Power, first rifle to take a high-powered .22-caliber cartridge, and in 1913 was first to be chambered for the .250/3000, the beginning of the flat-trajectory loads of today. At the time, the 3,000-feet-per-second velocity of the .250/3000 was almost unbelievable.

Soon thereafter, the bolt-action rifle was introduced, and coupled with the high-velocity cartridges, made an immediate hit. The autoloaders and pump-action rifles we know today are fairly recent innovations, coming into their own since World War II.

Nowadays the hunter can get a gun of his action choice in just about every deer-hunting cartridge imaginable. Bolt-actions are preferred by the hunters seeking an "all-purpose" gun, to be used under a variety of conditions for a variety of game, from varmints to big game like deer. The reliable bolt-action is also the most foolproof of all the actions. But strictly for deer hunting, the bolt-action never will be as popular as the lever-action, autoloader, and pump because of the speed factor. The lever-action is still far and away the most popular action among deer hunters. A rifle like the Marlin 336 chambered for the .35 Remington is lightweight and short enough for fast handling in dense timber, and the .35 Remington is a heavy bullet that plows through light, spindly brush. A combination such as this is ideal for the densely timbered deer woods of states such as Pennsylvania, New York, and Virginia.

But as mentioned in the previous chapter, the type of action is a personal choice. For whitetail-deer hunting there really is nothing to recommend one over another. Don't be influenced by what a buddy buys. Go to a sporting-goods store and try the different actions. Which feels best to you? Manufacturers produce different actions because of individual preferences among hunters. Otherwise, all hunting rifles would have the same action.

It is very important that you buy an action you are comfortable with and have confidence in. This confidence factor can't be stressed enough in deer hunting. It often is the difference between them-that-brags and them-that-doesn't.

When Elmer Payne killed his record-book buck (nontypical, 24 points) in Unicoi County of northeastern Tennessee, he credited much of his success to familiarity with his weapon. He explained, "For more than 20 years I had been hunting deer with the Model 336 Marlin lever-action .30/30 carbine that I was carrying, and I had come to know its capabilities as well as I knew my own."

Here's a brief rundown on the more popular rifles available.

LEVER-ACTION

Browning BLR. 4-shot detachable magazine, 20-inch barrel, weight 6 pounds 15 ounces, chambered for .243 and .308.

Marlin 336C. 6-shot tubular magazine, 20-inch barrel, weight 7 pounds, chambered for .30/30 and .35 Remington.

Marlin 336A. Same as 336C except has 24-inch barrel and 5-shot magazine.

Marlin 444. 4-shot tubular magazine, 22-inch barrel, weight 7½ pounds, chambered for .444 Marlin.

Marlin 1894. 10-shot tubular magazine, 20-inch barrel, weight 6 pounds, chambered for .44 Magnum.

Marlin 1895. 4-shot tubular magazine, 22-inch barrel, weight 7 pounds, chambered for .45/70.

Mossberg 472. 6-shot magazine, 20-inch barrel, weight 7½ pounds, chambered for .30/30.

Pederson 4700 Custom. 24-inch barrel, weight 7½ pounds, chambered for .30/30 and .35 Remington.

Savage 99E. 5-shot rotary magazine, 20-inch barrel, weight 7 pounds, chambered for .300 Savage, .243, and .308.

Savage 99A. Similar to 99E except with straight-grip stock and chambered for .250 Savage, .243, and .308.

Savage 99C. Similar to 99E except has detachable clip magazine and is chambered for .243 and .308.

Western Field 72. 6-shot magazine, 18- or 20-inch barrel, weight 7½ pounds, chambered for .30/30.

Winchester 94. 6-shot tubular magazine, 20-inch barrel, weight 6½ pounds, chambered for .30/30.

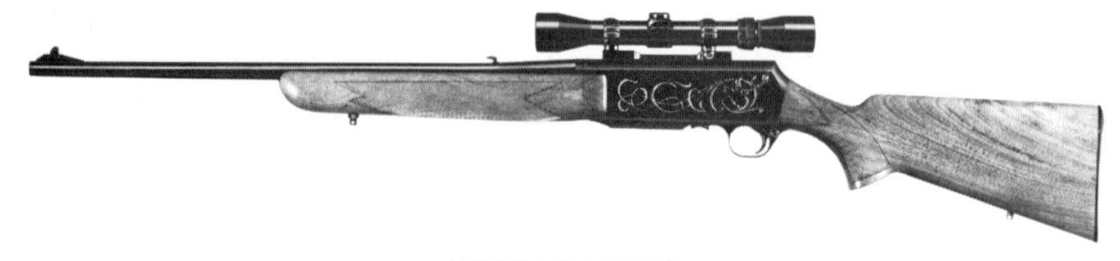

AUTOLOADING

Browning High-Power Auto. Detachable 4-round magazine, 22-inch barrel, weight $7\frac{3}{8}$ pounds, chambered for .243, .270, .30/06, and .308.

Harrington & Richardson 360. 3-shot magazine, 22-inch barrel, weight $7\frac{1}{2}$ pounds, chambered for .243 and .308.

Remington 742. 4-shot clip magazine, 22-inch barrel, weight $7\frac{1}{2}$ pounds, chambered for .243, 6mm, .280, .308, and .30/06.

Remington 742 Carbine. Same as 742 except $18\frac{1}{2}$-inch barrel, weight $6\frac{3}{4}$ pounds, chambered for .30/06 and .308.

Ruger 44. 4-shot tubular magazine, $18\frac{1}{2}$-inch barrel, weight $5\frac{3}{4}$ pounds, chambered for .44 Magnum.

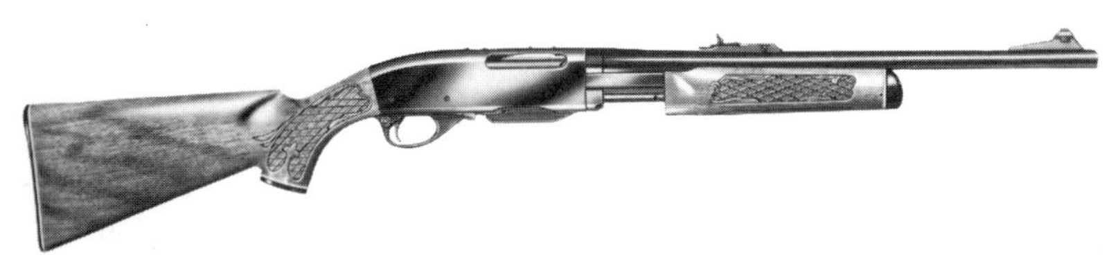

SLIDE-ACTION

Remington 760. 4-shot detachable clip magazine, 22-inch barrel, weight $7\frac{1}{2}$ pounds, chambered for 6mm, .243, .270, .308, and .30/06.

Remington 760 Carbine. Same as 760 except has $18\frac{1}{2}$-inch barrel, weight $7\frac{1}{4}$ pounds, chambered for .308 and .30/06.

Savage 170. 3-shot magazine, 22-inch barrel, weight $6\frac{3}{4}$ pounds, chambered for .30/30.

Savage 170C. Same as 170 except has $18\frac{1}{2}$-inch barrel.

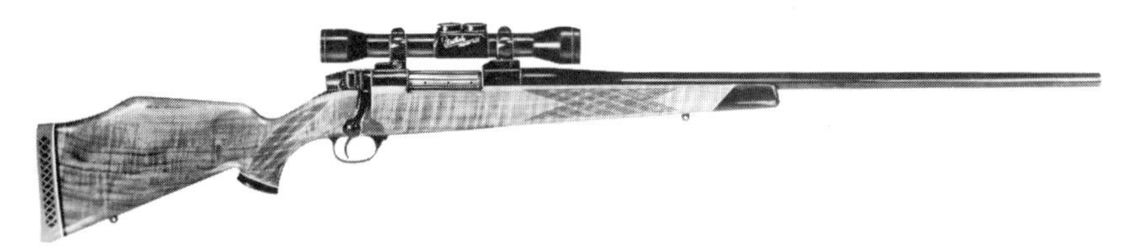

BOLT-ACTION

Harrington & Richardson 300. 5-shot magazine, 22-inch barrel, weight $7\frac{3}{4}$ pounds, chambered for .243, .270, .308, and .30/06.

Harrington & Richardson 301 Carbine. Similar to 300 except has 18-inch barrel, weighs $7\frac{1}{4}$ pounds.

Herter's Mark U9. 23½-inch barrel, weight 6¼ pounds, chambered for .243, 6mm, .284, .308, .270, .30/06, and .264.

Ithaca LSA-55. Detachable 3-round magazine, 23-inch barrel, weight 6½ pounds, chambered for .243, .308, 6mm, .270, and .30/06.

Mossberg 800. 4-shot magazine, 22-inch barrel, weight 6½ pounds, chambered for .243 and .308.

Mossberg 810A. 4-shot magazine, 22-inch barrel, weight 7½ pounds, chambered for .30/06 and .270.

Remington 700 ADL. 5-shot magazine, 22- or 24-inch barrel, weight 7 pounds, chambered for 6mm, .243, .270, .308, and .30/06.

Remington 700 BDL. Left-handed model, in .270 and .30/06 only.

Remington 788. 4-shot magazine, 22-inch barrel, weight 7½ pounds, chambered for 6mm, .243, and .308.

Remington 788 Left Hand. Southpaw model, in 6mm and .308 only.

Ruger 77. 5-shot magazine, 22-inch barrel, weight 6¾ pounds, chambered for .243, 6mm, and .250 Savage.

Sako 74. 23- and 24-inch barrel, weight 6¾ pounds, chambered for .243, .270, and .30/06.

Savage 110E. 4-shot magazine, 22-inch barrel, weight 6¾ pounds, chambered for .30/06 (also available in left-hand model).

Savage 110C. Same as 100E except detachable box magazine, chambered for .243 (right-hand model only), .270 and .30/06.

Savage 340. 3-shot clip magazine, 22- and 24-inch barrel, weight 6½ pounds, chambered for .30/30.

Weatherby Vanguard. 5-shot magazine, 24-inch barrel, weight 7⅜ pounds, chambered for .243, .270, .30/06, and .308.

Western Field 780. 5-shot magazine, 22-inch barrel, weight 6½ pounds, chambered for .243 and .308.

Winchester 70. 5-shot magazine, 22-inch barrel, weight 7½ pounds, chambered for .243, .270, .308, and .30/06.

4

Sighting In and Bullet Placement

HAVING A good rifle-sight combination doesn't necessarily make a hunter a better marksman. The rifle is just a precision tool. How well it functions depends on the man behind it. And knowing how to shoot properly is one of the glaring deficits among the modern-day hunting fraternity.

While researching this book, I talked to many people associated with deer hunters across the nation—outdoor writers, other hunters, conservation people—and almost to a man they voiced the same singular opinion: there just aren't many hunters who can shoot proficiently.

Seth Martin owns a livestock ranch in southern Mason County in central Texas, in the so-called hill country. Possibly this area has the highest density of whitetail deer per acre of any place of comparable size in the United States. Since Texas inaugurated its program of taking antlerless deer in 1953 to prevent overpopulations, Martin has supervised the taking of more than 1,000 deer off his land. Some of the hunters have impressed him with their know-how. Most have not. "There are too many incompetent shooters," he observed. "Many hunters who come to my ranch I suspect have never had a deer rifle in their hands before and they know absolutely nothing about using one."

Every hunter owes it to himself to be familiar with the sport of deer hunting before entering the woods; he should know his quarry and how to plan his strategy and tactics. And of course he should know how to skillfully shoot a gun once game is sighted.

It is a matter of decency. Each autumn a large number of deer are wounded. Although a few cripples are inevitable, the score would be reduced if hunters were more responsible. It is unforgivable when a hunter cripples a deer because he didn't take the time and effort to be prepared. Yet the ranks of unqualified hunters continue to grow because many people believe they become hunters the moment they buy a gun. These slobs are the ones who give this cherished sport a bad name. Don't be a slob.

To learn to handle a gun with some degree of success, the hunter must shoot it. He must become familiar with his weapon and know what it will do under varied circumstances. This means shooting several boxes of ammunition through the gun.

Shooting is like most skills—once you master the few fundamentals, you improve with practice. Admittedly, it is getting more difficult to practice. Urban life presents obstacles because shooting facilities and opportunities are limited. When I was growing up in a small rural community, I could roam the hills and fields and shoot a gun safely and to no one's distress. Not any more, even in this area of sparse habitation. Most of the private land is posted. Another deterrent to practice is the family budget; centerfire cartridges are expensive, and even if you reload your own, you are going to notice the cost "bite" if you do much shooting. An alternative is to plink or hunt small game with a .22 rimfire rifle. Anyone who can shoot a .22 with any proficiency will do all right with his deer gun. Just remember to use the same type sight on the .22 as your rifle has. If you prefer a peep, put the same thing on the rimfire weapon, or else scope both. Once you become familiar with the sight, your marksmanship will improve dramatically.

Nonetheless, every hunter owes it to himself to take his favorite deer rifle out of the closet or gun cabinet prior to the season opener, wipe off the year's accumulation of dust, and fire it many times. In doing so he could well stack the odds of success in his favor. Many hunters spend painstaking days looking for a legal target, only to miss with their shot during that moment of truth when the sights are aligned and the hunter slowly sq-u-ee-z-es the trigger.

Confidence is all-important in hunting. The shooter, I repeat, must have the utmost confidence in his weapon. Before he can practice with it and gain this needed confidence, he must know how it shoots, how accurate it is at different ranges. In other words, it must be sighted in properly.

Taking a gun out "cold" and trying to hunt with it is inviting trouble. It happened to me one time. An editor of a well-known regional magazine contacted me about doing a test story for his publication on the Ruger .44 Magnum rifle. He said he would personally deliver the rifle to me. Could I line up a place for deer hunting?

I got in touch with a rancher friend of mine and he agreed to take us out the following Saturday. We were going to hunt on a spread where there were many antlerless-deer permits available and the deer weren't spooky or wild. It was almost a dead cinch that we would get a reasonable shot at a deer. I told the editor to do the shooting and I'd take pictures.

Sure enough, we'd no sooner walked off into the pasture just after daybreak when a fat and sleek doe jumped from a knot of brush, ran out a few dozen yards, and stopped, in the classic broadside pose. I was already fidgeting with my camera, reasoning the shot and kill were only routine procedure.

The gun boomed. Dust geysered over the doe's back. She leaped frantically and dashed out of sight over a small knoll. My editor friend shook his head dejectedly.

Five shots and five misses later, with three different deer as targets, I was becoming perturbed. I was sure the editor had target-tested the gun and figured the misses were a result of his sloppy shooting ability.

Since I had one tag left on my hunting license, I told him to give me the rifle and I'd shoot him a deer for photos and a story. About an hour later I jumped a forkhorn buck that ran out about 100 yards and stopped, half facing me. I centered the open sights behind the buck's shoulder and tightened my trigger finger.

The bullet spun the deer completely around. Imagine my surprise when he leaped to his feet and took off as if he'd never been touched. I ran to where the deer had been standing and searched for the telltale blood droppings. But there was nothing but a hatful of hair. Bobby Burnam, the rancher, examined the hair and said it had come off the deer's back. What had happened, he imagined, was that the bullet had grazed the deer along the back, giving it quite a shock but inflicting no permanent damage.

This had me puzzled. I'd aimed at the lower part of the body, yet the bullet had sailed high. Could it be the sights? This prompted me to step off 100 yards and shoot at a prickly pear cactus pad. The bullet kicked up dust a full 12 inches above the target. Other shots confirmed my suspicions. The rifle sights were far off.

The embarrassed editor admitted he'd never fired the gun. He'd unpacked it from the factory crate only the night before.

Suppose we'd jumped a trophy buck. Think how we would have regretted the oversight of not checking the rifle out properly. Yet it happens every day of the deer season, somewhere. And it results not just in misses, but in maimed and mortally wounded deer that shame the sport.

A hunter should sight in his own weapon and field-test it regularly. Many nimrods simply turn their guns over to local gunsmiths and have them sight the weapons in. But there's always the possibility that the hunter and gunsmith don't see through the sights the same way.

Many years ago I was tied down with extra work just before the season opening, so I took a new rifle and scope I'd just acquired to a gunsmith friend of mine and asked him to check them out, sighting them in accurately. Afterward he assured me the rifle was zeroed perfectly for 100 yards.

The second day of the season I was pussyfooting along the side of a brushy header when I jumped a nice buck. He came from the brushy innards of the draw, turned abruptly, and ran almost parallel to me, perhaps 50 yards away on the opposite side of the header. I couldn't have asked for an easier shot. I pulled down on the buck and missed him cleanly three times.

Back in camp at noon I was really bemoaning the muffed opportunity. My hunting companions asked if I'd checked out my rifle. No, I confessed, but a gunsmith had, and I was sure the fault didn't rest with the rifle. But just to be doubly sure, I laid off a makeshift range and fired a half-dozen test shots. Not a one was near the bull's-eye. I was shooting a good 6 inches high and to the right, at one o'clock on the target. A few adjustments on the scope and I was back in business again.

Sighting in a rifle is no complicated engineering feat. Anyone can do it by firing less than a box of ammo. It is only a matter of following a simple procedure.

But before taking the rifle to a shooting range, you should have your sights mounted properly. If you use the factory-installed open sights, check to be sure they are aligned. Should you install some other sight, a peep or scope, have a gunsmith or some reliable person in a gun shop do the job. When I bought my first scope I put it on wrong, the windage adjustment up, the vertical adjustment on the side, and I wasted more than a box of ammo before my red-faced discovery of the mistake. Just recently I saw a scope with the internal adjustments frozen solid; the man who was installing the sight on his rifle tightened the mount-ring screws too tightly, bending the scope slightly. Another bought a new scope and used the mount and rings already on his rifle. Trouble was, the rings were just a fraction too large; they wouldn't tighten down snugly. The rifle's recoil moved the sight every time and this gent never could get it to shoot accurately.

Trying to work on your own rifle is false economy, unless you know what you are doing. The risks are too high. Take it to a gunsmith and have him put it in first-class working order. If he installs a scope, for example, he will "bore-sight" it and probably the first shot will be near or actually in the black. The Bushnell Boresighter has an arbor which fits into the gun's muzzle, putting a scopelike cylinder above the barrel, and the scope is aligned with this. More simply, bore sighting is adjusting the line of sight of the riflescope to be parallel to the bore of the gun's barrel. If you save a half-box of ammunition while sighting in, you've already offset some of the gunsmith's charge.

I always sight in my rifles at 25 yards. This way, by plotting the trajectory of the bullet, I can pinpoint where it will be "on" again and how it will perform at different distances.

The trajectory of the bullet is the curve it follows in flight. A bullet doesn't travel in a straight line, but rather in a curve. The term "flatter trajectory" means less curve of the bullet in flight.

At 25 yards the bullet will be striking the target the first time it crosses a horizontal plane. After this it will curve upwards, its midpoint trajectory being the farthest distance between the crest of the curve and the horizontal line. Then it will curve downward again, crossing the horizontal line again before dropping below it. When the lines bisect, this will be the point of impact again, the second spot where the rifle is "on." After this the bullet will drop, always shooting low in relation to the target.

By plotting the trajectory of your particular caliber rifle, you can determine the next point where the bullet will impact after the 25-yard mark. This will be about 175 yards for the .30/30. But at no place between the 25-

yard mark and the second point where the curve and horizontal plane bisect will the bullet be too far off the target. Certainly the aim will be more than adequate for deer hunting.

At the short range of 25 yards there is little doubt that the first bullet fired will be on the paper target. But should it miss, you can get it on by visually bore-sighting the rifle. Remove the bolt and steady the rifle on some kind of rest. Look through the bore until you have the target about centered. Then shift your gaze through the sight, adjusting it so the target is again about centered. This step only assures that you'll put a hole in the paper and will have some mark to work from.

From here the procedure is elementary. By changing the adjustments on your sights, you can move the bullet to hit where you desire.

On scope and peep (receiver) sights these adjustments come easy. But open sights are hard to change with any degree of accuracy. This is still another reason why either the scope or peep is the preference over open sights.

The scope and peep both have adjustments that are graduated in minutes of angle, or fractions thereof. A minute of angle means a movement of the bullet 1 inch at 100 yards. Therefore, if you were shooting 4 inches to the right at 100 yards, you'd want to move your line of sight 4 minutes of angle to the left. Most receiver and scope sights have two adjustments, one for elevation and one for windage, or horizontal.

Since the minute of angle means roughly 1 inch of movement at 100 yards (1.047197551 inches, to be precise), then it stands to reason that it will move the bullet only 1/4 inch at 25 yards. So if you wish to compensate for 4 inches at 25 yards, you'd move the adjustment dial 16 clicks, assuming each click represented 1 minute of angle. (Carefully read the instructions that come with the sight.)

With open sights there is a crude notched bar for elevation adjustment, but to compensate for windage the hunter must move either the rear or front sight by tapping it over in its grooved seat. *The rear sight is moved in the direction the shooter wants to shift his bullet.* If he is shooting high, then he moves the rear sight lower. The front sight, however, is moved in the opposite direction. Should the bullet be striking to the left, he'd change the back sight to the right, or the front sight to the left. There are no windage adjustments at all and moving the bullet by sliding the sight in its groove is simply a matter of trial and error.

After the rifle is zeroed in at 25 yards, it is best to check it out at a longer distance. One hundred yards is a likely choice. Any mistakes at 25 yards will be multiplied four times at the longer distance. At this range the rifle should be shooting a little high, as the curve of the trajectory has not bisected the horizontal line for the second time. But with reference to windage it should be in the center of the target.

The deer's most vulnerable areas are the spine, the neck and behind the shoulder in the lungs and the heart. Spine, neck and heart shots are difficult to make, though, so the hunter's best bet is a well-placed lung shot, roughly in the large shaded area shown. The heart is at the bottom of the shaded area.

After you have your rifle sighted in and you are all checked out on its operation, you are ready to go hunting. One of the most impressive things you learn in the hunting woods is that there is a marked difference between shooting at an inanimate target and live game.

The foremost tendency among shooters is to aim for the largest part of the deer. This is the midsection. Actually, it is the very worst place you could place your bullet. A paunch-hit deer may run miles without falling, and may leave very little blood to follow.

Deer have several vulnerable areas where a well-placed bullet will bring instant death. The three most popular are behind the shoulder, the neck, and the heart.

Probably the most logical thing to aim for is what is commonly referred to as the "high lung shot." This is just behind the shoulder, about 40 percent of the way down the body below the spine. Here the hunter has the greatest margin for error. If he is shooting either high or low, he'll still place his bullet in vital regions. A low shot will hit in the vicinity of the heart; a high bullet will penetrate around the spine. Forward, the bullet will shatter the shoulders; a little way back it will strike high in the paunch, which is much more deadly than a low paunch hit.

Many veteran hunters aim for the neck. A deer struck in the neck with a high-powered rifle seldom will run far. And in this region that is a minimum loss of edible meat. But the neck of the whitetail deer is very small and there isn't much margin for error. A bullet placed either slightly high or low will be a miss.

The heart of the deer is carried much lower in the body cavity than most people realize. The very location of the blood-pumping organ makes it hard to reach with a bullet without destroying excessive meat, save for the flat broadside shot. The heart is well protected with muscles and tissue. Any shot angled into this region is naturally going to mess up lots of choice eating venison.

And speaking of angles, this is something which every hunter should take into consideration. Seldom will a deer take a statue pose, still and broadside. Chances are much better that it will be moving away or standing at an angle. The hunter must mentally plot the path of the bullet to keep from completely ruining the animal for eating purposes.

Once I was sitting in a tree stand in central Texas, watching a long, open avenue which quartered off through the cedar brush. After a long wait of several hours an eight-point buck came slipping down the game trail. I was impatient after the wait and I didn't give the deer time to get out into the open, where I would have a clear shot. Instead, I tried to shoot over a small bush and angle a bullet into the buck's spine. When shooting from an elevated position, the tendency is to overshoot (a matter of parallax), and I didn't compensate for this. The bullet passed over the spine and nicked the deer's left shoulder blade. All I succeeded in doing was crippling the animal, a stupid blunder.

This composite picture of angles is another reason why the behind-the-shoulder shot is the best and most logical choice. Here the hunter has more leeway. Should the deer be running away at a tangent, a bullet placed behind the shoulder will angle forward, exiting just in front of the opposite shoulder, a surefire killing blow. From above, the bullet will angle down, through the chest cavity, also a vulnerable area. Entering from the front, it will angle back through the innards, or from below it will pass upward around the spine. Any of these shots will do the job.

When a deer is presenting itself at an angle, always think in terms of the shoulder bone structure. This is above the bottom of the body about a quarter of the way up, away from the foreleg bone. Any bullet placed around the shoulders this high is a good shot in a vulnerable area.

Probably the two most difficult shots are when the deer is either directly facing the shooter or is facing straight away. A deer in either of these poses doesn't offer much of a target. A running deer coming head-on or going directly away is particularly difficult to hit, since the small target area is bouncing erratically. Even when the deer is motionless there is only a tiny area to shoot at.

When a deer is facing head-on, aim for the spot where the neck merges with the body. A bullet placed here will expand in the chest, causing much damage. If you can only see the deer's rear, put the bullet at the base of the tail, driving the projectile into the body cavity, ultimately into the chest.

In shooting deer, placing the bullet is of utmost importance. It can't do its intended job unless it strikes vital organs. A correctly placed bullet should do one of two things: disrupt the nervous system, such as in the brain or spine, or stop the function of vital organs such as the heart or lungs. A gut or belly shot is the worst of all. It eventually will bring death, but the deer usually will run a long way before dropping, and it often leaves no trail you can follow.

Second to bullet placement is bullet action. I once saw a deer almost escape after being shot with a handloaded cartridge meant for target shooting. It ran for about 300 yards before we were fortunate enough to find it. The exit hole of the bullet was about the same size as the entrance hole.

Hunters seldom get a classic broadside shot like this. Usually it is some sort of angle picture which makes the aiming decision somewhat more difficult.

Since a bullet kills primarily by shock, this slug, by failing to expand or mushroom, was robbed of most of its effectiveness.

It is for this reason that I prefer a high-velocity cartridge like the 100-grain bullet in .243 (3,070 fps muzzle velocity) or 150-grain .30/06 bullet (2,970 fps) to the .35 Remington (2,210 fps with the 200-grain bullet) and the .30/30 (2,220 fps with the 170-grain bullet). I always go to the fast-moving bullets because of their shocking power. The whitetail deer probably is the most thin-skinned of all big-game animals. Not a whole lot of bullet penetration is necessary. Any big-game cartridge is going to get inside and do damage, rather than exploding upon impact with the skin.

A slower-traveling bullet like the .35 Remington sort of plows through the deer. The .243, on the other hand, hits with such devastating speed that any tissue will offer enough resistance to mushroom the bullet, creating tremendous shock waves. With the heavier bullets which leave the rifle muzzles at speeds between 2,200 fps and 2,500, I prefer soft-point bullets which tend to spread out rather than to force their way through tissue, doing little damage. Some cartridges designed for bigger game, where the accent is more on penetration, are not too satisfactory for whitetail deer. This is particularly true of bullets in the 200-grain class. A high-velocity deer cartridge, like the 100-grain Winchester Silvertip for the .243, is designed with both penetration and expanding ability considered. There is just enough outside protection on the bullet to get it through the skin, in where it is supposed to do its damage.

What this boils down to is that the deer's vitals are on the inside, not the outside. A bullet which passes through the largest segment of the body in the upper part, around the chest, is going to do the most damage. A shot that ruins less meat and still brings instant death is the perfect shot, but whenever there is doubt, shoot for a kill, toward the forequarters. Best to have a dead deer on the ground with a sizable chunk of damaged venison than a crippled one off somewhere in the woods.

5

Care of the Deer Gun

THE MODERN deer gun is a precision tool that never will wear out in a hunter's lifetime with normal usage. There is an old axiom that the shotgun or rifle is only as good as the man behind it. Equally true, it is only as good as the care it receives. Many rifle malfunctions have occurred at that moment of truth when the hunter puts the sights on a deer and squeezes the trigger simply because the gun hasn't been cared for properly.

Preventing rust is the most important consideration when caring for a gun. Unprotected steel, unless it is the stainless variety, rusts when exposed to air which contains oxygen and moisture. Acids, salts, and other corrosive substances, when touched to metal by some means or other, start a reaction that soon leaves the exposed surface layered with rust.

Cleaning a gun is no longer an arduous task as it was in pioneer days when cleaning materials were crude—hot water, ramrod, cloth, and hog fat. The smoking black powder left the bore in a mess and sometimes it required hours to completely clear the smudge out. The general procedure back in the days of my grandfather's youth was to pour boiling water through the barrel, continuously swabbing the bore with a cloth at the same time. The water had to be boiling so the non-stainless bore would dry instantly, and when the water ran out clean, the gun was ready to be heavily coated with hog fat.

Today, it's just as important to keep your deer gun in tiptop shape, but thanks to modern rust-resisting chemicals, the job requires only a few minutes.

I always carry an aerosol can of WD-40, SS1, or LPS in my field gear. And when I come in from the field I lightly spray my rifle with this space-age substance, and even give a tiny shot inside the barrel. If you handle your weapon with sweaty hands or get it wet, the metal begins to rust overnight. That is why this preventive maintenance is necessary.

But exercise caution when using these substances—especially when spraying them around sights. The liquid both lubricates and penetrates. And when it seeps around screws, normal rifle recoil will loosen them. I make it a practice to check the screws regularly to be sure they are snug.

This I discovered the hard way. A few years back I took my deer rifle to the range for its traditional preseason sight check and, much to my dismay, bullet holes were walking all over the paper target. It didn't take long to find the trouble. Screws holding the scope mount were loose, so the sight was moving with every shot.

One way to help prevent this is to seat the screws with some type of bonding agent, such as Loc-Tite. Also good is to merely dip the threads into cola before inserting the screws. Best of all is to have a gunsmith install the sight. He will use something like Loc-Tite, and he will also impact the screws by tapping on the screwdriver with a small hammer as he turns it, seating the screws very tightly.

However, before storing the gun away, you should give it a more thorough cleaning. Keep the firearm in a relatively dry place where the temperature is fairly constant; this lessens the chance of condensation. It is wise to check your gun every month or so for any sign of rust. Do not store the weapon in a sheepskin-lined bag. Such a case when zippered shut captures moisture inside. As the air inside the case warms, condensation invades the

When coming in after the day's hunt, give your gun a light application of rust-preventive spray such as WD-40, SS1 or LPS. However, when you plan to store the shotgun or rifle for any length of time, give it a thorough cleaning and oiling, not only to prevent rust but to make it function better.

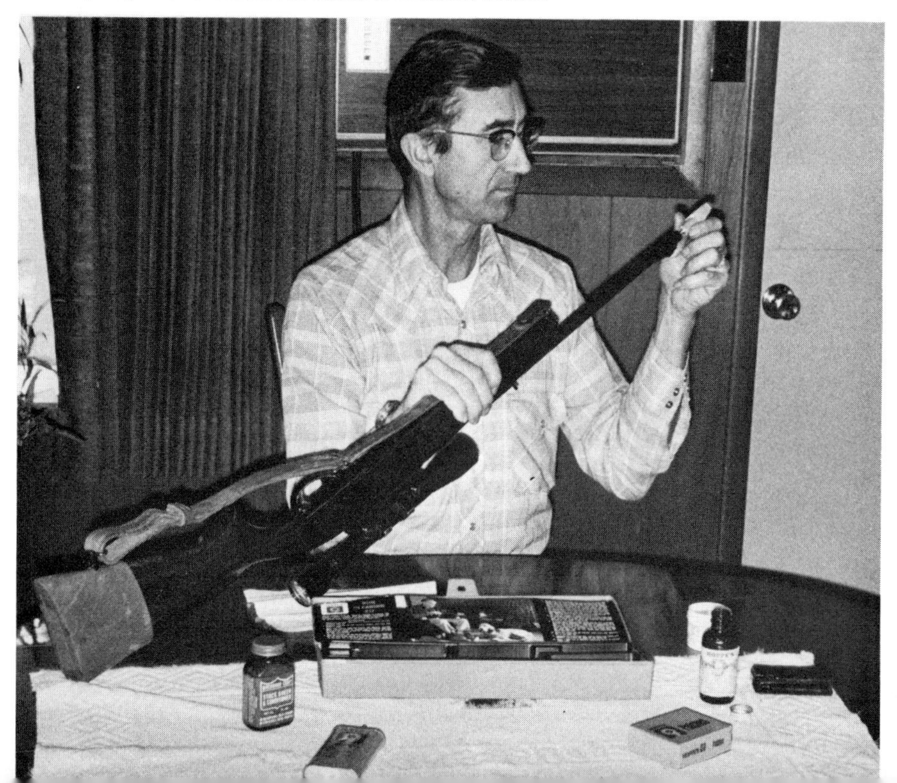

moving parts of the gun's action, causing rust. If you do store your gun in such a case even for a short period, keep the case unzipped and open, closing it only to transport the gun.

It isn't difficult to remove rust once it has taken hold if caught in time. Light rust can be removed with fine No. 0000 steel wool, usually without leaving any visible signs. If the steel wool does leave marks, they should be retouched with a bluing substance.

After excessive shooting, flecks of lead often show up in a rifle's bore. Unless this lead is removed it may impair the accuracy of your firearm. It usually can be scrubbed out with a brass brush, available in the proper caliber size at any sporting-goods store. The brushes should be free of dirt and lint. I have found it best to store them individually in plastic boxes. Those cylindrical tubes which prescription drugs come in make dandy containers.

Sometimes there is so much lead build-up in the bore that the lead must be removed chemically. Any chemical containing a large percentage of mercury will do as long as the other ingredients will not harm metal. Most well-stocked sporting-goods stores will carry the necessary chemicals, such as J-B Metal Fouling Remover. If this isn't available, see if the local drugstore carries blue ointment, which will do. Coat the bore with the chemical and leave it overnight. The mercury and lead form an amalgam which is easily wiped out. In some instances the procedure might have to be repeated several times.

Easiest way to obtain complete materials for gun cleaning is to buy one of the ready-made kits found in any sporting-goods store. A kit includes everything for a complete cleaning job, and usually the ingredients are packed in a sturdy container. It contains a cleaning rod, a light oil, grease, cleaning patches, solvent, and brass brushes. Usually the kits are packaged for individual calibers.

It always is best to examine the ingredients of such kits before purchasing one. Get nothing but the best materials, for any hunter is no better than the weapon he packs. Sometimes you may prefer to purchase each item separately and make up a kit of your own.

A good cleaning rod is a necessity. Metal ones are far superior to wood and brass. Many good ones are on the market, both solid and jointed. The jointed ones are much more compact and usually are quite durable. The better ones also have two or three interchangeable tips and a revolving handle.

Cotton flannel makes good cleaning patches. Flannel is tough and won't tear as easily as most other fabrics. Most commercial patches are made from flannel. A patch should be roughly 2 inches square.

An old toothbrush is a handy item in a kit; it will reach tight places inside the gun's chamber and action.

Any of the better-known oils and greases are good. I prefer 3-in-1 Oil and Gunslick, although there are many others just as acceptable. So that none of the items will be lost, it is best to store all of them together in a sturdy, compact box.

Cleaning a rifle is a simple procedure. First swab the bore thoroughly with a solvent such as Hoppe's No. 9 or Birchwood Casey Bore Solvent; then push through three or four clean patches to dry the bore. Follow with a thin coating of grease. Rub the outside down thoroughly and cover with a thin layer of oil.

Most people overuse the oil. Too much oil harms the stock and runs down into the action. An old cartridge case inserted into the breech serves as good protection against chemicals and grease finding their way from the bore into the firing mechanism. It also is advisable to store guns muzzle down so that excess oil will drain away from the action.

Firing mechanisms often have too much oil rather than too little. In very cold temperatures excess oil may congeal, causing the gun to malfunction. Oil should be applied to the mechanism by the drop, and only one drop to each part which requires a lubricant, or spray a fine mist of WD-40 over the parts with a pressurized can. Finely powdered graphite is a good lubricant that won't congeal in cold weather and it can be obtained in most hardware stores.

Caution is the keynote when cleaning a telescopic sight. A scope lens has a delicate coated surface which is easily scratched. I use contact-lens wetting agent, putting a drop or two on the glass and wiping it clean. Eyeglass-cleaning liquid is essentially the same thing. A specially treated cloth used for cleaning eyeglasses also is good for scope lenses and will keep them from fogging. The next best is photographic lens tissue. A substitute in the field is a badly worn bill of currency. Avoid using handkerchiefs or other rough cloths, for they tend to scratch lenses. Also be cautious when applying oil to the outside of the scope, and don't get any on the lenses.

With open or peep sights, ordinary match smoke will help reduce glare. The front blade sight should be checked from time to time to see if it has been knocked loose. Also a spot check will assure that the back sight is seated on the correct elevation notch.

The luster on dull stocks can be restored by rubbing linseed oil or Tru-Oil Gun Stock Finish into the wood. Several applications may be necessary to get the finish exactly as you want it. Any of the bluing chemicals such as Perma Blue found in sporting-goods stores are good for covering small worn parts on the metal. A full-scale bluing job can be done at home with a Birchwood Casey Gun Blue Kit, but a gunsmith with his specialized equipment will do a better job.

A pre-hunt check of the rifle's safety is a simple precaution that no hunter should overlook.

6

Equipment

One of the really appealing aspects of deer hunting is that no elaborate equipment is needed. Theoretically, a person probably could get by on what he's got in the closet at home, excepting his weapon. Of course, there are certain refinements which make the sport more attractive and productive.

Take binoculars, for example. Many hunters have a misconception that binoculars are designed for long-distance work, in the wide-open spaces. Since most whitetails are killed at a range of 75 yards or less, binoculars often are overlooked as a deer-hunting asset.

In the brushy habitat of the whitetail deer, a binocular can perform a specific job. A binocular with good light-gathering capabilities can aid in probing the dark areas where deer can stand quietly and remain undetected. The hunter sitting still and looking often can see much more than when on the move. Sometimes just a flick of the ear or movement of the tail will give the deer away. By probing the brush with a binocular the hunter might detect this telltale movement when otherwise he would overlook it.

A scope sight will not substitute for a binocular, despite what you may have heard. The twin-eye picture of a binocular gives more field of view and depth perception. The scope sight was designed to aim through, nothing more. A binocular accomplishes the job of detecting deer much more effectively, and without putting a hunter into your gunsight before you decide he's not a deer.

A standard binocular generally will have two numbers stamped somewhere on it, such as 6×30. The first number designates the power of the glass. Six would mean six power, or six times magnification. An animal 600 yards away would be seen through the binocular the size it would appear at 100 yards to the naked eye. The second number, in this instance 30, is the diameter in millimeters of the objective lens, the large one farthest from your eye.

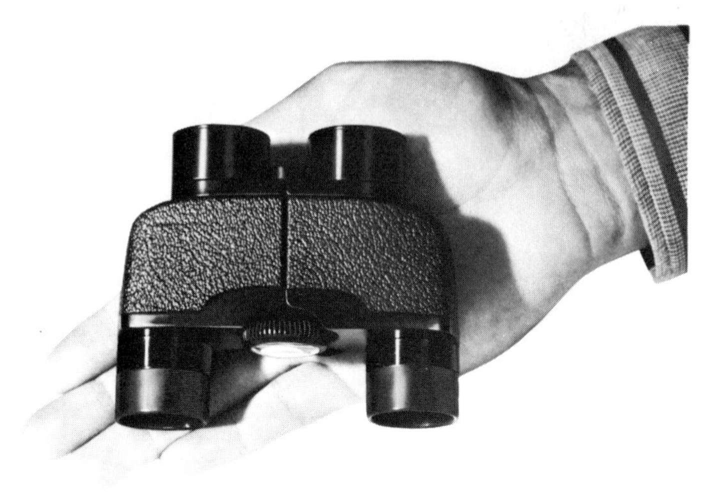

A compact pocket binocular, such as this Bushnell Custom Compact, will suffice for most whitetail terrain.

Divide the first number into the second and you get the light-gathering potential of the instrument, or the exit pupil as it is called. For the 6×30 binocular, the exit pupil would be 5mm. A 7×35 glass would also have an exit pupil of 5mm, a 7×50 one of 7mm, and so forth. The higher the last number the heavier the binocular, since the objective lens will be larger and will require a larger housing.

Since the eye won't dilate to more than 5mm under any normal hunting situation, a glass with a larger exit pupil won't be fully utilized. Something in the 6×30 or 7×35 class is more than adequate for whitetail terrain.

Notice that neither of the numbers has anything to do with field of view. This designation is stamped on only a few of the better-quality binoculars. It may be shown in numbers like 435′, which is the field of view in feet at 1,000 yards, or it may be in degrees, such as 7°. Using the formula of 1 degree field of view equals 52½ feet at 1,000 yards, you can determine the field of view for your particular instrument. The lower the power of the binocular, the more field of view it will have. (Some companies also market special wide-angle binoculars.)

The wider field of view is desirable in whitetail hunting since it will aid in studying areas of cover more extensively. In this kind of hunting you are searching for some specific part of the animal, rather than using the instrument to sweep across a vast swath of landscape simply looking for game. Often a binocular will reveal slight twitches of movement that will give the deer away, movement which would go undetected by the naked eye. A binocular also helps immeasurably when searching for the telltale antlers of a deer standing half-hidden in the shadows.

For most deer-hunting situations a compact binocular will suffice. Several companies make miniature models that will easily fit in a coat pocket and are lightweight. And the optics and field of view are surprisingly good. I use standard-size binoculars when I'm hunting in relatively open areas and will be glassing for deer hideouts most of the time. Otherwise, in heavier cover, I carry a compact model because I know I won't need to do as much glassing.

Hunting clothes will vary with the state, month, and terrain.

Well-known Vermont hunter Larry Benoit stresses that if the hunter is going to wait on a stand, he should dress warmly in order to remain in one place for as long as he wants without getting uncomfortable. But for walking, stalking, or tracking—which Benoit prefers—the hunter should not overdress. Benoit wears a T-shirt under a flannel shirt, wool jacket and pants, and well-fitting rubber boots that won't overheat in travel.

Underwear is very important, especially for the stand hunter who will be sitting motionless. The hunter with good foundation clothing will remain warm and comfortable, but the hunter with inadequate underwear will not. It is that simple.

Long johns are made from a variety of materials. Cotton is okay for moderate cold. But for low temperatures, thermal-action or quilted-type drawers are much superior. I like thermal-action underwear because it is less bulky and, for me, fits more snugly and comfortably. I also prefer the two-piece suit, since the top can be removed afield or simply left off on warmer days. Insulated underwear captures air between garment and skin to keep the hunter warm.

A lightweight down vest is a practical garment that affords freedom of arm movement yet keeps your torso warm. The torso and head have much to do with keeping your feet and hands warm. Mountain climbers and Arctic explorers have found that the torso pulls in blood (when it is cold) to keep the vital organs warm. If the torso is warm, it releases more blood to keep the hands and feet warm.

Wool still is the most popular material for outer garments. It has certain qualities which other natural and synthetic materials cannot match. For one thing, it is quiet—important for the hunter who is attempting to catfoot through the woods. For another, because of its porosity, wool provides warmth on the coldest days, yet is still fairly cool on warm days. Wool also dries from the inside out and retains some of its insulating power even when wet.

A good combination is a flannel shirt and wool trousers, or wool for both garments. Since I hunt in a climate where the temperature seldom dips below 25° during the deer season, I usually wear a flannel shirt and bluejeans. I feel more comfortable in the jeans and they stand up nicely against the punishment trousers take in the brush.

But be cautioned about denim or jeans. When dry, cotton jeans are comfortable and rugged, but if they get wet they lose about 90 percent of their insulating capability and even draw moisture to the garment's outside so that evaporation adds to the chill. The same is true of any cotton apparel such as sweat shirts and denim jackets.

Each year hunters die unnecessarily in the wilds. Sometimes deaths attributed to falls or other accidents might, in fact, be the result of hypothermia, commonly known as exposure sickness.

Hypothermia often strikes because a hunter foolishly tries to assume the role of he-man. He perhaps gets wet and instead of stopping to build a fire to dry out, he keeps pushing on. The victim, robbed of vital body heat by wind and dampness, becomes groggy, has difficulty making decisions, and might lose his sense of direction. This is why proper clothing is so important.

Jackets come in varied materials. That old standby, canvas, is still popular because it stands up well in brush and briers and can be waterproofed. Wool also is good. But most hunters prefer a quilted-type jacket which is warm, lightweight, and comfortable. The ability of a jacket of this type to do its job is determined by how much air it can trap, and that depends upon the stuff it is made of, how much of it is used, and how it is all put together.

The filler material for a quilted jacket will be either natural down or man-made fibers such as acetate, acrylic, and polyester. The manufacturer's label always should spell out the contents. (Quilted underwear has the same fillers.)

The function of a jacket of this type is to retain whatever heat is generated by your body without allowing the accumulation of moisture, which means it must breathe. Down, taken from mature northern geese, has the ability to trap more dead air per pound than any other material. It is expensive but you are paying for quality and comfort. Synthetics are the most popular because they will do the job for most situations at about half the cost or less. Some quilted jackets have tough nylon outer shells, both to break the wind and to keep the garment from tearing against brush. A few are made in blaze orange to satisfy hunting laws in some states. Otherwise, an orange vest must be worn over the shirt or jacket. There is a definite trend in most deer-hunting states to require the wearing of blaze orange for safety reasons. Connecticut, as one example, requires 200 square inches of the brightly colored material on cap and vest or jacket. Rhode Island has the same requirement, but nearby Massachusetts demands 500 square inches on chest, head, and back during the firearms deer season. Other states have similar requirements.

Gloves are optional. Personally, unless it is very cold, I prefer to go without them. I find handling a rifle with gloves is awkward. But if gloves are needed, I like a tight-fitting pair of buckskin gloves. In severe cold you can't go wrong with the Morris Feel Glove, made from waterproof wool with the ends of the index fingers and thumbs covered with a leatherlike substance to give a better "feel" when handling and shooting a shotgun or rifle.

Many states now require the wearing of blaze-orange for safety. This hunter is wearing a blaze-orange jacket and skull cap that fits atop a wide-brimmed hat. But the amount of blaze-orange varies by state.

Maybe the most important item of the hunter's apparel is his footgear. There is nothing more miserable than trying to sit motionless on a deer stand when your feet are aching from cold. Socks, as well as the boots, are important. Wool is good because the material cushions the feet and keeps them warm. Insulated socks also are popular. I like to put on a pair of thin cotton socks and cover them with wool socks, the cotton for comfort against itch and chafing, the wool for warmth.

When buying boots, always get them large enough to take the heavier socks and break them in before the season. Wearing a pair of new boots in the woods is just asking for blistered sore feet. A good hunting boot should be waterproof. I treat my leather boots regularly with either Snow-Proof or Original Mink Oil. Both soften the leather and also waterproof. For snow and wet weather, rubber boots are best. I wear leather when it is dry, rubber for snow or rain. The insulated rubber boots I own get warm if I do much walking and cause my feet to perspire. If I have a choice, I would rather wear leather. I like a spongy rubber sole since it makes for easier walking, especially on rocky soil. The height of the boot is a matter of personal preference.

The cap should be large enough so the ear flaps give adequate protection. For dry cold I like a stocking cap, sometimes called a watch cap. Bill-type caps should be waterproof. Cap color should be brilliant (some states require blaze orange) for safety. For severe cold, you might wear a full-face ski cap with eye slits along with a wrap-around wool neck muffler.

The importance of head cover can't be overemphasized. Tests reported by Holubar Mountaineering of Boulder, Colorado, reveal that even at a 40-degree temperature, as much as 50 percent of the body's generated heat can escape through the head if it is uncovered. At 5-degrees, heat loss can run as high as 75 percent.

Other than this, little equipment is actually needed. If you're planning on straying away from the road a good ways, always have a compass in your pocket and know how to use it. Another asset is a waterproof box of matches. You can carry them in one of those snap-top plastic containers that 35mm film comes packaged in. Just cut common household wooden matches to a length that fits.

Some sort of knife is needed to dress the kill. Most hunters like the common hunting knife, carried on a belt sheath which rests on the hip. Personally, I lean to an ordinary pocketknife with a 4-inch blade, because it seems my hunting knife is continually hanging on brush and deals me misery when I'm sitting on a deer stand. Also popular is the folding hunting knife which combines the best of two worlds, adequate size when open and compactness when carried. Again, this is simply a matter of personal choice, but remember that a big knife isn't needed to dress a deer. One with a 4- or 5-inch blade is adequate and lets you avoid packing that extra weight.

I always wear a wristwatch when deer hunting. It serves several useful purposes. For one, it aids me in keeping appointments, when I'm with other hunters. It also makes me more patient on a deer stand. Without this guide, I'm always inclined to move too soon.

A rifle sling also comes in handy at times. Not an elaborate shooting sling —just an ordinary carrying sling. A shooting sling is designed to steady the rifle for long-range shooting. Obviously you don't need that in deer hunting, at least not in most places where the whitetail roams. A carrying sling is nothing more than a strap of leather which fits on the swivels which come on many big-game rifles. A few temporary slings don't even call for the swivels; they snap on around the stock and rifle barrel. The sling allows you to throw the rifle over your shoulder when packing in a deer or maybe climbing into a tree stand. Caution: Unload the rifle first.

Here are some of the various fixed-blade and folding hunting knives available.

A hand warmer is particularly helpful to the stand hunter in cold climes. The stalk hunter at least gets to move about, keeping his blood circulating. The stocking-type protector mentioned earlier, one that slips over the head with holes for the eyes, nose, and mouth, also is comfortable. A hooded poncho that falls loosely around the body and is durable enough not to tear in the brushy habitat of the whitetail is best for rainy weather, although some hunters prefer the two-piece rainsuit. Whatever foul-weather gear you select, get material that won't tear easily and won't make a lot of noise.

A short length of rope is nice to have along when hanging up a dressed deer to keep it away from dirt and insects. Rope is also needed for tying the deer's feet together so a pole can be inserted for two hunters to pack the animal out. A sturdy plastic bag will carry the heart and liver of the deer, keeping fresh blood off your body and clothing. Another asset is a compact light-mesh deer bag, which fits over the deer and protects it from flies and other insects.

Remember, every piece of equipment you carry should be functional. Don't carry an item just because you feel you *might* need it. The hunter who travels light will travel comfortably. And in the deer woods there is no substitute for comfort.

7

Stand-Hunting

THERE IS ONE basic trait of deer behavior that every hunter should keep in mind: a deer's eyes are conditioned to movement and can be fooled by something which does not move.

The hunter who sits still, letting the deer move about and make the mistakes, is going to have much more success than the one who tries to carry the play to the sly creatures. The stand-hunter not only is going to see more game, he's also going to get better shots. This is particularly true in areas where there are a lot of hunters moving about, keeping the deer scattered. In most circumstances, the stand-hunter is going to get a shot at standing or slow-moving game; when moving around he might have to take a snap shot at one on the run. An immobile target naturally is going to be easier to hit and there's more chance for putting the bullet into a vital area.

Jerry Chiappetta, host of the television show "Michigan Outdoors," says his father taught him the wisdom of letting others do the work when hunting deer in crowded places. He explains, "On opening morning, get into the woods at least a half-hour before the crowd and be stationed on the best runway escape routes between hardwoods and brushy streambeds and lowland swamp where the deer like to take sanctuary when things get hot. Then in the afternoon, when other hunters are deep in the woods, get between the crowd and their cars on the road so that when they come thrashing back they will drive deer to you."

Deer trails, or so-called "runs," are used year after year, generation after generation. But deer will change their habits with the seasons, as the food sources change. One month they may be feeding predominantly on wild fruit; the next month on acorns. A trail may appear worn and well traveled, yet the evidence might be from the past. The idea, of course, is to locate a trail that is in use, or better yet, a spot where several trails come together.

A prime time to search for fresh tracks is just after a rain (left-hand photo). Soft ground allows deep hoof impressions that may give keys to the deer's size and sex. Look for signs of the rut (right-hand photo), such as where a buck has been rubbing his antlers against a sapling.

But a hunter doesn't simply wander into the woods and come to a likely spot by chance. There is too much country to cover. The wise hunter has a plan, a pattern he will follow. He knows the terrain and he knows the best spots for his ambush.

I can't emphasize too strongly the need for becoming familiar with the country you are to hunt. Take a day before the season and just walk leisurely through the woods, looking for deer sign and prominent landmarks. This serves a twofold purpose. It helps you locate your stands in the most strategic places and it might prevent you from becoming lost while hunting, when your mind is intent on something else.

"The main reasons why stand-hunters fail," says Mitch Rogers, "is a lack of knowledge about deer and failure to properly scout an area before hunting it." Rogers speaks with authority. He is a wildlife biologist with the Arkansas Game and Fish Commission and for almost a decade he has been in charge of the commission's experimental forest at Sylamore, studying the habits of whitetail deer in three square-mile pens. For another, in 23 years he accounted for 43 deer, just three short of his legal limit of two per year. Each season in Arkansas only about 10 percent of the hunters get their two-deer limits.

He explains that deer habitually follow the path of least resistance. Rather than walking over a hill, a deer will skirt around it in the hollow. The place to take a stand, Rogers goes on, is where there is a break such as where woods and field meet, or where pines and hardwoods meet, or where the mast (nuts from trees) stops, or near the edge of a road.

I like to get out about two days after a rain. This way all the tracks I find will be fresh. They'll readily stand out in the moist turf. Search along the worn avenues through the timber. Just a glance will ascertain whether or not deer are currently using the trail. Particularly good are trails leading into patches of dense cover, where deer likely will bed down. This way, if

Ground stands can be improvised from deadfalls, as shown above. In open country, any raised platform can be used. It's best not to silhouette yourself against the sky.

The stand-hunter should pick a spot near trails used by deer in their travels for food, water, and dense cover. Then he should get as comfortable as possible—and remain absolutely motionless.

you are on stand at daybreak, you can intercept any animal traveling from its feeding area to its bedding ground. Also good are trails leading to salt and mineral licks, where deer have been lapping on rocks to obtain necessities of their diet.

After finding a trail that deer are traveling you can then situate your stand. If you're at ground level, wait at a spot where you can see as much country as possible. If the area isn't too open, at least be where you can see through the underbrush, watching for the legs of a moving animal. Also situate your stand where the existing or prevailing wind won't blow your scent into the path of the oncoming deer.

Many persons have the misconception that stand-hunting requires no special ability. Nothing could be further from the truth. Successful stand-hunting is a true art, fully as demanding as other forms of hunting. One hunter might see numerous deer pass his stand; another a scant 100 yards away might not see anything.

The hunter can't haphazardly wander into the woods, idly search out a stand, sit down, and expect deer to start blundering over him. Position of the stand is vitally important. And there are other considerations, too.

The foremost consideration, of course, is to be hunting in known deer habitat. With any hunting, locating the game is half the solution to the mystery. The hunter in an area with an abundant population of deer is improving his chances tenfold for success.

Deer must have two basic things to survive: food and water. Protection also is important, but not nearly as much. Deer feed on such varied plants in various parts of the country that it would be impossible to chronicle them all here. The hunter seeking a prospective area to pursue his favorite sport should make local inquiries as to the best spots to hunt.

Once you have a general area pinpointed, look through it for more concrete deer signs, like tracks, droppings, browsed bushes, and telltale trails of travel. Try to situate your stand in an area where signs indicate a good concentration of deer. Locate it so that you command a view of a good deer run. Deer follow regular routes, and these "runs" can be distinguished where the grass is worn away, evidence of travel.

Arkansas deer-hunting expert Mitch Rogers says that when scouting he always looks for signs of rut, such as a rubbed sapling where a buck has been cleaning his antlers, or a scrape where the buck urinates and paws the ground around it to stake out his territory and leave his ready-and-willing calling card for any eligible does in the area.

Rogers adds that a buck will travel a circular route, rubbing and scraping as he goes. Sometimes the scrapes will be close together, other times farther apart. Should you locate such a fresh scrape, find a hiding place near it and watch patiently. Eventually that buck will return. He might come within a few minutes, or he might not come for days after. To get him you'll have to play the game on his terms.

Some hunters have the misconception that they must get as far away from camp as possible to hunt. True, in many instances it pays to get off the beaten path, back in the wilderness where there are fewer hunters. But in areas where there is less competition a stand a few hundred yards from camp might be as effective as one a mile away.

An acquaintance of mine was telling about a hunt he made some years ago in Jefferson National Forest, located in the mountainous part of western Virginia. On opening day of the season he slipped out of camp just at daybreak and walked for perhaps 500 yards when he came to a good deer run. Evidence showed that deer had been traveling frequently along this trail. Playing a hunch, the hunter found a good comfortable spot beside a tree, hunkered down, leaned back, and prepared for a long wait. But less than 30 minutes later a nice buck came tiptoeing down the trail and one shot put him down. It was a simple feat to drag the deer back to camp. The hunter had been gone less than an hour.

It isn't always that easy, of course, but you can never tell about deer hunting. One of the biggest bucks I ever saw killed in New Mexico was slain by a hunter sitting in camp. He was busy cleaning his rifle when he chanced to glance up and there stood this handsome buck in a clearing less than 100 yards away. The man gingerly fed a cartridge into the chamber, raised the rifle, and bowled the deer over.

Tom McNally, distinguished outdoor editor of the Chicago *Tribune* and a world-renowned hunter, will tell you that stand-hunting pays off—and he has one of the biggest bucks ever killed in Illinois to prove it. This one was bagged several years ago during a controlled hunt on the Horseshoe Lake Waterfowl Refuge near Cairo, at the southern end of the state.

McNally recalls that he'd found himself a likely spot in the swampy country to watch all about him. From his vantage point on a rotting log he could see clearly 60 yards in any direction through the cedars and oaks.

He had been sitting statuelike for maybe two hours, watching and listening, when suddenly he saw an immense buck step from the brush. The deer was perhaps 90 yards away—too far for a shot with the 20-gauge shotgun loaded with rifled slugs that McNally carried—and was angling across the swamp. McNally remembers that, at the time, he eased off the log and crouched behind it, hoping the deer, a monster of a buck with antlers like those of an elk, might come closer, but afraid it would walk right on by him.

Suddenly on the other side of the deer a shotgun boomed. The buck immediately swerved and came right at McNally, in a fast trot. Tom rested his shotgun over the log and waited until the deer passed into a clearing. Quickly he shot—once, twice. The deer sagged to his knees, then fell heavily.

This one had a 23⅜-inch antler spread, sported 14 points, and field-dressed 212 pounds.

The hunter who has a predetermined site for his stand has much better odds of scoring than does the person who tries to locate a likely stand the same day he plans to hunt. A stand should command a view of as much terrain as possible. In some areas this might be several hundred yards; in the brush it may be limited to seventy-five feet or less.

There are basically two types of stands, ground-level and elevated. A ground-level stand may be nothing more than the hunter leaning up

A tree stand allows the hunter to remove himself from the deer's natural direction of sight. Also, any scent he may leave will be blown high and away rather than along the ground where the deer can detect it.

against a tree, or maybe he'll construct a sort of enclosure of branches and brush for concealment. In areas where they are legal, tree stands are popular. By climbing back into the fork of a tree, the hunter has a wider view of terrain, he's up where deer seldom look, and any breeze tends to blow his scent high and away, rather than along the ground where deer can detect it.

In Florida, a hunter will pick a tree and erect a platform in it, sometimes an elaborate one, often nothing more than a board nailed in a fork. It is considered the lowest form of sportsmanship to get in another man's tree stand. In fact, it is almost sacrilegious.

A tree stand, legal in some form or fashion in every state, has certain advantages. From his elevated vantage the hunter can better see into the trees, briers, and thickets, especially if undergrowth is heavy. He is above the deer's normal line of sight and his scent normally will drift up and away rather than along the ground to spook any animals. And capricious wind changes seem to be the rule rather than the exception in the deer woods.

Ideally, the stand should be at least 12 feet off the ground. There basically are two types: permanent and portable. On some private lands the owners do not mind if hunters nail boards between tree forks, but this is prohibited in many areas such as state wildlife-management areas and forests owned by timber-growing companies. Some hunters construct platforms in trees to have room to either sit or stand or even move about to ease protesting leg muscles. A friend of mine built a platform in an oak, salvaged a bucket seat from a wrecked sports car, and bolted the seat to the boards. All the comforts of home!

Several types of portable stands can be bought. If you have the ingenuity and tools, you can build your own. Most commercial models are the seat or small platform type with some sort of bracket which fits around the tree and positions the stand securely. While these stands are portable, most hunters erect them in likely places and leave them during the duration of the season. One hunter might have as many as a half-dozen such stands.

Let me emphasize again that it is imperative to read the laws of the state where you intend to hunt before you use a tree stand. While the portable tree stand itself is legal in all states, most states prohibit portable tree stands and other climbing aids that damage trees.

Here are some random examples of present laws: Pennsylvania prohibits any tree-damaging stand, the exception being on private land where a person can construct a permanent stand provided he has written permission of the landowner. Arkansas law provides for permanent tree stands on private land only. In Georgia, on state-owned land or property leased by the state, only portable or natural tree stands are permitted. Kentucky allows permanent tree stands statewide except on the Land Between the Lakes Recreation Area. In Maryland, portable tree stands must be removed at night and they cannot damage trees. Virginia regulations provide for permanent stands on private lands only; no publicly owned trees can be damaged. In Florida permanent stands are restricted only in specified wildlife management areas. Permanent or portable stands in Minnesota cannot be more than 6 feet off the ground. In North Carolina it is "unlawful to erect or occupy, for the purpose of hunting, any tree stand or platform attached by nails, screws, bolts or wire to a tree on any state game land."

A prominent landmark in southern Texas is a windmill-like structure, a high tripod contraption, standing forlornly in the brush. Here, where, incidentally, all hunting is done on private lands, the artificial stands are erected to allow the hunter to get up high where he can look down in the patches of clearing scattered through the chest-high thornbrush. There are no trees here to speak of, certainly none high enough to climb into for a stand.

When you approach your stand, do so from upwind. Get right in and settle down, avoiding as much unnecessary moving around as possible, since this leaves your offensive odor spread everywhere. A deer's nose is its primary protection, and this whiff of human odor is one danger signal no creature of the wild ignores. And put any prevailing wind into your face, or blowing in at an angle, not to your back where your scent will be carried into the area you're watching.

These commercially made stands do not damage trees. The Baker tree stand, above, doubles as stand and climbing device for limbless trees. Note the safety belt—good idea.

Once on the stand, you must possess, above all things, patience and confidence and endurance. You might be tied to that spot for a long, uncomfortable wait. But at all times you must take the positive approach, confident that the next minute may be the magic time when that long-awaited deer walks into view. A man needs this self-confidence to hunt off a stand properly.

To have tenacity, the hunter must be comfortable. This means getting a stand where you can sit naturally and comfortably. Cramped muscles are the bugaboo of every stand hunter. Every time he moves for relief he is making movement and noise that an alert deer might pick up.

Wear warm, comfortable clothing. It is better to be overdressed than underdressed. If the temperature is low and a raw wind is blowing, insulated coveralls, such as those designed for snowmobiling, are very warm. These are easy to put on and take off, and all openings are tightly sealed with zippers. Get a pair large enough to fit over other clothing. You might want to wear the coveralls until the sun gets up, then shuck them if you get too warm. A chilled hunter is a careless hunter. Since much of the cold originates from the ground, take along something like a piece of tarp or heavy plastic to sit on. Also carry something to eat and a canteen of water. Don't try to push yourself unnecessarily. You're only defeating your basic purpose.

Many people can't adapt to stand-hunting. They simply don't have the patience. It is difficult to do a complete changeabout from the hustle and bustle of everyday life to simply waiting quietly, making like a statue. Ten minutes after the nervous hunter sits down he starts fighting the urge to move. He must brush at his nose or scratch his arm or sneeze or clear his throat—all giveaway sounds to the probing eyes and ears of a nearby deer.

Just remember that the stand-hunter's basic strategy is remaining absolutely motionless. If the human is moving, even when he's got terrain and wind in his favor, it is increasingly difficult to slip up on a wary, alert deer. You are challenging the animal in its own bailiwick. But when you are sitting still, it is the animal that is moving about, making the mistakes. In stand-hunting you are playing the odds.

Guy Clymer, a rancher friend of mine who has observed deer and their habits since the 1920s, said one of the animals won't pay much attention to a man out in the open, in the most conspicuous clothing, if he remains perfectly still. Yet sudden, abrupt movement is what gives the hunter away. A deer might not be overly alarmed by a slow, easy movement of an arm or leg, yet that flick of fast, unnatural movement may send a wily old buck pounding off into the brush.

Rather than fidgeting a little all the time, it is much better to sit absolutely still for as long as you can stand it, then move everything at once. Every couple of hours, or however, long you can endure the motionless wait, get up, stomp your feet, wiggle your arms to get the circulation going again, smoke a cigarette. Do this for a few minutes, then settle back down for another long-drawn-out endurance run. Perhaps it will be days before you even spot a legal deer. It is frustrating at times, but often very rewarding.

Arkansan Mitch Rogers says he will average from two to four hours per stay when stand-hunting. He also averages from 20 to 25 hours per deer—actual hunting time, not counting scouting—a fact that again stresses the importance of determination and patience. "I usually sit in one spot until I can't stand it any more, and then I force myself to stay for 30 more minutes," Rogers explains. "And I've killed a lot of deer in that last 30 minutes."

And remember to hunt with your ears as well as your eyes. Listen for any unnatural sounds. Listen for such things as the crunch of something in dry leaves, or the irritated chatter of a squirrel or the fussing of a bluejay—in short anything that might betray the whereabouts of your quarry. If you are prepared when the buck steps into sight, your chances of success are much improved.

A hunter who bagged one of the biggest bucks ever to come from the Black Hills region of South Dakota learned the value of stand-hunting quite accidentally. The hunter and his companion had separated and gone different ways into the densely wooded hills, in an area below Rapid City. All day they stalked through the draws and along the ridges covered heavily with pines and oaks without seeing a buck. Finally, just before sundown, the first hunter came to an old logging road where he'd agreed to meet his companion. He sat down on the thick carpet of fallen leaves, rested his back against a large pine tree, and waited, watching down the road for some sign of his companion. But instead, about ten minutes later, two deer came into view around a bend, walking leisurely up the road. The lead one was a doe, but behind her came a massive buck. There really was no time to get excited. The hunter threw up his rifle and put a .30/06 slug in the buck's brisket.

Who knows—the same could happen to you. That very next minute may be the climax to the long and muscle-cramping hours you've spent waiting and watching and listening. That's why it always pays to remain alert.

8

Stalking and Tracking

THE GREATEST challenge in hunting is getting out and meeting the whitetail deer on its own terms in its own bailiwick. Stalking, it is called. The hunter pussyfoots stealthily through the woods, always watching and listening. Being constantly on the move, he naturally looks at more hunting territory than he would stand-hunting. But at the same time, he's making himself more open to detection.

The hunter *can* sneak up on deer. I've done it numerous times. It only requires a special technique with accent on speed. Slow speed, that is. The slower the better.

I recall a buck I fooled this way some years back. I was hunting in west-central Texas, in Kimble County near the town of Junction, in wild and rugged country of canyons and deep-cut draws, liberally sprinkled with rocks. It was the type of country where a hunter must be doubly cautious to keep from announcing his approach to every deer within hundreds of yards.

All day I was continually on the move. Once that morning, a wise old buck outwitted me. There was an oval-shaped flat, studded with mesquite trees, fanning out in front of a sharp-rising hill. The deer had bedded down on the side of the hill where he could watch the flat and glimpse anything that suggested danger.

I was still a full 200 yards from the hill when I spotted movement up near the hogback ridge. I got my scope sight on it just as the fleeing deer topped the rise and vanished down the other side. As the deer crossed over I got a glimpse of antlers, a bragging-sized rack. This deer didn't live to enjoy old age by being dumb.

But actually, a deer isn't smart. At least not in the way we reckon smartness and intelligence. It is cunning and sly, all right, but not smart with the facility of gathering facts and reasoning a situation out.

The hunter can think. This is his one big advantage. If he knows deer habitat and the kind of terrain the critters prefer, he can, by simple deduction, know where to plan his stalk in order to assure the greatest odds for success.

Later that same day, near sundown, I'd dropped over a knoll and into a basinlike depression filled with persimmon trees and small cedar bushes. It was a likely-looking spot for deer, so I slowed up and really started concentrating and looking, taking each step as if I were walking on eggshells. I skirted a clump of brush and walked right up on a feeding deer. It was half-hidden behind a squat cedar, but when it heard me it threw up its head, above the bush.

The first thing I noticed was antlers. I threw up the rifle, aimed at the neck, and squeezed the trigger in one instinctive motion. The seven-pointer crumpled, a mere 22 paces from where I stood.

As we mentioned before, the deer's best defense is its nose. Always respect it. When stalking, hunt into the wind, or quarter into a prevailing breeze; never have it on your back.

The hunter should also keep in mind that deer habitually feed into the wind. The generally accepted explanation for this is that the deer's hair lies back and the animal prefers to have the wind blowing over the hair naturally, rather than under the hair from the back. This is the deer's protection against the elements. It also gives the deer the advantage in that anything which crosses ahead will have its scent blown right to the deer's nose.

The stalker should depend more on his eyes and less on his feet. Stalking may be described as stop-and-go hunting – moving a few feet, then stopping and unraveling the woods ahead, looking for anything that might betray the presence of a deer.

But take away its nose and the deer doesn't possess any super-plus advantage. Sure, its ears and eyes are sharp, with more latitude than those of the human's. Yet they aren't nearly as extraordinary as most people would believe. In the ordinary frequency of sound waves, in the range that humans detect, the deer can't hear a whole lot better than you or I. And the eyes are not so sensitive that the deer can stand off 100 yards and see you crook your finger.

So when you have the wind in your favor, your chances of success are almost 50-50, provided you plan your stalk properly. Of course, any deer is going to hear and see a hunter who blunders double-time through the noisy woods, making no effort to conceal his sound or movement.

The foremost tendency among run-of-the-mill hunters is to walk fast. It is literally impossible to hunt too slowly. Sensible strategy is to hunt a small stretch of woods thoroughly and correctly, rather than to cover lots of terrain haphazardly.

When stalk-hunting, take one step and stand still for the count of two. After each step this means to stop briefly and look and listen. A deer has wonderful camouflage which causes it to blend almost perfectly with the background, but it often gives itself away by movement, either the raising of the head or a twitch of the tail. The hunter can also actually hear deer, the noises they make while moving around, if he can learn to listen for all the sounds of the woods, disregarding those which belong naturally in the environment, and detect those which play an integral part in his hunt.

My hunting buddy Murry Burnham is about as good at this as anyone I know. He prefers to call it still-hunting. Whatever, he can glide through the woods almost like a ghost. His concentration is total. His eyes are quick to detect even the most insignificant clues that might betray a deer's presence.

"Still-hunting demands a lot of patience," Murry told me. "It is a mistake to call it walking. Walkers get their deer only by accident. You must learn to move in slow motion, or maybe I should say extra-slow motion. In a place where I have a strong hunch a buck might be, I probably will take an hour to travel 100 yards. Watch every step so you don't clink rocks, break sticks or rustle leaves. When you come to an opening, skirt it, like a deer; don't expose yourself in the open. Watch and don't move where you will be skylined, even in timber. Always be alert to what's happening."

I've been stalk-hunting ever since I was old enough to tote a rifle. In the beginning I always wanted to keep moving, hunting hastily, trying to see as much country as I could. My father was continually harping on me to slow down. Finally, when I did discover for myself that I could kill many more deer and expend much less energy, I did slow down my pace and start hunting the way I should. I've never regretted it.

Actually, hunting too fast can be harmful. For the man who is used to sitting behind a desk throughout the year, getting out in the woods and trying to walk five or ten miles a day can have serious repercussions. Many men die out in the woods each year from heart attacks. They simply weren't used to the extra exertion. So take it easy. You'll see more deer, come in at day's end feeling much better, and, who knows, maybe even save your life.

Footgear is important to the stalk-hunter. Choose a boot with a soft sole, something that will absorb noise rather than reverberate it. Bird-hunting pacs are ideal for this kind of hunting. My veteran deer-hunting friend Guy Clymer goes this one further. He wears ordinary tennis shoes. He suffers with the cold, but he's a very successful stalk-hunter. He'll bet you money he can walk right up on a deer, within 25 paces, and he'll win almost every time.

When hunting hilly country, learn to slip quietly to the ridges and peek over to watch for deer on the opposite side. Learn to approach behind bushes or rocks to break your silhouette. The stalk-hunter can't be too careful.

The best country, we repeat, for stalk-hunting is that where there are few other hunters. The real secret of successful stalking is to be able to sneak up on unaware deer, perhaps one that is feeding. In country where heavy hunting pressure keeps the deer stirring about, they are going to be more spooky and more likely to detect the walking hunter.

My friend David Barnett will argue that point. He is a regular visitor to northern Minnesota, near the Canadian border, each hunting season. And although he is a stalk hunter, when he goes into the woods, he likes company—companions of his own choosing, that is.

His party of five have been hunting together for almost a decade, and they score about as consistently as any hunters I know. Their technique is unique, something like drive-hunting, as described in the next chapter, yet there are no standers. Each person hunts alone, yet the presence of all five helps each.

It works like this. They pick a likely stretch of woods and, fanning out maybe 100 yards apart, they hunt facing or quartering into the wind. They stalk-hunt, taking one step or two, stopping and looking and listening, then moving and pausing again. Moving quietly and slowly like this, they don't frighten the deer. The animals only become a little agitated and attempt to double back into their home territory. Trying to elude one hunter, the deer often blunder into the gunsights of another.

But when hunting alone even in the most heavily hunted country, the wise deer hunter knows he can get a mile or so off public roads and have the country virtually to himself. The average American is a lazy and conservative hunter. He won't extend any extra effort toward getting his deer, and once out of sight of familiar landmarks, like the road, he becomes panicky because he fears getting lost. The hunter who is preoccupied with something else can't give stalk-hunting the concentrated effort and undivided attention it demands.

When you head into the woods always carry a compass, particularly in strange terrain where landmarks are not familiar. Learn how to use it. Even the most observant hunters sometimes become lost, however. It is no disgrace to lose your way in this environment. The disgrace is to panic.

Should you find yourself hopelessly turned around, fire the conventional three-shot lost signal and sit down and wait. Don't move. If someone knows where you are supposed to be, and this information should always be left with a relative or friend before you depart, then it won't be long before it is realized you are overdue and someone will come looking for you.

In this respect also remember to carry a supply of matches with you. They could come in handy, to build a fire for warming or for signaling.

In stalk-hunting, many hunters miss their opportunities because of fatigue. Stalk-hunting is walking, slow as it might be, and the hunter is on edge, always looking; here tension can sap a person's energy rapidly. It is very tiring, particularly if you've been sitting in an office all year and you're not used to the exercise. Fatigue can dull reflexes, and often just an instant of hesitation in that moment of truth when a deer is sighted may make the difference between success and failure.

The smart hunter gets in shape for the deer season, especially if he has an office job and is out of shape. Since hunting is mostly walking, this exercise should be engaged in regularly for several weeks before going afield. Instead of jumping in the family auto for a trip to the nearby grocery, walk. Perhaps if your office isn't far away you can walk to and from work. Begin

Float hunting is a possibility in many regions, and not only is it fascinating, it is also productive. Since deer usually are found along a riverbed, the floater should float quietly to keep from alarming the critters.

with a short distance and gradually increase it, adding a quarter-mile about every second or third day. At the same time, step up the speed of hiking. In two or three weeks you should be able to clip off three or four miles without strain. Walking is one of the most healthful yet least strenuous of exercises. It won't condition your heart the way jogging will, but it will get you in shape for hunting.

In the week prior to the deer season, wear your regular field boots or shoes. This serves a twofold purpose. You get the footwear properly broken in and you become accustomed to the added weight. Walking a few flights of stairs daily will bring still other muscles into play. One of the best exercises I've found is to jog up and down the steps of the local football stadium.

If you're overweight, it also pays to take off a few extra pounds. You don't have to cut down on your food consumption to accomplish this. Just follow a high-protein diet. Lay off starches and sweets. Eat plenty of meats and greaseless foods. The protein consumes fat. Being in shape for stalking not only intensifies the pleasures of the hunt, it also will make you more alert, quicker to spot game and take full advantage of your opportunities when they do beckon.

A popular method of stalk-hunting, particularly in some Midwestern states, is by canoe or boat. Hunters put in on streams, on public land of course, and float with the current, scrutinizing both shorelines for deer. It is best if two hunters work as a team, one watching the left bank, the other the right. This is one of the most fascinating of all ways to hunt, and also one of the most productive, since the hunter is covering lots of territory, yet making very little noise, and he's in wilderness country where there is apt to be much less hunting pressure.

The float-hunter shouldn't expect to cover much real estate in a single day. It is best to hunt a limited stretch slowly and thoroughly. A favorite system is to use a pair of vehicles, one for in, one for out. Get a map of the area you intend to hunt and attempt to find two public-access points about the right distance apart. Many hunters are unaware of the many different maps that are available. As for federal lands, information and maps can be obtained from any of the regional Forest Service offices, the addresses of which are listed below:

Write, Regional Office, U.S. Forest Service, at:

Region 1 (Northern): Federal Building, Missoula, MT 59801

Region 2 (Rocky Mountain): 1177 W. 8th Avenue, P.O. Box 25127, Lakewood, CO 80225

Region 3 (Southwestern): Federal Building, 517 Gold Avenue, S.W. Albuquerque, NM 87101

Region 4 (Intermountain): Federal Office Building, 324 25th Street, Ogden, UT 84401

Region 5 (California): 630 Sansome Street, San Francisco, CA 94111

Region 6 (Pacific Northwest): 319 S.W. Pine Street, Box 3623, Portland, OR 97208

There is no Region 7.

Region 8 (Southern): Suite 800, 1720 Peachtree Road, N.W., Atlanta, GA 30309

Region 9 (Eastern): Clark Building, 633 W. Wisconsin Avenue, Milwaukee, WI 53203

There also are other possibilities, such as a U.S. Geographical Service topo map. (See Chapter 13 for details.) Information on getting aerial photomaps can be had at the local U.S. Soil Conservation Service. A common state highway map is of some assistance, but even better is a county traffic-flow map, which is usually available from the state highway departments. Don't forget your state's conservation or game and fish department. It may be a goldmine of information, and it might have maps plus a list of public areas and streams which can be floated for deer hunting. Timber or tree-growing companies which open their lands to hunting usually have maps available. Don't overlook such areas. Many timber companies welcome hunters and some offer very good deer hunting. Their practice of cutting trees and encouraging new growth is conducive to large and healthy deer herds. These holdings are both vast and far-flung. (Some companies own lands in several states.) I've hunted in private forests owned by the St. Regis Paper Company and Brunswick Pulp Land Company, both in Georgia; on Union-Camp Corporation lands in South Carolina, and on lands owned by the Southland Paper Company in eastern Texas. While some of these lands are open to public hunting, others are leased by private hunting clubs.

Now you're ready to go. Take two vehicles, each hunter driving one, to the spot where you expect to terminate your hunt. Park one there and drive the other to the starting point. This way transportation will be available when you arrive. Some hunters plan on several days afloat, pausing on the way downstream to camp along the stream shore, maybe mixing in a little fishing with the hunting. But one note of caution. Before camping, check on local regulations. In some national forests, camping is restricted to supervised campgrounds, and in some, you must obtain a permit to build a campfire. Always be sure you're within the law before building a camp anywhere.

At times stalk-hunting can be very productive; other times, stand-hunting is the only logical way to hunt. Often, then, the ideal system is a blend of the two. Some hunters sit on a stand until they feel they must move, then stalk-hunt until their muscles unwind and their blood is circulating freely again, then they look for another stand to wait a spell.

Bill Klapp likes to tell about the time when such a plan paid off handsomely. Bill, now retired, was at the time of this hunt the owner of the Original Sight-Exchange Company in Paoli, Pennsylvania. Here's how he tells the story:

"Ralph Buffett, a gunsmith, and I were hunting in the Seven Mountains Range of the Allegheny Mountains in Center County, Pennsylvania, in Shingletown Gap. It was opening day of the season and we started hunting,

Ralph and I, up the side of a mountain. There was snow on the ground which made for quiet traveling. It also was about two degrees below zero, uncomfortably cold to sit on a stand for any length of time; so I figured we'd stalk-hunt a while, then sit down and watch until we got cold before getting up and moving again.

"I went ahead about 100 yards beyond Ralph, figuring that other hunters I knew camped up on top of the mountain might spook some deer down our way, and if one should come down and see me before I could get a shot, it might swerve and sneak across behind me, affording Ralph a shot.

"Here the mountains go almost straight up, to about 2,300 feet elevation, and it was tough walking. I also had to move very slowly to watch in the heavy cover. Hardwoods like hickory, beechnut, spruce, and pine grow profusely on the mountainsides, and there is a lot of rhododendron and laurel for ground covering. It is very difficult to see a deer in this underbrush.

"We'd gone up the mountain trail for maybe two or three miles when I heard a shot behind me. I turned around and hurried back and found Ralph bending over a nice six-point buck lying in the laurel at the edge of the trail. Our strategy had worked out perfectly and Ralph had dropped the buck with a single shot from his .32 Remington.

"We gutted the deer and took it back to the car. Then we headed up the same trail again. After walking this time for about five miles, I decided to sit down, catch my breath, and do a little stand-hunting. In a few minutes I heard a twig snap and shortly two deer, a small one and a large one, came into view, walking up the trail. I raised my .35 Remington, peered through the Lyman Alaskan scope, and noticed the big one had a large set of horns.

The author, armed only with a camera, slipped up on this buck in his bed. A stalk hunter can do the same thing during the deer season.

"One shot in the heart region did it. And I tell you, when we drove out with a buck on each fender of the car, we got a lot of envious glances from other hunters."

This is one instance when a contributing factor, the weather, dictated a combination of stand- and stalk-hunting. There are other such factors. Like the habits of deer, for instance. During a typical hunting day, the deer will be up and about early in the morning and late in the day, feeding and watering. The tendency then is for them to bed down in the midday hours. To allow for this behavior, the strategy would be to stand-hunt in the early morning and late afternoon, when deer are up and moving about, and stalk-hunt during those hours when the critters are resting in the underbrush, hoping to roust one from its bed for a shot.

Favorite bedding spots for deer are along timbered and brush-covered ridges and in the swamps. The hunter who jumps a deer from its bed can expect, usually, to get only a fleeting, running shot at the animal. This kind of hunting demands a hunter who can size up a situation in a split-second and adapt himself accordingly.

Most hunters overestimate the speed of a deer. They tend to lead running animals too much. The system I prefer is to swing the gun in the direction the deer is moving, pulling up until the sight centers on the neck before firing. This way the movement of the gun will be in synchronization with the running deer, and a bullet fired at the neck, discounting the time lapse it takes a hunter's reflexes to react, will usually hit the animal somewhere in the shoulder region.

Tracking is another method of hunting deer. In a way, it is an offshoot of stalking. It is, basically, nothing more than following tracks, hoping to get a shot at whatever is making those tracks.

This system is, at its best, only a long-shot affair in most places. I once read a newspaper account of a hunter in the Cedar Stream area of New Hampshire who spent almost two full days on a deer spoor. He got on the trail early one morning, kept after it all day, marked the spot near nightfall where he quit the track, returned the following morning, and dogged the deer for almost another full day before bagging a big buck just at sundown.

Me, I don't have that kind of perseverance. Yet that's what it takes. The hunter must stick with it if he is to track down a deer. It is no easy feat.

The trouble is, the hunter often doesn't know how old a track may be. Perhaps he will take out on a trail that was made the previous day. Naturally, his chances of getting a shot at that particular animal are almost nil.

There is one time, however, when tracking definitely pays off. Suppose you were driving down a country lane when a buck jumped across the road in front of you. This is a hot track. Get right on it and mind your ABC's of tracking and the odds are in your favor that you'll get a shot.

Another good time for track searching is just after a fresh snowfall.

Should a new layer of the white stuff be added to the ground overnight, you'll know that any tracks you come across are fresh.

And, with apologies for sounding too pessimistic, there is still another deterrent to the tracker. Often he doesn't know if he is trailing a buck or a doe. In areas where either is legal, this isn't important. But it is to the hunter out exclusively for a buck.

The male and female deer do make different tracks, but it requires an experienced eye sometimes to ascertain the difference. A big track doesn't necessarily mean it was left by a buck, yet usually it has been. But the main characteristics to watch for are toeing-out of the front feet, one mark of the buck, and a gait that shows the front feet wider apart. If there are two sets of tracks, doe and buck, you can readily tell the difference. A buck tends to drag his forefeet in light snow and sometimes swaggers, while a doe has this tendency only in deeper snow. The doe almost invariably puts the print of her back feet directly over those of the forefeet, while bucks often do not, and a buck will show some spreading between the two halves of the forefeet when walking naturally, while does do this only when running. A buck will dribble droppings as he walks but a doe deposits hers all in one spot. A doe will pass under a low-hanging limb; a buck will go around it.

Larry Benoit of Duxbury, Vermont, is recognized as a master of tracking. In fact, it is news when he *doesn't* get a trophy buck. He likes to get into the back country where he has things to himself, on remote ridges, deep in the swamps, in hidden basins. Nothing escapes his probing eyes. He is continually searching for clues that indicate a big buck has just passed this way. He says he can tell just by looking at tracks whether a buck will go better than 200 pounds. He also sees telltale signs that the novice would overlook, such as marks where a buck has dragged his feet, or antler-tine marks in the snow around a buck's bed.

Tracking is a fascinating way to hunt deer and is possible in any area where snow falls during the season, from Oregon and Washington across the Great Lakes states into the East. But remember that deer also are aware they are leaving a telltale traveling card with their tracks and they are much more wary and alert when there is snow on the ground. They are continually watching their backtrack, and the hunter must be doubly cautious.

Should the tracks lead into a thicket, this might be where the deer has elected to bed down. It often pays to skirt the thicket, searching for outcoming tracks. If there are none, the deer probably is still in there and you can work to spook him out where you stand the best chance of getting an open shot. Another thing to keep in mind is the wind. Perhaps while you are trying to circle the thicket, you'll cross the prevailing breeze, sweeping your scent right into the thicket. Should this happen, probably all you'll hear is a crashing noise meaning the buck has fled.

Larry Benoit says the tracker following a traveling deer should depend on his eyes, watching ahead for the buck, studying the track to see what the

If only suspicious and not frightened, a crafty old buck usually will try to sneak away from danger rather than run. But when spooked, a buck will take off.

critter is doing. If tracks indicate the buck is running, loping, or striding, you should crank up and get after him; but when you see indications that the deer has slowed, meandered, you should commence sneaking and eyeballing the woods carefully. This is not time to hurry. Look for anything that appears unnatural. The buck might be browsing or bedded down. You don't want to alarm him before you get a shot.

Tracking produced the biggest whitetail killed in 1963 and one of the largest typical heads recorded. Early T. McMaster of Columbia Falls, Montana, got this one in the foothills along the fringe of the continental divide near Columbia Mountain in Montana. He first saw the huge buck standing alongside the road. Later, he returned, located the deer's tracks, and stealthily followed the telltale spoor through fresh snow. Some time afterward he came upon the deer in a clump of brush and killed it. The antlers scored 191⅝ points in Boone and Crockett Club competition. (In 1973 the Boone and Crockett Club entered into joint sponsorship of records-keeping with the National Rifle Association of America (NRA). This alliance is now known as the North American Big Game Awards Program.)

Since a deer being tracked, and aware that a human is on its trail, has a tendency to keep moving and out of sight, often hunters combine tracking and stand-hunting to ambush the wary animal. This is a popular method throughout the Midwest. A hunter or two will remain on the deer's trail while other hunters circle ahead and take stands, hoping to intercept the deer as the trackers push it along.

There are many variations of this, such as the procedure that produced one of the largest bucks ever killed in Ohio. Arlee McCullough of Newark, Ohio, got him. He'd tracked the buck and some does for a few hours one afternoon. Just at dusk, the deer entered a large stand of brush. McCullough figured this was where the animals would bed for the night. Early the following morning he picked a strategic spot where he could watch the brush and sat down and waited. Soon something or someone spooked the deer. They came running from the brush. McCullough got on the big buck with his Marlin shotgun loaded with rifled slugs and hit it twice running.

As with conventional stalking, the tracker must accept the fact that most of his chances will be at running deer, unless he's particularly adept at setting up the animal for a standing shot. Usually the deer sights the hunter, rather than vice versa. The hunter will see the game, all right, but by the time he does, the deer will be on the retreat. Running deer aren't impossible to hit, but the hunter must have confidence in his ability and must know how to handle his firearm properly under such conditions.

During the summer months some friends and I like to play shooting games which condition our reflexes for the upcoming autumn deer seasons. To simulate a running deer, we insert a piece of cardboard in the hole of an old automobile tire. One man stands on the side of a hill and starts the tire rolling down. He then steps behind some sort of protection like a large boulder or tree, for obvious reasons. The tire comes bouncing erratically, building up momentum as it speeds on its downward course. The hunter stands off to one side and fires at the cardboard insert.

In some places, commercial ranges are being constructed to allow hunters, who pay fees, to shoot at realistic deer targets as they move in an erratic circular pattern on a track.

Another game we play is devised by painting silhouettes on large squares

Roused by a stalking hunter from its midday nap, a whitetail buck presents only a fleeting target as it bounds into the underbrush. Stalking is most productive during the day when the deer are bedded. *Courtesy Nebraska Game Commission.*

of cardboard (those cartons that mattresses come packed in are ideal). Normally, we try to paint up about twelve such silhouettes. On four cardboard squares are sketched the outlines of humans; on the rest are painted deer.

One person, in advance, goes along a game trail and hides the cardboard squares in upright positions, in inconspicuous places but still visible from the trail. Then the other person, armed, catfoots along the trail, searching for the silhouettes, which can be painted in actual colors to further simulate true hunting conditions. When he spots one of the silhouettes, he first must determine whether or not it is legal game, a deer not a human, and then, if it is a deer, he must get off a shot as quickly as possible (our time limit is ten seconds). The person who scores the most hits is the winner. Should there be a tie, then the person who puts the greatest number of shots in vital areas is declared the champ.

A friend of mine tunes his reflexes for the hunting season with some backyard practice every afternoon after work for about a month before the main event. First he checks to be sure his weapon is unloaded. Then he stands in the back yard and watches for anything moving overhead, a pigeon perhaps, or an airplane. He swings on the flying object, picks it up in his sight, and dry-fires a round. When he starts he says he has a problem picking up the object immediately, but after just a few days' practice he can shoulder the rifle and find it in his scope right away.

But shooting is just one facet of this game. It is equally important to make sure of your target before pulling the trigger. Just because there is no visible bright clothing is no reason for shooting. The hunter should never, never fire at an object just because he *thinks* it's a deer.

To protect himself, I repeat, the hunter also should take precautions to make himself readily visible to other hunters. This means wearing bright clothing. The time-honored brilliant reds and yellows are still good. But even better is fluorescent blaze orange. This was discovered in a series of exhaustive tests at Fort Devens, Massachusetts, to determine which colors afford hunters the best protection. The advantage of both these fluorescent colors is that they can be distinguished by color-blind people, who comprise something like 8 percent of the total population. That is why many states demand that blaze orange be worn.

To develop accuracy in leading running deer, practice with an automobile tire rigged with a target and rolled down a gentle slope. Most hunters tend to lead a deer too much. Swing with the animal and aim at the neck region for a hit in the shoulder area.

9

Driving, Rattling, and Calling

ORGANIZATION OFTEN pays off in deer hunting as well as it does in a business venture. Through teamwork, hunters frequently can get shots at deer when they'd only draw blanks if attempting to go it alone.

In some hunting areas, such as Pennsylvania, the hunter has his choice of using whatever method he prefers to get his deer. But there are some isolated instances when a well-planned drive is almost demanded if the hunters are to succeed. A good example is the Louisiana swamp country. Here men can't move about in pursuit of deer because of the quagmirelike terrain. Specially trained dogs are used to push the deer toward standers stationed in strategic positions to intercept any bucks rousted from the swampy marshes by the hounds, which can be of almost any breed. Such hound strains as Walkers, blueticks, and black-and-tans are among the favorites. In Arkansas, many deer hunters employ beagle hounds. They say these short-legged dogs are ideal for this kind of hunting since they keep the deer stirring, yet because they are slow, they don't excite the animals as much and don't drive them out of the country. One special kind of dog used in Louisiana is the Catahoula hound, named after Catahoula Parish, where it is used extensively by deer hunters. This hound was developed by the crossbreeding and interbreeding of many hound strains to get a dog especially adapted to swamp country.

Driving with dogs is frowned upon in most deer-hunting areas, but in some circumstances the canine assistance not only is helpful, it is necessary. And deer hunting in the wild and forbidding swamp country is about as exciting a sport as a person could find anywhere.

Noted dog expert and writer David Michael Duffey thinks the person who hunts deer with hounds has been unjustly maligned. He says, "When a man takes the time and effort to train a dog, he's usually more concerned with the dog's performance rather than with how much game is bagged or who kills it. As a result, he's more considerate of others and likely to observe niceties and self-inflicted rules."

Veteran Florida hunter Don Fox notes there is a difference between a good deer hound and just any hound. The quality deer hound has the ability to cold-trail and jump his own deer. Fox, like many Southern hound hunters, uses a good cold-trailer as a track checker before other hounds are turned loose. "I don't like a hound that will trail but won't open until the scent gets real hot," Fox explains. "I want to keep track of what is going on."

After some trial and error, Fox has settled mostly on July hounds because "these are dogs that can jump a deer and stick with it and tell you where it is and what it is doing even if it isn't running hot." But most prized is that "jump dog" which will find and unravel a cold trail and get things going.

Drive-hunting can be of various forms. As few as two people can drive deer successfully, or maybe as many as 20 or 30 will be employed.

Bill Klapp tells about a time when he and H. Wilson Orr were hunting in Huntingdon County, Pennsylvania. They were hunting around a large apple orchard where the farmer said many deer had been coming to eat the fruit and feed on his young trees. Along one side of the orchard were the foothills of the Allegheny Mountains. While hunting around the orchard, Klapp happened to glance up on one of the hills and noticed a large buck crossing through a clearing and disappearing into a thicket.

The hunters assumed the deer had entered the thicket to bed down. Hastily working out a strategy, the hunters decided that Orr would hide in some bushes down from the thicket while Klapp would circle to the opposite side and attempt to flush the buck out for a shot.

After reaching a point on the other side of the knoll, just down from the thicket, Klapp commenced to walk a zigzag course up the knoll, making as much noise as possible. Sure enough, in a few minutes Klapp heard a shot, and when he reached the place where Orr had been hiding, his companion was busy field-dressing the big buck. The strategy had worked out just as planned. Orr said the deer simply walked down the knoll, stopped, and looked back. A single shot from a .30/06 did the job.

One of the first deer I ever killed blundered unsuspectingly right into an ambush, a hastily conceived scheme where I actually had the buck driven to me. It was no great shakes of a drive, mind you, but nothing more elaborate nor more carefully planned could have worked out any better.

O. D. Tinsley, my father, and I jumped a group of deer, three does and a forkhorn buck, from a small brushy header. We caught just a flash of them topping the ridge and disappearing on the yonder side. Dad, being familiar with the country, knew the deer were crossing over into a deep-slashed canyon choked with cedar trees. If we gave immediate chase there would be little hope for a shot at the wily brush-wise animals.

But Dad, who has killed more deer in a lifetime of hunting than he'd care to admit, knows the behavior of whitetails, how they react under specific circumstances. This knowledge proved to be the downfall of the buck.

Dad instructed me to work down the header and circle until I came to the mouth of the canyon, find a vantage point, and watch the canyon mouth. Chances are the deer would stay in the cover, he explained, not moving any farther. At least that's what he was gambling on.

After 20 minutes, enough time for me to get into position, Dad would climb over the ridge and down into the canyon. He'd hunt slowly along the floor toward the mouth. The deer, he figured, would probably slip down the canyon, staying within the protection of the cover and moving quietly to conceal their retreat. If things worked out according to plan, the buck should pass just below where I waited impatiently in ambush.

Dad turned out to be a prophet. About halfway down the canyon, he must have spooked the deer, for I saw the three panicked does angling up the opposite side and topping out on the ridge. But there was no sign of the buck.

Minutes later, I heard a clicking of stones in the dry-washed innards of the canyon. Shortly, the phantomlike buck eased into view, stepping lightly, head tucked down, sneaking from the canyon. It was almost too easy. I guess that's why I missed with my first try—I overshot. But fortunately the deer didn't scare.

Instead, he threw up his head alertly, searching for whatever had caused the commotion. The second shot from my .30/30 staggered him. He ran a couple dozen yards before piling up limply against a small oak tree.

These are two examples of the crudest form of driving, employing only two drivers, the method most widely used by deer hunters. A successful drive can be organized by as many hunters as may be handy. In the pine barrens of New Jersey, a far-reaching drive might include 40 or 50 hunters.

Sal Urso of New York City, a member of the Pennsylvania deer club Whitetail Sportsmen, said his group's typical drive will include 16 to 20 hunters. They are divided into two teams by a drawing, and the groups alternate standing and driving. Drivers maintain a fairly straight line while moving through the woods, and every driver and stander knows where every other member of the party is at any given time. This is precise teamwork. Drivers are prohibited from shooting to either side, but can shoot behind the line if a deer shows there. Standers do likewise.

The success of these drives, says "One Shot" Urso, depends on experienced team captains who know the terrain intimately enough to position standers and drivers wisely. Yet that doesn't lessen the responsibility of every hunter, stander, or driver. Each must know what to do. The stander, for example, should sit quietly and still. The sound of human movement might spook a buck away from the stand. And the stander should learn to depend on his eyes. On dry days he usually can hear deer coming before he sees them.

As for the driver, Urso says he should stop occasionally to look and listen. Sometimes he will spot a deer sneaking ahead or attempting to double back through the drive line. Urso also stresses the importance of being able to *see* deer, picking the natural from the unnatural, a topic which is covered in the next chapter.

But no matter where it is staged or how many participants are involved, the drive has one basic purpose: to move deer in a designated pattern in order to set them up for standers situated at predetermined vantage points.

One variation of this is a drive where no standers are involved. A string of hunters simply fan out across the countryside. Perhaps each one will follow parallel logging roads or laid-out compass courses, traveling at about the same slow speed so the line will sweep across the deer habitat at an even pace.

The whitetail deer is an animal of fairly restricted range. It is reluctant to leave its home territory. Thus, when being driven ahead of the hunter line, it will frequently try to circle around and backtrack, sneaking behind the human to enter its bailiwick. This is just what the line of hunters hopes to accomplish. The deer skirting away from one hunter might cross paths with another hunter in the drive, and a mistake like this could be fatal. But

Organization and planning are keys to a successful drive. It is important that someone familiar with the country be appointed "captain" to plan strategy and place standers and drivers.

in a drive such as this, safety precautions should be stressed. One hunter should never fire in the direction of another driver. All shots should be out front or in the rear, never to either side.

In broken country of draws and headers, two or three persons can launch a successful drive. Deer always tend to move with the wash, exiting from either its mouth or its beginning. Therefore, should the driver enter the draw from above, the beginning, the stander should be set up in a concealed position where the draw opens its mouth.

At least one person in the party must be acquainted with the terrain. He should know the major deer runs, the likely routes deer will follow when fleeing the drivers. The very success of the drive depends on having the standers at the right places at the right time. A drive pattern is sort of triangular-shaped, with the standers set up at the apex of the triangle and the drivers fanned out along its base. The drivers should move not in a straight line but in a half-moon sweep, the outside drivers slightly ahead of the others to discourage deer from breaking through either side of the drive line.

Stands must be situated so that each one is out of the line of fire of the

A typical pattern for driving deer. The drivers move in a half-moon pattern to keep the deer from slipping around their flanks. The standers should be stationed along runs the deer are likely to take as they move ahead of the drivers.

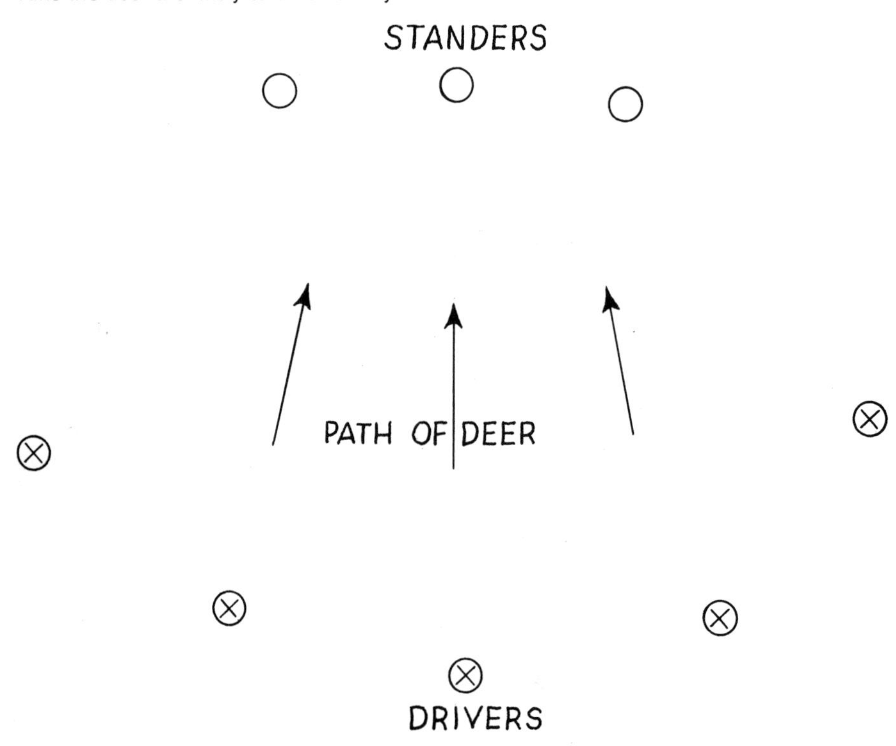

others. Shotguns are popular in this type of hunting since most shots tend to be at running deer at close range, and the short-range weapons are safer.

The drivers also should be alert for deer, not depending on them all to travel as predicted. Sometimes they'll try to double back. Doyle Johnson recalls a time when he was slipping through a thicket in Pike County, Pennsylvania, attempting to drive the deer out for others in his party to get shots, when suddenly three deer came running down the thicket-lined trail and nearly trampled him. The first deer sighted the hunter and tried to stop, planting both forefeet, but the other two crashed into the first, and the tangle of deer slammed into the thicket, scrambling frantically to escape. Doyle was too dumbfounded even to get his gun up for a shot.

There are, then, basically two ways to conduct a drive. One is to have the drivers steal along quietly, hoping to get a shot at deer themselves, and the other is to have them create a loud ruckus to move the deer on and prevent them from doubling back through the driving line. (Some drive-hunters use walkie-talkies for communication, but I am against the use of them or any other electronic gadgets.)

Tom Easterly, a Long Island resident, is an advocate of the quiet, slow drive. He admits he is prejudiced. Since he started hunting this way a few years ago, he's killed more bucks and bigger bucks than he had during all his previous hunting.

For many seasons he hunted the big woods of New York's Catskill Mountains. Only occasionally did he bag a deer, and typically he brought home a spike or forkhorn. Then a neighbor talked him into shifting his hunting bailiwick downstate, to the southern tier of counties west of Binghamton. Tom at the time was a dedicated still-hunter (stalker), but most hunters in this southern tier liked to participate in noisy drives, storming through the woods and running deer in every direction. Tom joined a few of these drives, and while he saw a couple of nice bucks, he had no trophy for the good fortune. "They were just blurs of motion through the trees," he recalled. "I couldn't have hit one with a machine gun."

Then something happened which changed his whole outlook on deer hunting. He was in a café with some local hunters and they invited him on a drive. But, as he was to find out, this was a new kind of drive. They did everything contrary to what Tom had been told about drive hunting.

"This area is mostly privately owned land," Tom said. "These fellows know of several places where they are welcome to hunt because they respect the landowner's rights. They have hunted the same areas many times and they know the terrain, which is important for their kind of driving."

There were six in the party and they divided into three standers and three drivers. The unofficial "captain" of the bunch had an aerial map and he showed everyone in the group his assignment.

A wedge-shaped chunk of woods was picked for the morning's first drive. One stander was put on either flank, one in the middle.

The "captain" explained the strategy to Tom. The standers would be given ample time to reach their designated spots and get settled. Only then would the drivers enter the woods, the reason being they would be moving *with* the wind. If standers and drivers went in simultaneously, the deer likely would smell the drivers and take evasive action and be gone before the standers were ready.

Once the drivers do enter the woods, any deer downwind will immediately pick up the human scent in the air currents. When a buck is presented with this danger signal, he will do one of two things: either attempt to slip back through the drivers, or sneak ahead or out one side, But unless a driver gets uncomfortably close, the crafty animal won't spook and run. He would much rather sneak. And this tactic gives either a stander or a driver a much better opportunity for a shot.

Tom was a driver and he was surprised to discover his assignment was no different from still-hunting, as he knew it. He moved very deliberately, taking a few cautious steps before pausing to look about him. That initial effort paid off with two bucks and Tom was fortunate to get one of them, an eight-pointer, only the second time in his career he had downed a buck this size. He caught a glimpse of motion as the animal tried to thread the needle between two drivers. Tom raised his Remington shotgun and trained the Weaver 1.5× scope on a narrow opening about 40 yards away. When the buck attempted to sneak through the clearing Tom whacked him behind the shoulder with a rifled slug.

The secret of a successful drive is organization. It is important that one or two persons be put in charge of the hunt, to organize and plan it, placing the standers and drivers in the most strategic positions. A disorderly drive not only cuts down on the deer kill, it also is dangerous. And everyone participating in a drive should wear a blaze-orange cap and vest, for safety.

Calling deer with commercial calls, blown by mouth, is too suspect for me to recommend it. Bill Klapp says he has used such calls with a good deal of success in Pennsylvania, but most reports from hunters I've received detailed only spotty results. But one form of calling—rattlin'—is almost as old as deer hunting itself.

Rattlin' a buck in close, within gunshot range, can be accomplished anywhere the rut or mating season comes simultaneously with the legal hunting season. It is particularly effective in that area called the brush country of south Texas, a he-man terrain of bushes with exotic Mexican names, plants that all have one thing in common—thorns.

The sight of a big buck "coming to the horns" is a drama that no deer hunter can forget.

Before daylight on one frosty, still December morning, Murry Burnham and I had walked almost a mile from where we'd parked the pickup, following the pencil beam of a penlight, trying to create as little noise as possible. We found a comfortable spot to sit on the side of a squat hill, among some clumps of prickly-pear cactus, a vantage which permitted us to see about 100 yards in three directions. Then we impatiently awaited dawn.

Rattling a pair of antlers during the rutting season will often bring a buck within gunshot range. The antlers are banged and twisted together, even rapped against trees and brush, to simulate the battling of bucks. At right, Murry Burnham bangs antlers together while the author watches from their stand.

Off in the distance a coyote howled, and as the eastern horizon began to brighten, I heard some scaled (blue) quail greeting the day.

When there was enough light to distinguish shape from shadow, I jacked a live round into the barrel of my slide-action Remington 6mm and Murry went to work with the horns. He rapped the two antlers together, twisting the tines, making it sound as if two bellicose bucks were squaring off.

Murry carried on this fake duel for perhaps ten seconds before putting the antlers aside. We raised our binoculars and looked around us. Sometimes a suspicious buck, especially an old and cunning one, will run to where he can look the situation over. If he sees anything that hints of danger, he'll turn and leave doubletime. We were hoping to see him before he sighted us so I could get a shot.

We were hunting on a huge cattle ranch in Webb County of southern Texas, not far from the Rio Grande River and the Mexico border. Deer normally start to rut in December in this part of the country, and a buck with love on his mind is susceptive to being duped. Of course there are many things that can go wrong when rattling, and something often does, but rattling is a fascinating challenge.

Anyway, Murry continued to rattle and I kept watching. Nothing. I checked my watch and discovered we had been at it for more than a half-hour. I suggested to Murry we change to a new location.

This is when experience paid off. Instead of getting up, Murry took one last look around him. His head abruptly stopped. Gingerly he reached over and grasped my shoulder.

"Easy now, look at about ten o'clock," he whispered. "There's your buck!"

I slowly moved my head. What a magnificent sight! The buck was standing in a flat among clumps of prickly pear. Sunlight from the low-hanging sun glistened on his dark coat and his antlers sparkled.

As I brought my rifle up, the deer started trotting, but he didn't seem to be alarmed, only curious. My heart was pounding as I waited for him to stop. In a large opening he paused broadside and looked directly at me. The crosshairs of the scope sight settled just behind the shoulder and I felt the jolt of the 6mm against my shoulder.

The buck never knew what hit him.

It is dramatic and thrilling, all right, but don't be fooled into believing that "horn rattling" is surefire. Most of my rattling has resulted in sore arm muscles and eyestrain and nothing more. Rattling is, at best, a hit-or-miss proposition.

Many factors are involved. Foremost, a buck must have a swelled neck, and he must be on the prowl for a willing doe. The hunting territory also must have a high ratio of bucks to does. Competition is keen for a female's interest. If there are numerous ready-and-willing females, there is no reason for a buck to be spoiling for a fight; he just enjoys the bounty. And

A young and eager buck like this often will barge in close as soon as he hears the first "horn rattling."

finally, a buck in the right mood must be within hearing range of the antlers and be fooled enough to be duped into an ambush.

Bucks seem particularly susceptible to rattled antlers just at the beginning and again near the end of the rut. The juices start flowing in a buck before they do in a doe. The buck is ready for action, and if he hears what he believes to be two other bucks fighting, he probably will rush to the scene, hoping to join the activity or lure the doe away while the others are engaged in combat. Toward the end of the rut most of the does are out of the mood, but a few bucks are still eager, and the sound of two bucks fighting is apt to bring a third to the scene looking for a doe.

Sometimes a buck in this frame of mind will do strange things. Once Winston Burnham volunteered to try to rattle a buck for A. W. McLaughlin, who never had killed a big one. Only a few minutes after Winston started banging the antlers together, the two men heard a sudden scrambling noise behind them. When they turned around they were face-to-face with a buck. He had his neck stretched as he looked over the low-slung bushes Winston and Mac were hidden in. He wasn't a large buck, just a six-pointer, but he was plenty steamed up.

"He was glassy-eyed and his nostrils were flared," Winston recalled later. "I could almost feel his hot breath, he was that close."

But it didn't take the buck long to realize this was no orgy. He vanished about as quickly as he had appeared.

There is no magic to rattling. Most neophytes at the sport worry more about creating the correct sound than about other, more important considerations. The sound really isn't that crucial. No two bucks will sound exactly alike when they are fighting. The only consideration is to slam the antlers together firmly, and pull them apart cleanly. When they are together they should be twisted and turned. As bucks fight they don't pull back and run together repeatedly. Instead they clash, then twist and turn, trying to gain an advantage by brute strength. This is why bigger, physically stronger bucks usually win. An instruction record on making the correct rattling sound is available from the Burnham Brothers (Marble Falls, Texas 78654).

I prefer fairly heavy antlers so the sound will carry farther. Some rattlers prefer matched mule-deer antlers rather than whitetail antlers, because the muley racks tend to be straight, while the whitetail's have a curve inward, making it more difficult to mesh them together without pinching a hand or finger. The antlers can be joined with a piece of cord about 2 feet long and slung over a shoulder for easy carrying.

The same set of rattling horns can be used year after year. After a few years they do begin to dry out, however. This can be corrected by treating them with boiled linseed oil or soaking them overnight in water. This restores the lost moisture and gives the antlers a firm, fresh sound rather than a ring.

Antlers can be banged together with the tine points of both beams pointed in the same direction, or they can be meshed with the points in different directions, the same way they are positioned on a deer's head. Just employ the method which seems natural to you. But I do advise wearing gloves. Catch a finger between the antler beams on a cold morning and you're apt to regret it.

More important than the sound itself is concealment. Even if your state law requires a blaze-orange vest and hat, cover your face with a camouflage mesh headnet and crouch or sit in front of a bush or other vegetation to break your outline. If I am hunting where there are no other hunters (in Texas hunters lease a tract of private land for their exclusive use), I wear complete camouflage.

The best time to rattle is just at daybreak on a cold, still morning. Rutting deer seem to be most active at this time. The sound will carry a long way in the calm, and there are no wind currents to spread human scent about. It isn't uncommon for an old buck coming to the horns to circle downwind, to check things out, before barging on in. With a young buck it doesn't seem to make much difference. During the rut he is downright stupid.

Some rattlers like to use scents to short-circuit this downwind-circling tactic. Pure skunk musk is about the best human-scent-overpowering agent I have tried (I discuss the use of scents in Chapter 14). Another practice is to obtain the musk pads from a buck's hind-leg hocks, pads which are dark and smelly where the buck has been urinating on them, and put them in a sealed coffee can. Before rattling, the hunter places the can slightly downwind from his position and removes the snap-on plastic top.

There is no established pattern for rattling. Trial and error seems to be standard. Each rattler has his own pet technique. One might prefer to bang the antlers together almost constantly, while another will rattle a few moments, then wait a minute or two, then rattle again. I believe constant rattling will bring in bucks quicker, but a buck may arrive so abruptly that he sees the hunter and reacts before the hunter can get a shot. Constant rattling also seems to bring more young bucks. Periodic rattling, about five to ten seconds at a stretch with a time lapse of a minute or two between rattles, will bring a buck toward the hunter at a slower, more deliberate pace, and the buck usually won't immediately pinpoint the rattler. In short, the rattler should attempt to sucker the buck into making a mistake and then take advantage of it.

When you are rattling constantly, about 15 minutes in one spot is sufficient. But if you use the rattle-and-stop method, it is best to stick around at least a half-hour. Sometimes it takes that long for a cautious buck to show. Walk about a half-mile to a new location to try a new territory.

And finally, perhaps most important of all, do your homework and find areas where signs indicate rutting activity, especially scrapes where a buck has urinated and pawed the ground. If the sign is fresh, this buck won't be far off. And he'll likely come to horns, unless he's already with a doe. An alternative is the hit-or-miss method, moving through likely country and pausing occasionally to rattle, hoping you are within hearing distance of a juiced-up buck.

Texan Bob Ramsey has the reputation of a rattler par excellence. He has written and lectured extensively on the subject. He says that while some people have the misconception that horn rattling seems to work only in Texas, it will produce anywhere the hunting season coincides with the rut.

"I have letters from hunters in New Hampshire, Pennsylvania, Georgia, Florida, Michigan, Iowa, Louisiana, Arkansas, and three provinces in Canada, all claiming to have rattled up one or more bucks," he says. "One man from New Hampshire, who has been down to Texas to compare notes with me twice within the past five years, went to Maine and rattled up and bagged a buck sporting 12 large points and dressing over 300 pounds."

Again, rattling isn't surefire. Sometimes it produces, sometimes not. It is like feeding coins into a one-arm bandit; the anticipation is half the fun. And once you hit a jackpot, you're hooked—but good!

Murry and Winston Burnham, the brothers of game-calling fame who have done much research on the behavior of wild animals and which sounds cause them to react, tell me that whitetails sometimes will come to a mouth-blown call, though the results are unpredictable.

The tone of a deer call is similar to that of the dying-rabbit predator call, but the pitch of the deer call is much lower. This pitch is important. The deer caller has to create just the right sound to entice a deer to come a-running.

The call the Burnhams have developed to bring in the bucks is a weird-sounding thing, violent and loud with an anguished squeal. This is a startlingly different sound from the one the brothers first started with, an imitation of a soft-bleating fawn. The distressful bleating, they discovered, will often bring a wild-eyed doe in fast, but it never enjoyed much success on bucks. The loud, panicky sound is much more effective, which is odd since the deer is one of the least loquacious of all wild animals. The Burnhams' theory is that the call arouses the curiosity of a buck.

Numerous times I've had deer answer the squalling of a rabbit-in-distress predator call while hunting in my central-Texas bailiwick and in Mexico. It isn't unusual to have a pugnacious doe come bolting out of the brush, run up close, and start pawing the ground and snorting. Probably she associates the gosh-awful noise with some sort of danger to her young.

One thing the Burnhams found was that the calling should be abruptly terminated when a buck approaches within view. Calling when the animal has approached fairly close often drives him off, rather than luring him. The distress call normally works best in the fall on the bucks, but at times the males will come to a soft, bleating sound, like a doe often calls during the rut.

The Burnhams said one Pennsylvania game-calling enthusiast, James S. Seibel of Pittsburgh, wrote them that he has called and kept records on more than 900 deer in his home state, which proves that the system can be effective if the caller knows what he is doing.

The caller should use all the caution of the stand hunter, staying concealed and completely still, with the wind blowing in his face. A day with little or no wind is best for calling, the Burnhams explain, because a stiff breeze muffles the call, and also it throws the human scent away where deer can detect it. And one note of caution. Be sure and check the game laws in your state to see if deer calls are allowed. In some states they are illegal.

No matter which method you may choose to seek your deer—stand-hunting, stalking, tracking, driving, or calling—always take the positive approach and have confidence in your own ability. If you follow the rules outlined here, there is no reason why you shouldn't get your deer this season. Every year beginners with no prior experience go afield and score, some of them with quite spectacular results.

Orrie L. Schaeffer of Corning, Missouri, is a living example of this. On his very first deer hunt in Holt County, Schaeffer downed a ten-point buck which weighed nearly 300 pounds. Just getting a deer on his first hunt was significant enough, but Schaeffer had the added distinction of downing a record-book head, at that time the largest ever taken in Missouri.

10

The Art of Seeing Deer

A CRAFTY WHITETAIL DEER is a master of the vanishing act. In fact, many never are seen at all, standing motionless in the shadowy undergrowth until danger passes.

Learning to see deer is one of the most important keys to successful hunting. Or it's as a friend of mine describes it: "Scanning a chunk of woods and separating the unnatural from the natural."

Trained eyes see *something* that just doesn't belong: the glint of sunlight on an antler tine, the flash of a white rump, the horizontal curve of a deer's back in vertical vegetation, the contrast of a reddish-brown coat against somber green or maybe snow.

Despite what you might have been led to believe, man's eyesight is better than a deer's, for a couple reasons: depth and color perception. Depth perception enables the hunter to see and isolate opposing or conflicting lines; color perception negates much of nature's camouflage. If you take a photograph of a deer in both natural color and black-and-white, you will see that it is easy to distinguish the animal in color, but in black-and-white, as one colorblind animal sees another, the deer blends in, becoming almost invisible, often as if it is standing in a shadow.

But this advantage is of little value unless the hunter is looking and concentrating, and in this instance the two words are virtually synonymous. The hunter must first be able to pick the deer from the overall clutter.

Something that doesn't belong catches your eye. Quickly, the word "deer" flashes through your mind. Is it a doe or buck? If it indeed is a buck, how big is the rack? You must be almost computerlike in response time, for deer hunting requires split-second decisions. He who hesitates isn't going to eat venison.

My friend Gene Powell will testify to that. He and I were hunting in brushy south Texas near the town of Pearsall, and Gene was standing close to a bush and watching an active trail. At twilight, Gene shook the kinks from his protesting leg muscles and prepared to walk the half-mile to the pickup truck.

As he wiggled a leg he heard a startled snort from behind. He turned just in time to see a deer jump from the trail into adjacent thornbrush. Gene listened. A hush fell over the scene. Obviously the confused critter had stopped to try to figure out what had alarmed it.

Some quick searching pinpointed the deer's body. As luck would have it, a fast-fading sunset provided just enough illumination to faintly silhouette the animal. Gene's eyes zeroed in on something that just didn't belong in the scene. He raised his binocular for a fast look. Antlers were protruding above the low brush.

All this took no more than a few seconds, a chain reaction. Powell raised his rifle and, squinting through the scope sight, aimed below the antlers about where he though the head and neck should be. If he connected he would have a dead animal; if he missed, he would miss cleanly.

The .30/06 bullet whomped. There was a loud thrashing in the brush. My friend raced the few yards to where the neck-shot buck fell.

I called him a lucky son-of-a-gun, but I knew better. It took trained eyes to pinpoint a deer in the dim underbrush. But once Gene established it was a buck, he took advantage of the situation. Of a fashion, Gene was lucky: That's when preparation meets opportunity.

Most hunters do not exploit this eyesight edge. They either hunt too fast, walking a lot of countryside, or if on stand, try to spread their vision too wide, wanting to watch too much terrain.

In dense undergrowth, look for horizontal lines of a deer's body. In other words, distinguish between animal and vegetable lines.

Sometimes a flick of a tail or a glint of antler will betray the quarry.

As an illustration, I recall a hunt I took with an acquaintance on a cattle ranch not far from my home. It was a hastily planned hunt and we didn't arrive at our destination until midafternoon. I directed this man to a tree stand I knew about while I went in the opposite direction to still-hunt along some brush draws.

Shortly after sundown I detoured toward where my companion was hunting so we could walk together to our automobile. As I catfooted down a trail, I noticed motion ahead. Dropping to one knee, I looked through my binocular. A doe crossed a narrow clearing not 25 yards from my buddy's stand. Shortly another doe came into view, then another.

I waited impatiently for several minutes, hoping a buck might be following the group. After satisfying myself that no buck would follow, I continued on and got to the tree as my colleague was climbing down.

"See anything?" I asked.

"Just one doe right after I got in the tree," he reported glumly. "Deer weren't moving."

"How 'bout those three that passed near your stand a few minutes ago?"

"What three?"

I told him about the deer. He sheepishly admitted that he had been watching some large patches of clearing in the distance, almost 200 yards away. The deer crossing nearby had gone unnoticed.

Whether walking or sitting, the wise hunter mentally divides his territory into segments, thoroughly scrutinizing each section before focusing on the next. In short, he pinpoints his concentration rather than allowing it to make a shotgun pattern.

While the whitetail of Alabama is pretty much the same critter found in Pennsylvania, as habits and behavior go, they do inhabit different terrains, and this difference, along with weather conditions, dictates the hunting method.

Again, the whitetail is very adaptable and might be found in fairly open country with scattered trees and brush, or in small woodlots around fields and even in the fields themselves, or back in the thickest tangles and brush.

In more open country the hunter can use a binocular to study the landscape, letting nothing escape his probe, but in dense woods he must depend primarily on his unaided eye, because any deer sighted will be at close range. The hunter must also adapt to the situation, maybe getting high—in a tree perhaps—to look down onto openings and trails scattered through the trees and underbrush. Or maybe a high browse line will make visibility better at ground level.

Seth Martin will tell you that an old buck knows all the wily tricks of survival. Seth, as I mentioned earlier, owns a cattle ranch in central Texas which supports an uncommonly large population of deer, many of them bucks. On several occasions, while riding horseback to check his livestock, he has passed close by a buck bedded in the underbrush. If the horse continued its steady gait, the sagacious buck most likely would drop his head

The hunter will see more if he moves less and looks more.

and lie perfectly still, thinking that he hadn't been detected. But if Seth reined his mount to a halt, the deer, feeling he had been discovered, would immediately explode from his hiding spot and run for cover.

I am convinced that the ability to see deer is an acquired art, not something which comes naturally, although some people have better eyesight and are more perceptive than others. One method for improving ability is to practice by getting into the woods at every chance just to look for deer.

Any preseason time spent in the woods is particularly worthwhile. For one thing, you become more familiar with your hunting territory, which later will enable you to concentrate on areas where you most likely will find deer. By observing them you learn what to look for, to actually train your eyes. And you can "pattern" bucks (figure their routines) in order to return during the season and attempt to outwit them.

Like humans, deer acquire certain habits. Unless disturbed, each animal will develop a fairly predictable routine: bedding in a specific area, following a trail or trails to a food source, drinking at the one waterhole.

But habit doesn't eliminate the deer's regard for survival. The older the animal, the craftier. That is why there is a premium on the hunter's woodsmanship, including his ability to see and thus find deer.

This sort of heightened perception includes curiosity. One commuter can drive back and forth along the same road every day and be oblivious to the details en route. Another person may continually see new things, for his curiosity makes him more observant.

As you get into the woods or drive backcountry roads to look for deer, you will begin to notice things you never were aware of before. And as you become more curious about these things, you find that you are seeing more deer.

Yet even if you have superior eyesight, don't fail to take advantage of any optical aid that might help. Two of the most difficult times to see deer occur during prime moving periods—early and late in the day when light is feeble. If possible, always try to hunt with the rising or setting sun at your back. A deer's coat and antlers will reflect light, giving the critter away, and the glare will blind the deer rather than vice-versa.

Even in thick brush, a binocular is an aid. Quality lenses gather and intensify light. Ditto a scope sight. Yellow-tinted shooting glasses will brighten the landscape, bringing everything into sharp focus, when unaided eyes have difficulty separating shape from shadow.

The problem with total concentration is that after a while everything begins to resemble a deer. You find yourself getting excited over a bush or stump. That's all right as long as you are positive of your target before raising your weapon. Some hunters use scope sights in lieu of binoculars. But it is frightening to find yourself looking at a rifle trained your way as another hunter examines you with his scope.

I'm so cautious about this that I've missed opportunities for a few really big bucks because I looked at them first through a binocular, only to see them escape before I could drop the glass and raise my rifle.

Occasionally I will forget to carry my binocular. And I nearly always regret the oversight. I remember one such incident quite vividly. I was slipping along a brush-lined ranch road, looking and listening, when ahead, at the edge of a large clearing, I noticed something unusual which prompted me to pause and peer more closely.

It was a deer, partly obscured by morning shadows from trees to the left of it. I don't know what gave the motionless animal away. But some insignificant clue must have caught my attention.

The range was roughly 150 yards. It was shortly after sunrise and the shifting shadows played tricks with my eyes. But after a moment or two of intent looking, I could faintly distinguish the deer's whole outline. I found myself wishing I'd brought my binocular, but I'd left it in the pickup to lighten the load.

The deer removed the doubt for me. The animal was looking at me too. After a few brief seconds, his suspicion won out. He wheeled and with one quick bound disappeared into thick brush. As the critter turned I saw the antlers—big, heavy, and wide—but by then I was too late. The old bull of the woods was gone, the largest buck I saw that season.

So sometimes just seeing a deer isn't enough!

Crouching at ground level, the hunter may see legs or even a buck in his bed.

11

The Weather and Deer Hunting

MANY OF THE whitetail's actions still remain a mystery. One old adage has it that deer normally are active at night, early and late in the day, and that they take a midday siesta.

Arkansas wildlife biologist (and hunter extraordinary) Mitch Rogers doubts the adage. When asked which was the best period to hunt, early or late, Rogers admitted that most of the time he goes in midday.

Now wait a minute! Surely he must be kidding. Deer just aren't out when the sun is high and bright. Or that is what many hunters have been led to believe. Yet the small majority that consistently get bucks, season after season, are well aware that deer often are active around noon, in addition to early and late.

Actually, according to a study by the wildlife department of Texas A&M University, whitetail deer are even less sophisticated than people believe.

The research was conducted at the Welder Wildlife Refuge near Sinton in southern Texas. Several deer were shot with tranquilizer guns, and each got a collar containing a tiny radio transmitter. The deer then were "tracked" with remote sensing equipment. Each transmitter emitted a steady beeping sound when the deer carrying it was still, but there was considerable variation in the tone when the animal was on the move.

Among the observations of the year-long study was that deer bounce out of bed at daybreak, *become most active around noon,* again a little before dusk, and finally at midnight. There was little or no movement from 9:00 to 11:00 p.m.

But there are some days when deer are moving about almost continuously. They bed down either not at all or for a very short time. It may be a mild, sunny day, not unlike the previous day when the deer followed their regular routine, yet there will be evidence of movement everywhere. It is a phenomenon which every observant hunter takes into consideration when mapping his strategy.

I remember one of those rare days at the opening of the deer season several years back. It was a beautiful, sunny fall day, clear and still. My stand was in the high fork of a gnarled oak tree overlooking a well-traveled deer run. I can't recall ever seeing more deer than I did that morning. In fact, by noon I'd glimpsed four legal bucks; each time something crossed me up and prevented me from getting an early, auspicious start to the season. Three times I had no control over the matter, the deer being in situations which handicapped me, such as the time one walked through a sliver of opening allowing just a quick glimpse for identification, but not enough time for a reasonable shot. But the other muffed opportunity was of my own doing. I had a deer standing about 75 yards away and blew the golden chance by overshooting.

For every buck I sighted, however, I must have counted at least four or five does, fawns, and yearlings. Hardly was there a time when I didn't have at least one deer within my vision. Often there were two or three feeding near my makeshift tree stand.

Soon after noon, around 1:00, I was preoccupied with watching a pair of female deer grazing off to my right, when a noise of hoofs on rocks behind me quickly diverted my attention. I looked around just in time to see a nice buck scrambling through a dry wash, kicking rocks as he jumped in and out. He was walking directly away from me as I put the sight on his back, just this side of the shoulder, and touched 'er off. The bullet struck fair just where I was aiming, angled down through the chest cavity, and exited in front of the shoulders. The buck was dead before he hit the ground.

That shot abruptly terminated my hunting for the day, but all the other hunters I talked with later remarked about the unusual deer movement, right on through the warm midday hours, when normally the animals would be lost in the cover.

The next morning I knew the answer. The kind of storm that we Texans have come to call a "blue norther" came snowballing in from the north, gaining momentum as it went, a severe storm for so early in the year. An icy wind sent the temperature plummeting below the freezing mark, and for three days the storm raged.

It explained the deer movement. A creature of the wild seems to have a built-in "sixth sense" when it comes to forecasting weather. The deer, with its limited protection against the elements, owes its very existence to its ability to foretell what weather the days ahead will bring. The deer on this particular season opener were up and about throughout the day, feeding, to get ready for the lean storm days ahead when they would be relatively confined.

That season opener was one of the best in history, with a heavy kill of deer. Yet the following day the number of animals being brought into the small deer-hunting towns dropped drastically. The deer had migrated back into the dense cover, seeking protection from the storm, and there was only limited movement.

After the weather front moved on southward, skies cleared and temperatures began climbing again, and the deer ventured back out to browse and water. The day after the severe storm was a time of movement again. The weather was 15 to 20° colder than it had been opening day, yet still not severe enough to keep the deer in the cover. Right on through the noon hour, the animals were still milling about, feeding.

Again, the deer were following a predictable pattern based on the weather outlook.

Just prior to a severe storm, whether a dry front or a blizzard, and again right after, there will be concentrated deer movement. Before the bad weather, the deer are storing up food, filling their bellies, in anticipation of the lean days ahead, days when they will be relatively confined. After the storm, the deer will come out to stuff their empty stomachs. This behavior is particularly noticeable before severe fronts which bring abrupt changes in weather. Perhaps the sudden change will be in the form of cold severe weather, or maybe it will be torrential rains. If it is the kind of weather which will interfere with the deer's daily habits, then it will aid the hunter, helping him to plan his strategy according to the anticipated reactions of the deer to the weather change.

A deer is a whole lot like humans in this respect. Weather dictates what its routine will be, not vice versa. Everything it does is directly influenced by weather, because in the wilds an abrupt change in the elements often is fatal to the less hardy creatures.

Suppose a severe storm blows in, bringing with it snow and hard-freezing temperatures. In this kind of inclement weather, a deer isn't going to feed much early and late or at night, because it would rather bed down to find some protection against the cold, and feed when the sun is up.

The duration of the storm also is a determining factor on deer movement. With storms of short duration, two or three days, the deer will remain restricted to a fairly limited area, not moving around much; but should the storm last for many days, the deer will venture out to feed and water at times, though the movement won't be nearly as pronounced as it is during more typical weather, unless it is an early cold snap which helps trigger the rut.

Sometimes there is an overlap which brings phenomenal hunting. Just after a storm hits, for example, the deer might be at the peak of their feeding spree, heading for cover only as the storm gains in intensity.

There are many hunters who swear by the barometer. Their philosophy is this: high barometer, good hunting; low barometer, poor hunting.

A barometer, of course, is only a device for predicting weather. Generally, a high barometer will mean fair weather, a low barometer will indicate bad weather. It is this elementary.

Immediately after a storm, when the barometer is rising steadily, there is often a time for exceptional hunting. I remember one particular New Mexico rain storm, a steady wintery drizzle which lasted for two miserable days.

On the third day the black clouds scattered and the skies opened up as blue as the eyes of a newborn baby, and the sun sparkled like diamonds on the rain-splattered trees.

Right after a rainstorm is one of my pet times for still-hunting. The ground is soggy and quiet, making for silent traveling. And the deer are moving about freely, exposing themselves in a more vulnerable position.

On this morning in the woods, the first thing I noticed was the unmistakable evidence of deer movement. Fresh tracks were everywhere. In the moist earth, after the storm, the telltale tracks showed up vividly, and since the rain had washed all past evidence away, I knew the tracks had been made at most the night before, no sooner.

Throughout the day I sighted untold numbers of deer. Many of the feeding animals I walked right up on. This was in the pine forests of Lincoln National Forest, near Cloudcroft, an area where I'd hunted only a week earlier and found very little evidence of deer.

The weather had made the difference. It had prompted the deer to move about more, to track up the area.

Weather also influences the hunter's strategy. As a general rule, stand-hunting will be more productive immediately prior to and immediately after the storm, since these will be times of active deer movement. During the storm, the hunter must still-hunt back among the dense cover, hoping to jump deer from their beds.

The wise hunter keeps close check on weather reports. He knows when the fronts are moving in, the nature of them, and how to incorporate the anticipated weather changes into his hunting strategy.

In populous areas where deer-hunting pressure is greatest, the weather is a definite asset. A deer preparing for unsettled weather, or regrouping after a storm, is going to be less cautious and more vulnerable to the hunter. The more severe the incoming storm, the more concentrated and heavy will be the deer movement, and the easier and more predictable is the hunter's job.

Yet we also know that weather patterns influence deer behavior even if there is no drastic change.

In some areas, for instance, weather often is unseasonably warm during the deer season, or at least during a part of it. Deer are a lot like humans: Comfort dictates their daily routines. If it is shirtsleeves-warm, the critters likely will be quite active very early, around daybreak, and again very late, about dusk, but they won't be moving much when the sun is up. So if you hope to stalk one and maybe roust it from its bed in the day, you must figure where the deer will lie down, a spot where it can find both security and have the benefit of any cooling prevailing breeze.

Master hunter Larry Benoit has observed that when the wind is howling, nothing moves in the woods.

I have discovered the same thing. Wild animals especially dislike high, gusty winds. One reason perhaps is that the tree-rattling wind makes it more difficult to detect danger. And probably deer are just plain uncomfortable. A dead-calm, bluebird day is almost as bad. Why, I don't know. It is just something I accept.

The moon phase also influences deer behavior. I personally have found that hunting is best during the dark of the moon and poorest during a full moon. Also, it seems to me that daylight moons affect deer activity. Should the moon rise late and still be visible in the morning light, deer will be most active in the morning, compared to other periods of the day. If it rises early, before nightfall, just the opposite is true. And deer don't move much in the day if there is a full moon at night, even if the moon is obscured by a heavy overcast.

But much of the relationship between deer and weather remains unknown.

Deer behavior can vary from week to week, and indeed even day to day, although there has been no discernible change in the weather. I have observed this many times.

On a typical early-autumn day, that is shirtsleeves-cool with just a light breeze, you can drive a backcountry road and find that deer will stand off, watching the vehicle without showing any fear. Some act almost as tame as domestic livestock.

Later, maybe the following day, with the weather virtually the same, you might find that the deer are spooky. They run from the vehicle—just white flags waving in the underbrush. In more open country, you may sight them hightailing before your vehicle approaches within 200 yards.

Why the change? I wish I knew. It would make me a better hunter. Yet in a way I am glad I don't. If we knew everything there is to know about the deer and its everyday habits, hunting wouldn't be nearly as much fun.

12

Advanced Deer Hunting

WHEN DEL AUSTIN bagged his world-record whitetail (archery nontypical) in the Platte River bottoms of Nebraska, south of Shelton, he afterward attributed much of his success to luck. In 1962, Austin and a companion, Charlie Marlowe, decided to go after the big buck one afternoon. Austin stationed himself alongside a good deer run, in a tree blind, on the Dan Thomas farm. Some 30 minutes later, he heard a crashing noise in the brush and shortly the big buck stepped into the open. When he was a scant 20 yards away, Austin pulled back on his bow and let an arrow fly. It was a solid hit behind the front leg and—presto!—Austin had himself first place in the Pope and Young Club archery record book.

True, Lady Luck does play an important role in deer hunting, particularly when a man collects a record trophy head. It is the old axiom of being at the right place at the right time. But it goes deeper than that. Occasionally, a novice will bag a big buck, but usually such a specimen will fall before the seasoned veteran hunters, those who have the know-how and skill to outwit a super-sly whitetail.

Take Austin and his record kill, for instance. The hunter knew enough to station himself along a known deer run, where he had the best chance of spotting deer. He knew enough to conceal himself thoroughly and avoid detection. But more important, he was aware that the big buck roamed the area. Austin had been told by Al Dawson that he had seen the giant buck for the five previous seasons in the Platte River country, in the vicinity where Austin elected to hunt.

This incident points up something about the behavior of whitetail deer which few hunters realize. The whitetail is an animal of a limited area. When it homesteads on a certain place, usually the area where it was born and raised, it remains mostly within that area, never ranging far away. This is why one tract can have a serious overpopulation of deer with a drastic die-off because of a food deficiency, while maybe a mile away there might be a comparable area with only a nominal population.

Dr. William B. Davis, a professor of wildlife management at Texas A&M University, says that "normally when food conditions are adequate, deer tend to stay in one locality for long periods."

Just how limited this locality usually is was revealed in a study of trapping and retrapping deer by the Texas Parks and Wildlife Department. One particular example was a buck that was killed within sight of the trapping site where it was caught, banded, and released five years earlier.

In another phase of this program, 102 deer were captured, tagged, and released. Of this number, 43 were caught again, and all but three were taken in the same traps. Another time, 49 deer were retrapped from an original 66 tagged, and not one was taken more than a quarter of a mile away, many in the same traps.

Nineteen deer were tagged in another phase, and in 12 retraps, the average distance between point of release and recapture was a mere 63 yards. In three specific examples, deer were in the same traps with time lapses of 15½, 15, and 16½ months respectively.

In a similar cooperative study by Auburn University and the Florida Game and Fresh Water Fish Commission, battery-powered radio transmitters were strapped to deer by means of stout dog harnesses, and deer movements were plotted by telemetry. The home ranges of nine Alabama and Florida deer varied from a low of 147 acres to a high of only 243 acres.

According to another radio-tracking study conducted by the wildlife science department of Texas A&M University, the range of undisturbed deer, both bucks and does, "was much more restrictive than we ever dreamed." In fact, the deer on the Welder Wildlife Refuge in southern Texas "never moved out of a home range of a one-fourth square mile area."

The researchers did discover that one doe moved quite a distance. Her range was in a small bottomland area along the Aransas River for four months, but a hurricane and high water forced her into higher country. Even so, she sort of took her range along. Once she was established in new territory she never once ventured outside a quarter-mile-square area.

What this means to the hunter is that if he can pinpoint the spot where a shootable deer is ranging, he can fairly well assume the deer will remain within the area where it was sighted.

Although the whitetail is not a migratory animal, in the popular sense of the word, it may move during the winter months in places of severe weather, to locate available food. However, it will not wander about for long distances, as the mule deer will. Deer sighted in a certain area a week or two before the season opening will remain in that area, unless there is a heavy snowfall to move them to more suitable browse. This latter situation is rare in the fall during the big-game season; it is generally a winter occurrence.

Scouting your potential hunting territory is a vital key to success. Look for any sign of deer, such as fresh tracks. Also look for fresh droppings, especially along trails that deer have been using regularly.

Incidentally, whitetails show this home-range tendency even when deep snow forces them to yard up in places where there is suitable browse. Only about 10 percent of the northern whitetail's total range may be used in winter. In these yards deer feed on twigs and buds. White cedar is preferred but aspen is excellent browse. During deep snow it doesn't take long to strip off all available browse, and then starvation begins. In a state like Michigan, as many as 50,000 deer might be lost in one winter. Yet the deer are reluctant to leave an area they have established. While they will beat trails within their yarding area, they rarely will leave it, even though men may break trails to unused areas nearby.

These tests only confirm the beliefs of veteran hunters who have learned the same thing by observation. Take Joe Ralston. He's a confirmed city slicker, having been born, raised and employed in New York City. Yet Joe never misses a deer season. And he's a doggone good hunter, too. He's a firm believer in scouting out an area before hunting it. He says if deer are there before the season, they are going to be there during the season.

Joe told me about a hunt he took many years ago in Coos County, New Hampshire. A week before the season was to open, he drove over one weekend to look over his prospective hunting site. While he was motoring down a back dirt road, he jumped a deer that ran off a few dozen yards and stopped. Joe braked his car and looked the deer over carefully through a binocular. This was a three-pointer, with the typical forked horn on the left, but the right antler was long and smooth and bent over at a crazy angle.

The season was in its second day before Joe sighted a deer. He jumped a buck from a swath of dense timber flanking a dry creekbed and dropped him with one shot as the deer crossed a clearing.

There was no doubt about this deer. It was the identical three-pointer with the same crooked right antler Joe had sighted just a week earlier. And from the spot where he downed the buck, Joe almost could have thrown a rock and hit the site where he previously had seen the whitetail.

The whitetail may range at times, particularly during the rut and in times of food shortage. Yet its range probably is less than a mile, with the deer habitually returning to its familiar homestead to bed down. I once killed a buck which had corn in his stomach, although the nearest cornfield was almost a mile away. But the deer had returned, undoubtedly, to his regular haunt after eating.

This means, then, that the person who scouts the area he plans on hunting prior to the season opening will be improving considerably his chances of success. This scouting serves a dual purpose. The hunter can search for deer, either by visual sightings or wildlife signs, and look for likely spots to situate his stands or map a pattern to follow while stalk-hunting.

Food, of course, will determine the best spots to hunt. Master the food situation and you've taken more than half the guesswork out of deer hunting. A deer must eat, every day. By locating regular runs between feeding and bedding areas, you often can ambush the deer.

The forage of deer will differ with different locales and sections of the country. The New York Conservation Department, in its pamphlet "Food Preferences of the White-Tailed Deer," found that deer in that state ate things like apples, wintergreen, witch bobble, cherry, red maple, basswood, dogwood, and staghorn sumac. Beechnuts are a favorite food of deer in New Hampshire. In a study in Missouri it was found that something like 75 percent of a deer's diet is composed of oaks and acorns. In southern Canada and the far Midwest, various conifers and hardwoods are eaten. Georgia deer feed mainly on oaks. In a five-year stomach-sample study of

Another key is to pinpoint the deer's current food source. One of the most favored foods nationwide is the common acorn in its many types.

deer in Florida, it was found that 20 foods constituted 85 percent of a deer's diet. The foods in order of preference were: oak acorns and leaves, palmetto berries, mushrooms, bamboo briar, deer's tongue, gallberry, titi, blueberry leaves, holly, Virginia willow, sweet bay, legumes, horse wicky, ferns, sumac, willow, elderberry, black haw, yellow jessamine, and blackberry leaves.

While some food sources are fairly dependable—witness that certain areas provide a high deer harvest year after year—a change in a particular food will dictate where the deer will be or where they will not. As an example, a favored deer food in north-central Pennsylvania is the apple. During one recent season the apple crop there was poor to nonexistent. Several late-spring killing frosts aborted the fruit's development. Thus when the hunting season arrived the deer were not in their customary areas around apple orchards, but instead were back in the woods where there was a bountiful nut crop. Hunters who realized what had happened and who made the change to new country with the deer were the ones who generally were successful.

Farmlands also offer a vital source of deer food, and good hunting around agricultural areas is becoming a rule rather than the exception. The reason is obvious. There is a ready-made food supply every year, not just of domestic crops, but also on small woodlots, scrubs, and fence rows. When Kent Price bagged his record-book typical whitetail (archery, Pope and Young Club), it wasn't deep in seldom-hunted dense forest, but along a millet and corn field in Maryland. Traditionally, the biggest deer in almost every state come from agricultural areas, due primarily to this bountiful food supply. Farm crop residues which supplement woody plants provide more nourishing food than does overbrowsed woodlands. In fact, crop depredations in many areas have become so acute that the deer are looked upon as pests by the farmers. Nutrition determines the size and numbers of whitetail deer.

The record Missouri deer, weighing 369 pounds on the hoof, came from farm country; and in a comparison made between deer coming from forested counties in Missouri and those from farm country above the Missouri River it was found that the largest deer, both in weight and antler size, were bagged in the farmlands of the northwest part of the state.

In Mississippi, the biggest deer are found along the Mississippi River, from Tunica County south to Wilkinson County, in the heart of the agriculture belt. The better hunting for whitetails in West Virginia is concentrated through the western countries of Ritchie, Gilmer, Calhoun, Wirt, Jackson, and Roane. This is open farm country.

Dr. Vagn Flyger of the University of Maryland's Natural Resources Institute once made an exhaustive study of deer weights in Maryland, comparing animals taken in the western mountains against those of agricultural Kent County, and he discovered the ones from the latter area were heavier and sported larger antlers than those which browsed solely in the forests.

It also should be stressed that quality and quantity seldom go together.

Areas with large deer herds generally produce smaller bucks. The trophy heads often come from locales with a low density of deer and minimum hunting pressure.

Your state's game and fish department keeps statistics on where the most and largest deer are killed. This agency is a source of information not to be overlooked. While the prime trophy-deer areas can change, the same regions seem to produce the big bucks season after season.

Consider the information I have compiled over the years. While not complete, it does pinpoint some places in the various states where I might go and get a buck worthy enough to hang on the wall.

The northwestern-Wisconsin counties of Ashland, Beyfield, Douglas, and Sawyer. The cornfield country of southern Michigan, counties of Clinton, Gratiot, Barry, Jackson, and Ionio. Schuyler County, Illinois. In Ohio, the timbered hill country of the southeastern counties. Nebraska management units Keya Paha, Plains, Loup, and Pine Ridge. Koochiching County, around Craigville and Littlefork, in Minnesota. The Rangeley area of Somerset County, Maine. The White Mountains region, especially Jefferson-Twin Mountain country, of New Hampshire. In Vermont, the northern counties of Essex and Orleans. The farm country of Worcester County in Massachusetts. The western and central regions and the Adirondacks in New York. Crawford and Susquehanna counties and also the north half of Wayne County in Pennsylvania. In Virginia, the Philpott Reservoir area of Patrick, Henry, and Franklin counties, along with western Giles County. The Harmon Den area, about 25 miles north of Waynesville, in North Carolina. The so-called brush country of deep south Texas—Webb, LaSalle, Dimmit, and other counties of this area. The hardwood bottoms of the Atchafalaya River basin in Louisiana.

Once you've pinpointed a general area to hunt, get a map of the area (see Chapter 13). The general topography will give you some inkling as to the best route to follow when hunting. Now you are ready to go into the area before the season opening to scout things out, to get familiar with landmarks and look for deer and deer sign.

The whitetail is primarily a browser, eating twigs and branches of trees and scrubs, but it also likes domestic crops and weed plants. If you learn the foods deer favor in your area and then locate them, you are apt to find whitetails there too.

Visual sightings are best. When a hunter sees a buck he knows one actually roams the area. It gives him added confidence. But even if he fails to see deer, he can get some inkling as to an area's population from obvious signs such as tracks, droppings, and regular runs. One of the better indicators for determining whether or not bucks are present is to look for the rubs where the males have honed and polished their antlers on sapling trees.

Sometimes it is, indeed, difficult actually to see the deer. A man gets more respect for the sagacity of the whitetail when he realizes that even though a deer does live out almost its entire life in such a limited area, there are instances where some old and wise bucks have escaped the wandering horde of hunters for years. In a unique experiment in Michigan many years back, 34 deer were released on a square mile of ordinary forest land surrounded by a deerproof fence. Hunters were then allowed to go into the confines of the square mile of deer habitat. When deer of either sex were legal game, it required 14 hours of hunting for each deer bagged. For bucks only, the ante went up to 51 hours of hunting for each deer killed. From this, it is easy to see why killing a deer is no simple feat.

Once you have established that a buck, or more than one, is in a certain area, either by visual sightings or reading telltale signs, then you must make something of a scientific appraisal of his "home" and attempt to speculate as to where he might be at any given time of the day. In short, you must learn to think like a deer. Where is he feeding? Where is he bedding? What trails does he follow? Sometimes you can actually smell the strong odor of urine in a buck's scrapes. If you find big tracks you suspect were made by a buck, attempt to confirm this be searching for other clues. A buck often will hook at overhanging limbs. So look for broken branches. Also rubs on saplings. Unless disturbed, for that brief period just before and during the season, a buck will have a primary feeding area, main bedding areas for both night and day (not necessarily the same), and main trails which connect these areas. In some instances the buck might also have a night feeding area (such as an open field where he feels secure in darkness) and a day feeding area in heavier cover. Probably he will be in about the same areas at the same times each day. Thus if you sight a buck traveling a certain trail at, say, sun-up, that would be a likely place to situate your ambush point for early-morning hunting. If there are indications a buck has been feeding in a field, look for his established route or trail into the field. Stand-hunt along this trail. A cagey old buck probably won't enter the field until dark. And stay put until the end of legal quitting time or when it is impossible to see any more. That last five minutes of weak light, just enough to illuminate a scope sight, might make the difference.

It is this kind of preseason research and preparation which distinguishes the serious follower of the sport from the beginner or average haphazard hunter. The person who studies the deer and its habits is going to stand the better chance of putting venison on the dinner table, simply because he'll know where to look for deer and can predict what one will do under different circumstances.

Here bucks are feeding along "edge," where a grassy area meets a line of brush and trees. Such edges are good places to watch.

This is particularly important for the trophy hunter, the man who seeks a bragging-sized rack and antlers. Big bucks exemplify the survival of the fittest. While their brethren have fallen before hunters' guns, they somehow have survived, and become much wiser to the ways of the human predator. With trophy hunting, a lot depends on hunting where deer with record antlers are known to be. The North American Big Game Awards Program chronicles world records for firearms hunters. In thumbing through the record book, issued about every six years, you can pin down where the big heads have been coming from. Recent editions are dated 1971 and 1977.

The skilled deer hunter has studied the everyday habits of deer and often can predict what one will do simply by the way it acts. Every movement a deer makes means something. A deer will, for instance, look at another deer differently from the way it will look at a human. Often a person who really knows deer behavior can tell, simply by watching a deer's reactions, whether it is alarmed or simply curious about something natural to its environment.

A deer that is looking about occasionally, just idly watching, will hold its ears almost straight up and cupped slightly forward. When alarmed, when listening intently for some danger signal, the ears will stand out at about a 45-degree angle.

The learned deer hunter also can distinguish between the infrequent sounds which deer make. Almost always the sound will come from a female, the bucks being relatively mute. If it is a low, pleading bleat, the doe probably is communicating with other deer, perhaps a buck that has come courting. But if it is a loud, abrupt snort, she has detected something out of the ordinary and is giving a warning signal.

A snorting doe won't always flee, however. I've had one stand off in the brush and snort loudly over and over again. I stayed put and waited quietly. Soon the deer got over her sudden fright and started feeding again, often wandering out in the open where I could see her.

Yet if there was a buck within hearing distance he likely took off, not waiting around to determine whether or not it was a false alarm. A buck usually doesn't take the unnecessary chances that a doe does.

Another thing the serious hunter soon learns when studying deer is that tail movements betray what the deer is thinking. If you watch feeding deer for any length of time, you'll observe that each one is glancing up periodically, searching the landscape for anything out of the ordinary. If it twitches its tail back and forth a few times, that means everything is okay and the deer will start feeding again. But if the deer raises its tail it probably means the animal is suspicious.

How far it raises the tail depends on how suspicious it really is. If it throws it straight up, it probably is getting ready to bolt; should it only ease it up halfway, it means it is leery, all right, but not quite suspicious enough to run. When you see a deer do this tail raising, be extra cautious to avoid detection, particularly if only does are in sight and you believe a buck might be lingering out of sight in bordering brush. Also watch for the stamping forefoot. A deer that is picking the foot up and dropping it sharply is suspicious of something. When a deer is scared into running, it often will alert every other deer within hearing range.

A doe is much more observant than a buck. Watch deer of both sexes feeding together and you'll note the doe is almost continually raising her head to look around briefly, while the buck seldom raises his. Also notice that when crossing open places, the buck seldom leads the herd. He lets a doe go first, to determine whether it is safe for him to pass, just as he lets her watch and look while they are feeding.

The hunter also can usually ascertain whether a deer moving through the cover is a doe or buck merely by observing the manner in which it is traveling. A doe tends to run in rapid steps with her head up; the buck keeps his head tucked down, to avoid tangling his antlers in low-hanging limbs and brush, and he takes shorter steps, more of a slip than a run. Of course, the hunter shouldn't shoot at a deer because it *looks* offhand like a buck, but having an idea that it is legal game will aid him in moving around to intercept the retreating deer for a shot.

The idea of studying deer, naturally, is to learn something about their behavior which will give you an advantage when planning your hunt. The deer must be the one that makes the mistakes, not the hunter. It is a battle of wits, in a way, with the hunter's intelligence and reasoning trying to offset the inherent wariness, or woods wisdom, of the whitetail.

As we mentioned earlier, the deer's foremost defensive weapon is its nose. It depends primarily on its use of air currents and smelling ability to detect any enemy. The slightest whiff of human scent is all that is needed to scare one off. When it smells the human it won't be merely suspicious, it will be frightened.

For this reason, contrary to popular belief, it is much better to hunt on a day when there is a light (not strong) prevailing breeze rather than on a still day. By putting the wind to sensible use, the hunter can keep his scent blowing away from the area he hunts. On a still day he may be lured into false security, since it doesn't take even a noticeable breeze to carry human scent around. But the hunter must always be on the alert for sudden wind changes which will stymie his strategy.

On still days, the hunter is in a precarious position unless he knows how to counteract the lack of air currents. A man who has done extensive experimenting with catfish baits, of all things, proved this. In a still pool of water, the bait lying idle in one spot will give off a scent that slowly seeps outward like concentric circles from a pebble dropped in water. How fast it spreads depends on water temperature. In warm water the scent travels much farther and much faster than it does in colder water. Conversely, the colder the water, the less it travels.

This same pattern holds true with deer hunters and surrounding air. If a hunter is on stand during a warm and still day, his scent will radiate outward, moving eventually far enough to forewarn any deer that is approaching the hunter's concealed position. (This is important in dense timber and brush when the hunter has a confined field of view.) On a cold day, the scent will move much slower and within a more limited area. It stands to reason, then, that the stand hunter on the calm and warm days must move occasionally, to hold this scent pattern in check. Scents help mask the strong human odor (see Chapter 14). The hunter should remain in one place about an hour or two, at the most, on warm days. During colder weather, he might move only every third or fourth hour.

The hunter who makes a serious study of deer behavior is going to be a better hunter than the person who approaches the sport with a haphazard attitude. Learning the habits of deer and how the animals react to various circumstances is the graduate study of deer hunting. The person who takes the time and effort to study his quarry will spend much less time in the woods in relation to the number of deer killed, and in the long run he will bring in much larger deer with bigger antlers than will the person with a lackadaisical approach to the sport.

Every deer hunter dreams of killing a trophy. Because of increased hunting pressure over the years, few bucks live to a ripe old age any more. Standards are high and record-book kills are rare. But a few still are made each season.

The Boone and Crockett Club, named in memory of those legendary hunters Daniel Boone and Davy Crockett, was established in 1949 to compile world-record big-game trophies. Probably the man who did most to champion the cause of the trophy hunter was the late Grancel Fitz when he was with the Boone and Crockett Club. In 1973 Boone and Crockett affiliated with the National Rifle Association to form what is now called the North American Big Game Awards Program, a title that better interprets the organization's purpose. Minimum standards have steadily increased through the years as more and more trophy hunters have become aware of the record lists and have sought recognition. Nowadays it takes a score of 170 points to make the typical whitetail listing, 195 points for the non-typical listing.

A trophy head cannot be measured until 60 days after it is killed, to allow for shrinkage. A typical head, basically, is one that scores about the same on both sides and has the symmetrical balance of the classic whitetail head. Many whitetails, no matter how old they may be, will have no more than ten points, four on either side and two brow points. Should a set of antlers have four points on one side and only three on the other, this would not make it nontypical. This wouldn't be freakish, since the animal simply failed to grow the extra matching point. The head would be graded as typical, but the head would lose credit due to imbalance or lack of symmetry.

In a typical head, all points grow off the main beams. When another point forks from a typical point, this is abnormal. Also, if a head has two brow points on one side it is freakish. When the score of a nontypical head is entered in the record books, it will be a compound score, such as 187¼:251¼ or 212½ total points. The second number indicates the length of abnormal points while the first is the score of the typical version of the antlers. The second number may be a conclusive determining factor as to whether or not the head makes it into the record book.

If you do not know the official measurer in your community, most taxidermists are familiar enough with record-book measurements to give you some idea as to whether you should write for an official entry blank and locate an official measuring representative. The official scorer in my town explained that he lets the hunter, using instructions from the entry blank, measure his head, and if the score is close or above the minimum standards, then he will take an official measurement. There is a $20 entry fee if you wish to submit a head for possible recognition. An official entry blank can be obtained from North American Big Game Awards Program, National Rifle Association of America, 1600 Rhode Island Avenue N.W., Washington, D.C. 20036.

The Pope and Young Club, named after two of bow hunting's earliest pioneers, Dr. Saxton Pope and Art Young, was established in 1957 to give credit to bow hunters, setting up a record list similar to that of the Boone and Crockett Club, but with slightly lower standards—125 points for a typical whitetail, 135 for a nontypical. The same measuring and scoring system developed by the Boone and Crockett Club is used. Any deer bagged with bow and arrow in fair chase can be submitted to either or both organizations for possible inclusion on their record lists. When the first record book was published in 1975, more than 591 heads qualified for the typical antlers list. Information and an official entry blank are available from Carl M. Hulbert, Executive Secretary, Pope and Young Club, 600 E. High Street, Milton, WI 53563.

What are your chances of making either the North American Big-Game Awards or Bowhunting Game Records of North America lists? Probably much better than you imagine. Despite popular belief, the "good old days" have been since 1955 – records reveal that a majority of the top 100 heads, typical and nontypical, have been added to the lists since then. So many, in fact, that both record-keeping organizations have had to raise their minimum standards.

Consider the Pope and Young Club. Since the bow-hunting boom is a modern-day phenomenon, virtually all the top heads certified have been added since 1960. An initial minimum score of 115 points was established for a typical whitetail head, and when the club published its first record book in 1975, more than 591 heads had qualified, prompting a boost in the minimum score to 125.

Of course, record heads are few and far between. Even under the most ideal conditions, few bucks grow massive antlers, just as few humans exceed 7 feet in height. But it is known that two critical factors are required to grow a record-book buck: age and nutrition of the right kind.

Whitetail bucks generally develop their largest antlers when they are from five to eight years old. In many areas of intense hunting pressure, few bucks live that long. Also, in many places the deer are overprotected to the extent that an overpopulation results and the range is overbrowsed and there is not adequate food to grow huge antlers.

The North American Big Game Awards list gives a better reading on what has happened to whitetail deer hunting because its records date back to the turn of the century.

An inkling of what can and has happened is best symbolized by a region I

Kent Price with his record-book whitetail, killed with bow and arrow in Maryland farm country. Agricultural regions provide abundant deer food and for that reason often yield better deer hunting than woodlands.

am intimately familiar with, the so-called brush country of deep southern Texas. Many of the top heads listed in the first Boone and Crockett Club record book came from this region. Now in the best 100 heads the area is mentioned only occasionally.

A study by the Texas Parks and Wildlife Department in Webb County (Laredo is the county seat) revealed that the typical buck was getting progressively smaller in both physical and antler size, the culprit being a combination of "overkill of bucks" and "overprotecting the herd generally." In sum, this indicates a deterioration of the range and too few bucks able to reach full maturity. In a program that may turn the trend around, the department established a buck permit system to limit the number of bucks which can be taken from this county once noted for its record-book heads.

A quick rundown of the North American Big Game Awards lists shows that a record-book head might originate from almost anyplace. A few examples: Peoria County, Illinois; Randolph County, Missouri; Monroe County, Iowa; Christopher Lake, Saskatchewan; Lyman County, South Dakota; Flathead County, Montana; Dakota County, Nebraska; Linton, North Dakota; Lynd, Minnesota; Council Grove, Kansas; Frio County, Texas; Wirral, New Brunswick; Crook County, Wyoming; Ashtabula County, Ohio; and Thompson Creek, Washington.

Most record-book heads are, in addition to skill, a matter of fate: a hunter being at the right place at the right time. But some hunters seek only trophy heads. This is a game which demands a big dose of self-restraint, passing up lesser bucks in hopes of getting that coveted big 'un. A person might go an entire season or seasons without taking a shot. But that is the price the trophy-head hunter must pay.

13

The Adaptable Hunter

NOW THAT WE HAVE discussed the various hunting methods and something about the behavior of the whitetail deer, it is a matter of putting this knowledge and know-how to best use.

Occasionally I come across a stubborn hunter who extols his pet technique and can't be convinced that it isn't the best, all things considered. True, self-confidence plays a significant role in eventual success, but don't confuse confidence with stubbornness.

There is, of course, no one best method for hunting whitetails. In a way, hunting methods are similar to shotgun chokes: each does a specific job better than the others, depending on the circumstances. Praising one method over another must be done with some qualification. The wise deer hunter learns the strengths and weaknesses of each method, analyzes the situation which confronts him, and *adapts* accordingly.

Personally I would rather still-hunt or stalk than hunt by any other method. It is challenging, fascinating hunting. But, I hasten to add, not always practical.

The scene: De Soto National Forest, southeastern Mississippi. Time: mid-December. The setting: a thick carpet of dry leaves from deciduous hardwoods. The situation: hunting alone. Any forward motion sounds like stepping into a bowl of cornflakes, magnified many times. The choice is clearcut: I sit on a stand and hope that an unsuspecting deer will pass my way. Conditions and circumstances dictate it.

Generally, as I've pointed out in earlier chapters, you can play the percentages by stand-hunting early and late and around noon, prime periods of deer movement, and either stalk-hunt or drive-hunt at other times. That really, however, is too much of a catch-all statement to adhere to religiously. You must play the game on the deer's terms, not vice-versa.

I remember a trip that Winston and Murry Burnham and I took to northern Nebraska, the sand-hills country. My first impression was one of disbelief. It didn't look like deer country.

But some time later, as we turned off the highway, the answers began falling into place. We followed a dirt road along the winding Calamus River. Bordering the river were fields. The riverbed was brushy with a few trees. Deer could bed along the river, moving into the fields periodically to forage. From a deer's viewpoint you couldn't ask for more convenience.

One possibility was to find a stand and wait in ambush for a deer to come to a field. But there was lots of country and it would be easy to be at the right place at the wrong time. Considering the topography of the river and nearby so-called shelter belts, drive-hunting would be the most practical, controlling deer movement to our benefit.

There are no trees native to this country, other than those growing along watercourses. The shelter belts, or narrow bands of timber found elsewhere, were planted by man. Some deer bed along the rivers; others hide in the narrow woodlots found near the fields.

There were five in our party: we three, plus Gene Hornbeck of Omaha and Bob Harrington, the ranch foreman. I got my buck from a shelter belt. I was positioned to watch the south side of the timber, Winston the north side. The other three fanned out and walked slowly through the trees.

The buck came slipping gingerly from the trees, but once he hit open

This is the type of undergrowth encountered on a hunt along the Calamus River in northern Nebraska. About the only way to get deer to expose themselves is to run them out by making an organized drive.

country he started running. He was about 50 yards away when I sighted him. I swung on him with my 6mm Remington and piled him up, a fat forkhorn.

Later we made a drive along the river. Winston and Murry got ahead of us, one on either side of the Calamus, up on the banks where they could look down into the brush tangles where Gene, Bob, and I were walking, trying to rouse any hiding deer into the open.

On this drive a seven-point buck came crashing from the riverbed and hit the open country under full throttle. One slug from Winston's .264 sent him cartwheeling.

Murry got his deer the next day while driving another stretch of the river. This was a wily, heavy-antlered ten-pointer that was wise to the facts of survival.

Gene practically stepped on him before he flushed from his hiding spot. Instead of heading toward open country he hit the water and swam toward a brushy island. Fortunately Murry sighted him before he gained this new sanctuary. We had to wade in and drag that buck back to shore.

In less than three days of hunting we three nonresidents all had collected our bucks, thanks to the expertise of our hosts, who matched the method, drive-hunting, to the topographical conditions, narrow strips of brush and timber where deer had no place to run off and hide. If the drive was organized properly, they virtually had to show themselves, either moving ahead or attempting to slip back through the drive line.

Larry Benoit and his son Lanny have made quite a reputation for themselves by their adroit snow-tracking of trophy bucks in remote areas of Vermont, New Hampshire, and Maine. They get far off the road into places where bucks grow old and big and are undisturbed. It is a system they have worked hard to perfect, and it pays off for them because they are dedicated hunters and are willing to pay the price.

In the part of Texas where I live, however, if we waited for a snowfall during the hunting season we might never get a chance at a deer. Here a deer either hides in a thicket or runs for its life if it wants to survive.

Another example, this in the Ouachita National Forest of western Arkansas. Normally an abundance of crunchy dry leaves would make stalk-hunting virtually impossible, but on this late-autumn day the forest was saturated from an overnight rain. Leaves were mushy and quiet underfoot. So I waited on stand until midmorning, then got up and started creeping through the timber. I surprised a fat forkhorn and headed back to Texas with lots of venison steaks.

Get the idea? The successful hunter is adaptable. He makes the best of opportunity.

He starts with some sort of "game plan." It begins, as mentioned previously, with his homework, getting in the woods before the season, eyeballing for fresh sign, collecting a mental picture of the terrain, selecting specific spots for stands, areas for stalking or maybe even an organized drive. He prepares for any contingency.

I hate to keep harping on this point, but scouting is so vital to success. My dad used to tell me that it was important to hunt the same terrain for several seasons running in order "to learn the place." What he meant was finding the best deer habitat, including feeding areas, and concentrating on places that likely would pay off with the highest returns. In other words, you should gain familiarity with your hunting territory, by preseason scouting or some other means.

If you are in unfamiliar country you would be wise to make judicious use of a compass and map. A topographic map gives all the facts and figures for planning a successful hunt. Each map is called a "quadrangle" and the most practical is the 1:24,000 scale. Contour lines show the lay of the land. Colors represent different map features: green for woodland cover; blue for water; brown for relief features and contours of the land (with symbols for some unique terrain); red for roads, built-up urban areas, and public land subdivisions; and black for man-made features such as a cabin. Indexes of published topo maps (specify which state) are available free by writing Map Information Office, U.S. Geological Survey, Washington, D.C. 20242, or Federal Center, Denver, Colorado 80225. Indexes outline the surface area covered by each quadrangle, its name, the scale, and the year of survey. An order blank comes with each index.

Maybe the locale is lush with undergrowth and stalk-hunting would be a waste of effort. Even from a ground-level stand it is difficult to see more than a few yards in any direction. The logical solution would be to gain some elevation for better vantage, perhaps a tree stand. I even know hunters who use 10- or 12-foot stepladders as portable stands, painting the aluminum with something to dull the shiny finish, and standing the ladders beside trees or tall bushes to break the outlines.

Should the early part of the season be abnormally warm, deer might move in the cool of night, bedding down by daybreak and not arising until dusk is washing the last light off the landscape. Stand-hunting is a maddening game of frustration. The thick cover makes stalk-hunting impractical. So utilizing the topo map and prevailing wind currents, hunters organize a drive to move the deer.

The success of any particular method selected depends chiefly on the hunter's ingenuity. While he has formulated his "game plan," he nonetheless must be prepared to improvise, to deviate from it when need demands, to take advantage of specific conditions and circumstances. Since the whitetail deer has a marvelous defense system and intimately knows its home range, about your only hope is to use your God-given intelligence and simply outsmart the deer.

And that, my friend, is indeed a formidable assignment.

14

Bow Hunting

I've been in close proximity with whitetail deer all my life. I was raised in the heart of Texas' finest deer country. My current home is surrounded by prime deer habitat. My first deer was killed when I was nine years old and I've gone very few seasons since without getting at least one deer.

That's why about a decade ago I unhesitatingly accepted a challenge from a friend of mine to try bow hunting. I reasoned that I knew deer behavior well enough to get close enough to bag one of the critters easily with this primitive weapon.

I wasn't naive enough to believe I could go out during the peak of the rifle season and expect to get a buck with bow-and-arrow. But I got a permit for an antlerless deer, a doe, and figured I could at least kill one of the less suspicious females.

Was I in for a rude awakening! I'll never forget my first shot at a deer with a hunting bow. I doubt that I did anything right. The doe came tiptoeing down the game trail, across a small clearing from where I crouched in hiding behind a makeshift blind of cut bushes. Instead of shooting from the downed position. I tried to rise up and draw the 51-pound Bear bow. The deer glimpsed the movement and bolted. I fired hastily and the arrow whished harmlessly over her back.

When I trudged campward that evening I was a frustrated and exasperated hunter. For I'd gotten three chances, and three times I'd fouled things up royally. Mentally I was exhausted. I'd been too tense and too keyed up all day to relax. My nerve ends were rubbed raw.

But there was one consolation. I'd gained a new respect for the bow hunter. This, I decided, is the ultimate in deer hunting, the true challenge. While I'm not planning to discard my trusty rifle for the bow, I'm still fascinated by bow hunting and usually I try my success with the Indian weapon several times every year.

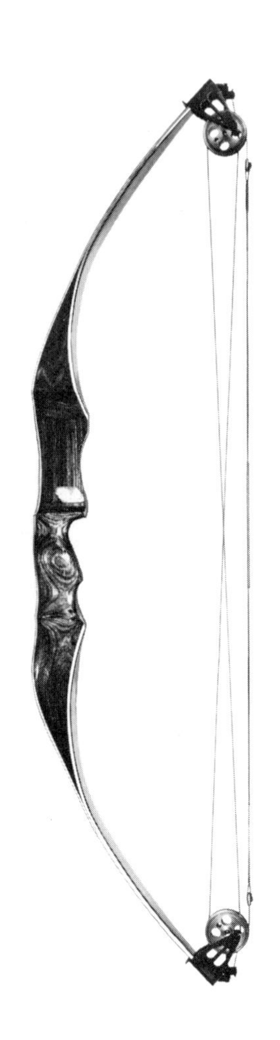

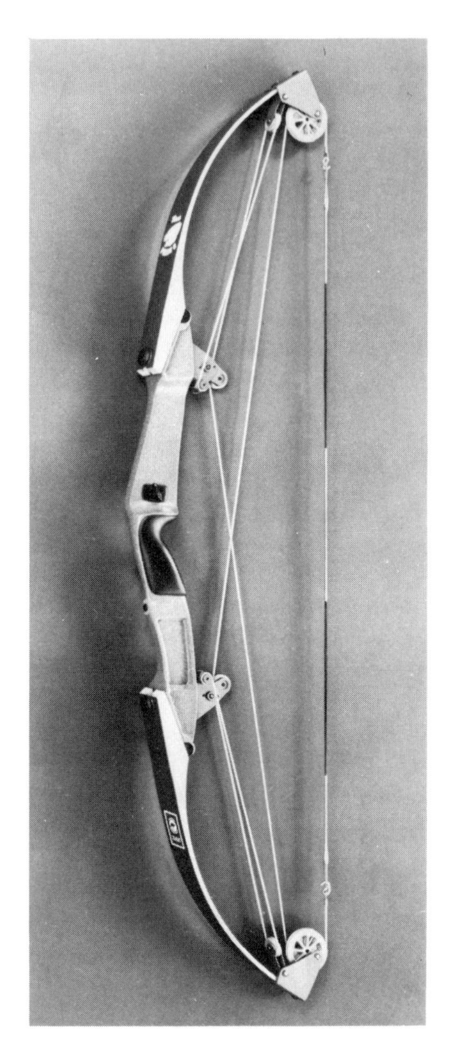

Here are two of many different compound bows available. The bow at left has only tip-to-tip cabling. The one at right has a more complex pulley system for added mechanical advantage.

The Indian, whose very existence depended upon his homemade weapon, both for protection and for providing food, would not recognize the modern bow, especially that mechanical marvel called the compound bow with its wheels and cables. In fact, bow hunting has been in a state of almost constant change in recent years as modern know-how and technology have brought this challenging sport into the space age.

At the same time, the number of bow hunters is increasing at a phenomenal rate. For example, in Pennsylvania, the hotbed of bow hunting, only 17,318 archery licenses were sold in 1955; by 1975 more than 215,000 were sold.

More efficient equipment—or tackle, as some call it, might be one impetus for the amazing growth, or perhaps the equipment might be only a reflection of the demand. Other factors include the challenge of bow hunting, more emphasis on the chase rather than the kill, liberal special seasons which permit the "two-season hunter" to extend his hunting time (using both bow and firearms during legal seasons), and areas off limits to firearms that are open to the bowman, such as some state parks and national wildlife refuges.

In my home state of Texas, I, like numerous others, hunt with both bow and gun, the first during the special month-long archery season (in some states it is much longer), the latter during the regular season—although in Texas, unlike most states, a person can hunt with a bow even during the regular season.

With bow-and-arrow I feel I earn every deer, even if it is only a doe. There is no long-shooting rifle to compensate for some of my human errors. In bow hunting there are many things that can go wrong, and something usually does. Frustrating at times, but fascinating and challenging.

When the recurve-bow principle was married to rugged fiberglass-laminated finish, it was thought this was the ultimate bow-hunting weapon. Then came that weird-looking contraption called the compound.

H. W. Allen started it all when he invented the bow with eccentric wheels and block-and-tackle principle and named it the compound. His company, later joined by Jennings Compound Bows, gradually but slowly laid the foundation for the mushrooming business of today. Major companies such as Bear, Ben Pearson, and Wing were slow to develop their own compounds. One drawback was archaic state laws which prohibited "mechanical bows." Only after Pennsylvania legalized the compound did compounds with different brand names really start rolling off the production line. At this writing only Georgia continues to outlaw the compound during its special archery season, although the compound is legal during Georgia's regular deer season.

The compound does have certain advantages. With a 50-pound-pull recurve (poundage needed to draw a standard 28-inch arrow full length), the shooter at full draw is pressing to contain that much force and at the same time remain steady for a good sight picture and then a smooth release, vital to accuracy. Unless his arm and back muscles are strong and in shape, the archer can't hold such a bow at full draw for very long—only a second or two, if that much.

But with the compound principle the bow "relaxes" at mid-draw, as much as 50 percent on some models, especially the so-called "trim compounds" with only two wheels and tip-to-tip cabling (the classic compound usually has two wheels and two pulleys). These bows require some straining to draw the arrow about halfway; then the eccentric wheels turn over and much of the resistance magically disappears. At full draw the shooter is holding only about 25 pounds or slightly more, and if you don't think there is much difference between that and 50, just try the two weights and find out! I can hold my 55-pound Bear Polar II at full draw for more than a minute and never get unsteady, even if my shooting muscles have been inactive for a month or longer.

A compound will also propel an arrow faster than a comparable recurve, and greater arrow speed means flatter shooting—up to 50 yards, arrow drop will be negligible. This improved performance is possible, explained inventor Allen, by application of three basic principles of physics: increasing foot-pounds of energy applied to the arrow; reducing inertia or the resistance of weight in motion; and reduction of projectile weight.

Without getting too complicated, the foot-pounds of energy are increased for the same reason that a long rifle barrel will provide greater muzzle velocity than will a short handgun barrel; the rifle applies gas pressure from the cartridge for a longer distance. Since the compound has peak pull-weight poundage at mid-draw, this means as the string is released it moves forward to peak, then decreases, providing a significant increase in foot-pounds of energy for direct application to the arrow.

As for inertia, the arrow is only one factor involved. The total weight which must be put into motion also includes the bow string and that portion of each bow limb which moves. So simply reducing arrow weight does not contribute that much to speed. With the compound's block-and-tackle principle, however, a 50-pound bow will have limbs equal in strength to a 150-pound recurve, now often referred to as a "stick bow." Limb-tip travel distance also is reduced to 3 inches rather than the 8 inches of a recurve. In sum, 150 pounds are available to move the limbs and pulleys a distance of only 3 inches, while the remainder of the 50-pound force at the bow string moves only the arrow and string. Thus much of the limb-motion inertia is eliminated by the tripled force used to move the limbs and the shorter distance they must travel.

And finally, because the bowman is holding less weight at full draw, the acceleration upon release is gradual and the arrow already is in motion before the peak push, at mid-draw, is applied. This permits the hunter to utilize a lighter arrow than he can with a recurve of comparable weight.

Another advantage is the draw-weight adjustment of some compounds (but not those with only tip-to-tip cabling). My Bear Polar II, for instance, is factory-set at 50 pounds, but peak weight easily can be increased to 55 or even 60 pounds. As the shooter gets stronger and can pull more weight, he can adjust his bow accordingly. And any hunter is going to get better performance from the heaviest bow he can adequately handle. I stress *adequately handle* and not what he can pull.

Which brings forth an obvious question: Does the compound signal the demise of the recurve bow?

Certainly not. A recurve in the hands of an accomplished shooter is a lethal weapon. Many hunters prefer its simplicity; there is less that can go wrong with it in the field.

I'm sold on the compound. I believe it is the best buy. Yet I still recommend that the beginner learn with a recurve. The "stick bow" in conventional sizes of 48 inches and longer is more tolerant of errors in the shooter's form, especially in the release. With the recurve the factors of arrow weight and spine, fletching, and broadhead design are now so critical. The recurve also strengthens back and arm muscles so vital to a steady hold and accuracy. Once you master the recurve you can graduate to a compound and keep the "stick bow" as a spare. It always is wise to have a backup bow on a hunting trip.

When shopping for a compound, be alert to what you actually are buying. With so many new models available it pays to shop wisely. Some compounds come bare, while others will be predrilled to take accessories such as a bow quiver. The simplest compounds do not permit adjustment within a wide range of draw weights, while the more sophisticated models do. Some compounds can be adjusted only at the factory. What type of guarantee does the bow carry, and do you have access to a service dealer? These are important considerations to keep in mind. The more sophisticated the compound, the more you will pay for it and the more complicated it will be should you need to make emergency repairs in the field.

The dramatic emergence of the compound is certainly the most important development in bow hunting. Yet there have been many other innovations as well.

Consider arrows. When I first got into bow hunting, the deer hunter needed at least two types of arrows, one with a field point for practice, another with a sharp broadhead for actual hunting. If the archer happened to buy two different brands, there might be a weight difference of just a few grams between the practice point and the broadhead. Get accustomed to one and how it performs at different ranges, and then change to the other, and everything is off enough to encourage misses. Also with permanent heads is seemed sensible to buy the cheapest arrows because of the variety and number needed.

The beginning bow hunter needs all the help he can get, and cheapie arrows don't help but hinder. Wood arrows are apt to warp; they break easily if they meet much resistance.

Aluminum arrows are the best because each shaft can be milled to the same wall thickness and weight. Aluminum does cost quite a bit more than wood. But when you take into consideration the quick-change feature of some arrows, the price difference isn't that overwhelming. A dozen quality shafts should last a long time. Buy a few of the the different kinds of heads needed. Simply screw in a field point for practice, and when you are ready to go hunting, substitute a broadhead. Since the head weight is identical, there is no significant difference in arrow trajectory once it flies off the string. Fiberglass arrows are rugged and nearly as good.

Since an arrow kills by hemorrhage rather than shock, it is imperative that a broadhead have razor-sharp edges. Some heads, such as the Savora Super-S, will accept replaceable, presharpened surgical-type steel blades. Other than the Super-S, quality broadheads I can recommend are the Bear Razorhead, Ben Pearson Switchblade, Mohawk Magnum II, and Zwickey Black Diamond Delta.

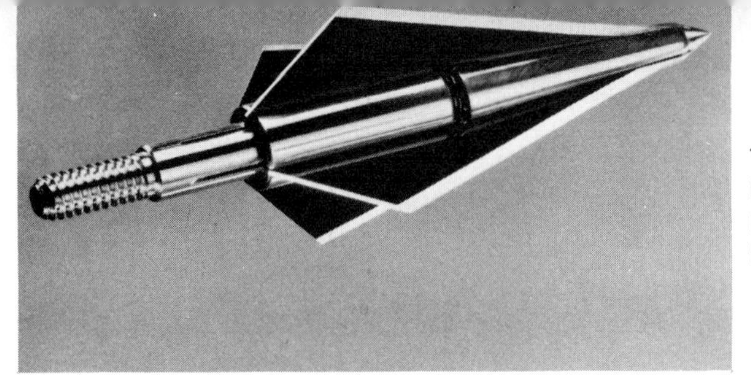

This Savora Super-S IV broadhead has razor-blade edges for maximum sharpness.

But once the hunter has several broadhead arrows sharpened and ready, he needs some sensible method of transporting same as he moves about in the woods. The best device, I am convinced, is a quiver which fits snugly to the bow. Formerly, most quivers were "universal models" which clamped to the bow, never fitting any one model with much permanency. Such a quiver was apt to slip or vibrate when the arrow was drawn and released. Now many models, both recurves and compounds, are tapped to accept personalized, adjustable quivers, easy to put on and take off by twisting a couple of oversized screws. Extra arrows are quickly available, yet when shooting, the bowman is hardly aware the quiver is there.

Getting properly equipped is just the obvious and most basic first step, of course. Then you must learn to handle the equipment with some proficiency.

Bow hunting is usually a waiting game, staying in one place and hoping a deer comes within arrow range.

Well camouflaged behind a blind made of cuttings and bushes, noted bow hunter Jim Dougherty takes up watch.

Despite what you might have heard, learning to shoot a bow and arrow is not difficult. Once you master the fundamentals, a few hours of backyard practice will make you accurate enough to hit a deer's vital organs at 20 yards or less. After that it is merely a repetitious thing, practice. The more you shoot the better you will become. There are no shortcuts.

The most important step is learning the fundamentals. Preferably get someone who knows about the sport to help you select the proper equipment and show you how to shoot it (most larger cities have pro shops which give lessons), or obtain a book on basic archery from the local library and read it studiously. The person who follows the basic steps will attain fair accuracy almost immmediately.

One fundamental complements another, so you must master each and every one for consistency.

With *draw,* the arrow should be pulled full length smoothly every time, and for this reason it is imperative that arrow length be selected to suit your specific physical measurements (any sporting-goods dealer who knows his business can fit you properly).

Anchor point or simply *anchor* is pulling the arrow to the same place every time, such as the corner of your mouth, which makes each shot virtually the same, adding to accuracy and consistency.

The *release,* or turning loose the string and sending the arrow on its way, should be smooth, not herky-jerky; you just open your hand and let the string roll off your fingertips.,

Practice these basics until each one merges into one subconscious move. When pulling on a deer you want to concentrate solely on a specific point you wish to hit with the arrow; you can't be thinking about accomplishing each of these steps individually and properly. Accurate shooting should become a habit that requires no involved thought.

Some bow hunters prefer to use a sighting device as shown in the left-hand photo; others use none. The right-hand photo shows a camo glove and a quick-change arrowhead that screws into an aluminum shaft.

There are a couple of ways to learn to shoot: with two fingers below the arrow and one above, at the nocking point on the string; or with all three fingers below the arrow, the so-called Apache style. In either case you will need a shooting glove to keep from burning your fingertips with the string. Some shooters prefer a tab (a small piece of leather to hold the string), but it is more awkward than the glove, although you might want to try both and find which you prefer.

The archer can also shoot instinctively, the same way he'd aim a slingshot, or he can use some sort of sight. There is no reason to recommend one or the other; each shooter has his own personal preference. So this is one good reason for patronizing an archery pro shop, if there is one in your town. The different types of equipment are available and you can try it all to satisfy your needs and/or wishes. Otherwise, get a beginner's book on archery and read it carefully. One I can recommend is *Bow Hunter's Guide* (Stoeger). I wrote it.

But learning to shoot the bow-and-arrow is no guarantee of success. I have known many archers who were crackerjack shots who never killed a deer. Much more important is being a skilled hunter. To bag a deer you must have it close—nationwide statistics show that the average whitetail killed with a bow is at a range of less than 30 yards. Getting that near to a crafty, vigilant whitetail deer is no easy feat. Bow hunting is not a sport for the careless, haphazard hunter.

Most whitetails, I would suspect, are killed from tree blinds. Such a vantage puts the archer above the critter's normal line of sight, and up high like this there is less likelihood of telltale scent spooking the animal before it approaches within bow range.

When I first started bow hunting I either found a spot to sit on a limb or I nailed a board in a fork. Nowadays there are commercial stands easy to erect and take down with no damage to trees. Most states allow tree-stand hunting, yet at the same time no tree-damaging stands are permitted on many public and timber-company lands, and indeed even some private lands. On some kinds of trees, such as pines, stands of the platform type which snug solidly against the trunks are mandatory.

The typical stand-hunter attempts to locate a well-traveled trail—or a juncture where several trails come together—and he situates his tree vantage to ambush any deer traveling this route.

Murry and Winston Burnham, the brothers who manufacture and sell a popular line of game calls, and I had selected what we considered three prime traveling areas along the Niobrara River in northern Nebraska. It was the first day of the archery season, and Murry and I arrived back at the camp trailer almost simultaneously. Darkness had settled quietly over the landscape.

I had sat in the fork of a leaning oak and watched a well-traveled run for the better part of the day, and I had seen nothing. Murry had improvised a blind atop a haystack in an alfalfa field and had seen a doe and fawn, but the deer were a long way off, at the opposite end of the field.

It was some time later that Winston came trudging in. He was smiling.

Each bow hunter finds his own comfortable "anchor," the spot near his face to which he draws the arrow each time—for consistency and accuracy.

Most hunters armed with bows and arrows prefer to hunt from trees, putting them above the whitetail's normal line of sight.

"Think maybe I got me a buck," he said excitedly.

Murry and I pressed for details.

"This buck eased out of the brush right at dusk," he told us. "I was sitting on that board nailed in the fork of a cottonwood tree and watching to the left where I expected any deer to show. I heard a rustling in the leaves and I half-turned and immediately saw this buck. He hadn't seen me. I had to swivel about, cant my bow almost level with the ground, aim down the arrow the best I could, and shoot. I lost sight of the arrow in the gloom of the underbrush but I heard it whomp against something and the buck whirled and ran into the trees. But I think I hit him."

We hurriedly dug around in our equipment and came up with a pair of flashlights and walked the 500 yards to Winston's stand. Winston showed us where the deer had been standing, perhaps 25 yards from the tall tree, and Murry flashed his light along the leaf-covered ground.

"You hit him all right," he said, pointing to large splotches of blood glistening in the beam.

We followed the liberal blood trail for maybe 50 yards before coming to the buck sprawling prone. He was a fat eight-pointer. The arrow had caught the buck in the throat, severed the jugular vein, and angled down to completely penetrate the shoulder bone.

In a way you might call this luck. Winston was at the right place at the right time. But he was in his stand during a prime traveling time, late afternoon, and when opportunity presented itself, he was able to capitalize. That is what successful hunting is all about.

In this instance the high vantage undoubtedly helped Winston avoid detection. When the bow hunter decides to make his move, he faces a twofold problem: his quarry is close and quick to pick up the slightest danger signal; and raising the bow and drawing the arrow are going to generate a certain amount of telltale motion. If a nervous whitetail homes in on the hunter and sees an arrow coming, it can move quickly enough to evade the projectile.

But for one reason or another it is not always possible to hunt from a tree. So the archer hides at ground level and improvises the best he can. He respects the whitetail deer's formidable defense and pays attention to details: having the air currents in his favor, using endemic materials to make some sort of blind, remaining absolutely still until he is prepared to draw the arrow. At that critical moment the archer attempts to negate the critter's perceptive eyesight by watching until the deer's head is turned or is behind some object before he raises his bow.

Mel Johnson was hunting from ground level when he bagged his world-record buck in a soybean field just a few miles north of Peoria, Illinois. Johnson had seen a pair of large bucks in the field previously and had spent many hours of many days waiting and hoping before he "got lucky."

It was late October, a bright and clear day. Johnson was crouched in a brushy area of the field not far from bordering timber. It was nearing sundown when he spotted movement and shortly, from the shadows, a magnificent buck walked out of the woods into the field. As the buck approached his position, Johnson froze, almost afraid to breathe, realizing the slightest mistake now would spook the wary animal.

Here is where experience and patience paid off, and considering the impressive size of the buck's rack, any hunter can only admire and envy Johnson's self-restraint.

"There was only one thing to do," he explained later. "I let the buck pass me, and as soon as his head was turned away I got to my feet, notched an arrow, and got off my shot—all in one continuous motion."

Johnson's buck, incidentally, scored 204⁴⁄₈ points, a Pope and Young Club record and, for a time, the biggest typical whitetail taken by fair chase in the North American Big Game Awards Program's record book. (If you submit your kill as an outstanding example of its kind, to be considered for record-book inclusion by either of the organizations above, or both, you must sign an affidavit certifying that the whitetail deer was taken under the Rules of Fair Chase.)

Most archers, like Johnson, get their infrequent chances by waiting impatiently in ambush, stand-hunting, which puts a premium on woodsmanship, knowing deer behavior, and being able to read sign. This is not hunting for anyone who discourages easily. I once spent an entire week stand-hunting in Nebraska with bow-and-arrow, and I didn't see a deer within arrow range.

Some archers prefer drive-hunting, attempting to move whitetails by a stand where a companion can get a shot, but it is almost mandatory that it be a patient, quiet drive, not frightening the deer into running, but rather keeping them slipping ahead, diverting their attention to the drivers and making them oblivious of any danger they might sneak into.

I remember one such Mississippi drive that paid off. A half-dozen of us were hunting a part of the De Soto National Forest, some 50 miles south of Hattiesburg. Three circled ahead and got hidden, and the rest of us, spread apart, proceeded quietly and slowly toward them. A fat doe came catfooting by Hershel Howell and that was a fatal mistake.

Now this trio of random examples also points up another fact: the archer must adapt to make the best of any situation. Whitetail deer are unpredictable. No two will act or react exactly alike. One might approach your stand from any direction. There is no anticipating the "perfect opportunity" when everything falls neatly into place. Perhaps the archer might have to release an arrow from a sitting position, or while on his knees, or when twisted around in an awkward pose. Learning to shoot from unorthodox positions like this demands practice under actual field conditions, maybe even off a ladder to simulate a tree stand. The conventional feet-spread-comfortably-apart stance used in target shooting doesn't have much practical application in bow hunting.

The wise archer also takes advantage of the many aids which swing the odds a bit more in his favor. Such as string silencers, for instance. They attach to or slip on the bow string to soften or deaden the twang. Since sound travels faster than an arrow, a nervous whitetail sometimes hears the string noise and moves a split-second before the projectile arrives, resulting in, at best, a clean miss, and at worst, a wounded animal.

Many manufacturers now offer soft cases for their bows, recurves and compounds, both for protection and to satisfy state law. A couple also market sturdy, hard protective cases. (In some states a bow must be unstrung or in a case when being transported.)

Ancillary equipment for the tree-stand hunter includes a safety rope, to prevent a fall should he slip, and a special rope for raising and lowering equipment once the bow hunter is in his stand. Razor-sharp arrows are wicked instruments and the archer should never attempt to climb with them, even if they are in a protective bow quiver.

Camouflage certainly is not new, but refinements continue to be made. Camo rain gear has been quietened considerably, Camouflage grease paints still are popular for obscuring the hunter's face, but many bowhunters prefer to use a camo mesh headnet. The trouble with most headgear is they disrupt vision somewhat, and this bothers the hunter's concentration. One solution is simply to cut eye holes. But the net has a way of slipping so that the holes are not aligned with the eyes. Penn's Woods Products markets a headnet with a pair of eyeglass frames sewed in; the frames hold the eye holes securely in place. And there are mesh camouflage gloves.

Perhaps the most difficult camouflage job is with equipment, however. Manufacturers make bows glossy and handsome to sell, yet in the woods these weapons sparkle in the sunlight and stand out like a bald head in a barbershop. Camo cloth sleeves and camouflage tape are available to cover the limbs of both recurve and compound bows. A few companies offer painted camouflage bows. Bow Dull, by Martin Archery, is a spray-on paint in earth and leaf colors which won't harm the finish of a bow. It is easily removed with Brite Bac, from the same company.

Even some aluminum arrows are made with a dull finish. Special dip-paint kits are also available from several mail-order outlets for camouflaging your arrows.

Fact is, anyone who browses in an archery-equipment or sporting-goods store will be amazed at the diverse number of products available to the bow hunter, everything from scents to obliterate human odor to slings for packing the heavier compounds into the woods to improved bow sights.

The bow hunter of today takes advantage of the many accessories that can put the odds a bit more in his favor.

Many bow hunters use scents. A deer depends on its nose as its first-line defense. Confuse it, even briefly, and you might get a shot. There often is a very thin line between success and failure.

I often employ scents even when rifle hunting, where I am watching a limited amount of terrain and wind currents are capricious and unpredictable.

There are many types of commercial scents available. I have used those made with cedar oil, those with a sweet apple smell, and some with a strong odor that I couldn't identify. A few are advertised as "attractors"; they actually are supposed to lure deer to the hunter. But to me such claims are suspect. I use a scent for one primary reason: to mask the human odor, a danger signal that no cautious whitetail ignores.

One of the very best scents for this is common skunk musk. No, you don't put the malodorous stuff on your clothing. You simply uncap a bottle of musk and place it downwind of your position. I have had deer cross where a breeze was blowing my scent their way, yet the strategically set skunk musk kept me effectively hidden. Or at least the deer showed no concern or alarm. One source for skunk musk is Burnham Brothers, P.O. Box 100, Marble Falls, Texas 78654.

When bow hunting and using a scent like cedar oil, I will sprinkle it liberally on my stand and even put a few drops on my clothing. If I also have a bottle of skunk musk with me, I'll place this downwind and will use it in addition to (rather than in lieu of) other scents. I figure that I can't be too cautious.

Yet despite the many innovations and improvements, bow-hunting equipment and accessories are only tools. The main ingredient continues to be the human who uses them. No amount of equipment will provide a magic shortcut; success only comes from dedication, hard work, and patience.

Surprisingly, nationwide statistics indicate that the odds of bagging a deer with bow-and-arrow are actually increasing, despite increased hunting pressure. One reason no doubt is that the bowman, realizing the limitations of his weapon, spends a lot of time and effort to become an adroit hunter. But he also has the benefit of increased deer populations in many places and superior equipment.

Bow hunting was a real novelty back in 1923 when Dr. Saxton Pope wrote his book *Hunting with Bow and Arrow.* But his writings, along with those of his hunting companion Art Young, kindled an interest in the sport, and by the 1930s hunters were beginning to take to the woods with bows and arrows in hand. Finally, in 1934, interest reached the point at which Wisconsin decided to open a special archery deer season, to find whether it would work and whether there were enough bow hunters to support it. Michigan followed suit in 1937, and a grand total of 186 hunters turned out for the first archery season.

From that inconspicuous start, bow hunting has just grown and grown and grown. And the end is not yet in sight.

15

Hit or Miss

MANY HUNTERS who shoot at deer and subsequently see the animals run off assume their shots were misses. Untold hundreds of deer are left to rot in the woods each year for this reason. The hunter doesn't take the time or make the effort to find out that his shot actually was a miss.

Sometimes a deer will be knocked over as if pole-axed when struck by a high-velocity bullet. Other times it will hunch or jump if hit. But I've seen deer that were hit solidly in a vital area bolt off spiritedly as if they'd never been touched.

I was once hunting with a friend who fired at a deer and swore till the earth looked level that he'd missed the deer cleanly. I insisted we go look, to be positive. That buck, struck squarely through the heart, had run less than 100 feet before folding.

Occasionally, a bullet placed in the deer's most vital organ, its heart, won't bring instant death. Of course it is eventually fatal, but the deer may run for considerable distance, carried along only by a spurt of adrenalin. The more frightened a deer is before hit, the farther the boost of adrenalin will carry it. This might be 200 yards or farther.

There are too many intangibles involved in hunting to assure an instant kill every time. The hunter shooting from a draw up an incline tends to undershoot, unless he compensates by aiming higher on the animal, while the person firing from an elevated position, such as the top of a hill, will often overshoot unless he aims low. The hunter pulling down on a running deer might hit the animal too far back for a quick kill. A deer standing at an angle to the hunter may receive only a glancing shot that perhaps cuts through the flesh of the hindquarter without striking bone. A deer so hit might run for a long way, but often the painstaking hunter can follow the spoor until he either jumps the animal again for a finishing-off shot or finds it dead.

I witnessed a remarkable trailing job by Miles Bingaman, a deer-hunting veteran with wide experience, on a ranch in South Texas many seasons back. One of the hunters on the Diamond H near Catarina had crippled a deer. The only spoor was scattered droplets of blood. Bingaman started unraveling the trail, combing the ground with infinite care, sometimes going for yards between tiny pin-top drops of blood. Every time he'd lose the trail momentarily, he'd mark the last spot he had discovered blood and start circling, each time around gradually increasing the size of his circle until he'd scouted the territory for dozens of yards in each direction. He'd eventually pick up the trail again. After more than three hours and many miles, he finally came to the animal, down but still alive, too sick to continue farther.

In some Southern states, dogs are permitted by law to be used in trailing crippled deer. If there is any fresh blood at all, a trained dog will quickly run down the wounded deer. Dogs prevent loss of many cripples, but the anti-dog faction says there is too great a tendency for the canines to chase and kill healthy deer, by getting off the original trail and onto the track of another animal which just happened to pass in the same vicinity. Most persons experienced in the use of trained dogs for trailing wounded deer say this is fallacy. Very seldom will a dog get off the track of a crippled animal to chase one that is healthy and spry, they tell me.

If a deer is hit solidly in a vital area, there probably will be a very distinguishable blood trail to follow. But let the bullet strike in some place like the hip bone or low paunch and the animal might not bleed at all at first. Often a deer so hit will run quite a distance from the original spot where it was hit before beginning to bleed.

Some years ago, a hunter came in to the landowner's house on a ranch he was hunting and announced that he had wounded a deer, but he couldn't find anything but some scattered hair, no blood. I was visiting with the rancher at the time, so I accompanied him to look-see around the vicinity. We found the spot where the deer was standing when hit, all right, and tracks where it had crashed off into the brush. Painstakingly we followed the tracks. Perhaps 100 feet farther we came to a pool of blood which looked as if it had been poured from a bucket. Evidently the deer had paused momentarily and the blood had started flowing freely. Not 50 yards farther along we discovered the deer dead, piled up in a clump of brush where it had lain down.

The hunter should never take anything for granted when he shoots at a deer. He should always check to make sure he actually missed. Sometimes the deer might be dead nearby, or crippled.

Actually, the hunter who knows or even suspects he might have hit a deer has to be something of a detective. He searches for clues and, by fitting the pieces of the puzzle together, attempts to determine where the animal was hit and how damaging the wound might be. It is, for instance, possible to trail and maybe eventually get a deer that has been hit in a hindquarter; but one crippled in a foreleg probably will escape. It can travel on three good legs about as rapidly as it can on four.

When a high-speed bullet strikes an animal with tremendous force, it will leave some evidence of that fact, if nothing more than some loose hair on the ground.

Once I shot at a buck and spun him completely around. He didn't go down but I knew I had hit him. I marked the spot and went to get my hunting companion, Winston Burnham. Down on our knees we examined the ground where the buck had been standing. Winston finally found some loose hair. From its length and texture we determined it had come from the back. We followed the buck's tracks for some distance and discovered no blood. The tracks seemed to indicate the deer was running in normal motion. From all the facts we finally concluded that the bullet had only grazed the critter's back, causing no permanent damage.

If there is any blood, attempt to determine from it where the deer was hit and how badly wounded it might be. Foamy red blood indicates a lung shot. If there is considerable blood the animal probably is hurt badly and won't travel far. Absence of blood could indicate a paunch or "gut" hit. Look closely and try to find something else other than blood, perhaps pieces of bone or dabbles of partly digested food from the animal's stomach. By examining a piece of bone you sometimes can tell from where it came—maybe a tiny chunk of round leg bone or part of a rib.

A common tendency, especially with a running deer, is to simply shoot at the animal rather than at a specific spot on him. This usually results in a midsection hit. A paunch-shot deer normally will hunch and sort of hops off rather than running. A bullet in this region usually results in little if any blood. Since there is no way to trail it, leave the animal alone for at least a half-hour. It probably will travel just a short way and lie down and eventually die, unless it is spooked and starts moving again. Push a crippled deer and get its adrenalin to pumping and it can go for an unbelievable distance before succumbing.

A hip-shot deer usually bleeds quite profusely. It will take off in a fast run but after a short distance will slow to a walk. Again, be patient and give the animal time to get sick and stop.

In any case, do not immediately charge after the animal. This only makes it run faster and farther. Go to the spot where the deer was standing when you shot it and mark it so that you can always return to it should you lose the trail and need to start over again.

On hands and knees, examine the direction the blood trail and tracks took and periodically mark the spoor with some type of marking material. Folded toilet tissue or paper towels carried in a pocket will work well. Don't give up until the trail completely peters out or you find the deer. If you find no more blood, go forward in the direction the deer was last headed and cut back-and-forth arcs, always looking. Sometimes a deer stops bleeding only to start again a short distance away. Watch not only the ground but also ahead. You might see the deer struggling to sneak away or lying down, and there is the opportunity for the *coup de grace.*

A couple seasons back I was hunting with first-rate bowman Jim Dougherty. Our party was making a drive, and a doe made the mistake of running near where Dougherty was hiding. He hit the animal solidly but he instantly knew he had not led her enough. She took the arrow somewhere back in the body.

Since his weapon kills by hemorrhage rather than shock, a bow hunter soon learns the value of being a skilled tracker. Jim Dougherty is one of the best.

After a wait of about an hour, we got on the doe's trail. When tracking any wounded animal, hit by either bullet or arrow, two or three hunters working together can solve the tough ones, Dougherty told us. One person always stays at the point of the last sign while the others track. In this way a line always can be established on the back trail which will help in establishing the direction the animal is going.

A common mistake, Dougherty explained, is to confine the search to the ground. At least 25 percent of trackable signs will be above ground level on foliage, rocks, or logs. Dougherty marks the trail about every 10 yards or so; he said this helps establish a pattern.

"A blood trail which goes uphill for any distance sometimes indicates the animal is not seriously hit, but never assume this and give up the track," Dougherty went on. "*Never* quit a trail that is leaving any sign."

He said also to always consider the possibility on a hard track that the animal may circle or backtrack on you. This is common when a deer is followed too soon and becomes aware of the pursuit. If the trail is lost, this is where persistence pays off. From the last sign a circling patrol is started to cover the area meticulously for 100 yards around. Sometimes a deer that is completely bled out will stagger a few more yards before going down.

Under Dougherty's guidance we stuck to the trail and before long we came to the dead doe. She had taken an arrow in the hip.

Every hunter owes it to himself and his fellow hunters to exert every effort to find deer he may have crippled. Leaving a deer to rot needlessly in the woods is, in my opinion, the most loathesome sin a hunter can commit.

16

Field-Dressing and Butchering

You have a deer down in the woods. It is an exhilarating moment, the climax of a long and tedious search, the legendary pot of gold at the end of the rainbow. But it is no time to let excitement overwhelm common sense. That deer lying there innocently may be potential danger, if it isn't dead. Always approach a downed animal with caution from behind. Punch it with your gun barrel in an attempt to detect any flickering sign of life.

Whenever I approach a downed deer, I recall something that happened to a friend of mine, one Carlton (Buzzy) Keller. He walked up to a fallen animal which he assumed was dead, straddled the buck, and started to dress him out. Unexpectedly, the deer came to life and started struggling frantically, trying to free himself from the hunter, shaking his antlered head and flailing his sharp hoofs. Buzzy held on desperately with his left hand and with his right hand punched at the deer with his knife. Fortunately, he killed the deer, but not until he was skinned and bruised and given quite a scare.

Murry Burnham once approached a large buck he had shot, assumed the deer was dead, leaned his rifle against a nearby tree, and reached for his knife. Unexpectedly the deer wobbled to his feet, staggered in a drunken circle, and toppled again, only this time against Murry's rifle, splintering the stock.

Another time I was hunting on the last day of the season, still looking for that elusive "big 'un." I had all my license tags and my dad told me if I saw a fat doe to get her for venison. Shortly after leaving my parked vehicle I was walking along a trail when ahead, a doe coming my way strolled around a bend. We sighted each other almost simultaneously. Startled, the deer stopped and threw up her head. She was no more than 20 yards away. I shouldered my 6mm, found her neck in the scope, and fired, a quick reflex response. The doe fell heavily.

I ran to her. Immediately I saw she was still breathing and I cut her throat and jumped back. If I'd tried to field dress that deer I would have been asking for trouble. The slug had just grazed her neck, stunning her.

After the deer is dead and harmless, then comes the routine labor of any successful hunt. The deer must be field-dressed immediately to assure prime steaks and chops on the dinner platter. The taint of the meat is particularly evident when the innards of the deer have been shot and the animal isn't gutted right away.

A handy item for any hunter to carry is a short length of rope to tie a hindleg to one side, making dressing easier, or maybe two ropes to spread both legs. Otherwise, just turn the animal on its back and prop it with logs or rocks, anything to steady it. Your knife should be very sharp. With a sharp blade you will do a better job and there is less risk of injury. A pocket whetstone or sharpening steel is a handy item to have along.

A hunter should approach a downed deer with extreme caution. If there is any life left, the animal can indeed be dangerous.

You can first cut away the pad (tarsal glands) on the inside of either hindleg, but this is optional and not really necessary. The pads of a rutting buck will be stinking and foul, saturated with urine. If you handle the pads there is a possibility you will taint the meat as you gut the animal.

Unless state law requires that the genitals be left attached to the carcass for sex identification, cut them off if the deer is butchered in camp and carried home sans skin and head, or if the head is detached from the body. In the hole left where the genitals were, insert your knife blade and cut back to the anus. Reversing the blade, go forward, slitting the abdomen from aitchbone to breastbone. (If the head is to be mounted, stop the incision before you reach the forequarters, to assure an ample cape.) While slitting the belly, some hunters like to reach inside the body cavity with one hand and press down the intestines while cutting with the other hand. This is a wise precaution. Nick an intestine and you've got a mess. While performing this operation, position yourself behind the deer and cut forward, the blade's sharp edge going away from you, as a safety precaution. I have seen hunters get nasty wounds from careless knife handling.

Gently squeeze on the bladder, if it is full, to free its contents. Cut around the anus to clear the intestines from the pelvic arch or aitchbone, where the hipbones are connected. Draw the intestines into the body cavity. Inside the abdomen, at the breastbone, cut the membrane which holds the innards to the deer, being particularly careful not to puncture the stomach or intestines. Just below the head, cut the windpipe and esophagus, and with both hands pull them downward until everything is free to the midsection. Now you can turn the deer over and shake the innards out. Just before this last step, remove the heart and liver if you wish to save them. The prepared hunter carries a large and stout plastic bag in his hip pocket for transporting the liver and heart back to camp. If two men are packing out the deer on a pole, the heart and liver can be carried inside the body cavity.

Yet once the field-dressing job is over, your work isn't finished. Somehow you must get the animal back to camp. If it is just an average-size deer and the terrain isn't too uneven and rough, grab it by the antlers and start pulling. Always drag it this way, head first, so the body hair folds back naturally and gives some protection against dirt and dead grass and leaves. Move the weight just a short distance, then stop and blow. Probably you are unaccustomed to this sort of strenuous activity. To overextend yourself is asking for a strained muscle, at the least, and maybe even a cardiac arrest, at the worst. Each year quite a few hunters die from heart attacks because they ignored common sense.

I recommend dragging rather than carrying. A carcass even from a small deer is heavy and hard to manage. You might fall and break a leg or arm. It is almost impossible to backpack a deer without getting your clothes bloody messy. And walking through the woods with a deer on your back is asking for someone to take a shot at you. If you must carry the carcass, take the precaution to tie a bright-colored rag around the antlers.

But the most sensible way to get a deer from here to there is to go for help. Enlist the aid of a hunting companion. Drape the gutted animal spread-eagled over a stump or bush so the body cavity can be draining until you return. Two people can manage the pack-out chore much easier than one with a lot less exertion. Tie the carcass on a pole, a hunter at either end, and carry it. Or each of you can grab an antler and drag.

Despite what you might have heard, the shortest distance between two points isn't always a straight line. Unless camp is close to where you made the kill, consider any accessible point nearby. If there is a road, head for it, even if it might not be in the direction of camp. Stash the carcass here and go for a vehicle and drive to pick it up.

If it is seasonably warm weather the deer should be taken immediately to a locker or cold-storage plant. This may be impossible at times, however. Should the nights be cold and the days warm, it is imperative to capture and hold as much of the chill as possible. Skin the deer promptly. The hide acts as insulation and prevents the meat from cooling properly. Prop the carcass open with a stick so that air can circulate inside. After it cools at night, cover it with a light mesh deer bag to protect it from flies. Hang it in a cool, shady spot. Swab the inside with a damp cloth and remove as much of the bullet-damaged flesh as possible.

If the temperature remains below 50° night and day, the deer will keep indefinitely if hung in a shady place. Skinning is still a good idea to cool the carcass throughout. Put the skinned carcass in a mesh deer bag, but never use anything like canvas or plastic as a permanent cover; air trapped inside gets warm and the meat will quickly spoil.

Should you plan to hold the deer in camp for only a brief time, one or two days, and the temperature is low enough to sufficiently cool and keep the meat, you probably will wish to leave the skin on. It help keeps the meat clean while the carcass is in transit from camp to home. Even so, prop the body cavity open with a stick or sticks to ensure good air circulation.

Although the near-universal method of skinning a deer is to hang it by its hind legs, I prefer to do just the opposite—to tie the animal up by its neck or antlers. This way the hide slips down with the grain of the meat and underlying fat. But if you're going to mount the head, hanging by the hindquarters has an obvious advantage, since you can slip the hide completely to the head before severing the neck.

When it is hanging by its neck or antlers, cut an incision around the deer's throat, just below the head, and start peeling the skin downward. With the alternate method, cut around each hind leg just below the hocks and start pulling the hide off, using your knife whenever flesh starts to give with the skin. After the rear legs are skinned, cut the tail at the base and strip the hide off the body down to the shoulders. Skin the front legs and peel the hide to the base of the neck. Remove the feet by cutting the flesh and tendons at the knee joints and bending each leg back sharply until the joint snaps. Sever the neck tendons and twist the head off. If you've hung the animal by the neck to skin, you'll have to rehang it by the rear legs for

If the temperature is cool enough to allow adequate cooling of the carcass without skinning, the body cavity should be propped open with sticks, as shown at left, to permit optimum air circulation. But in warm weather, the deer should be skinned promptly—easiest to accomplish with the deer hung from its hind legs, as shown below left. Below right, a mesh bag protects the skinned carcass from dirt and insects. Here again, the body cavity should be propped open to cool.

cooling. This is done by splitting the membrane under the tendons of the hindlegs, inserting a gambrel stick to spread the hindquarters, and hanging from the garage rafters or a tree limb.

Most hunters simply drape their deer on the hoods of their autos, or the front bumpers, and head homeward. On long trips, this is the worst possible thing to do. Engine heat soon transfers to the animals and spoilage comes quickly. Probably the best spot for transporting the deer is on the auto's top. This is where a station-wagon rack comes in handy. Otherwise, carry the deer in the car's storage trunk. If the weather is warm, get a bag of crushed ice at the first stop and lay it inside the carcass. This will keep it cool. Another method is to wrap the carcass in a heavy piece of tarp. This insulates the coolness inside.

If you're on a lengthy trip and stop for the night, remember to lift the trunk lid and allow the animal to cool during the night. Heat from the road and automobile collects in the trunk. It is even better to remove the animal completely and hang it up, propped open, and allow it to cool thoroughly. When in doubt, always use ice liberally to keep the animal chilled.

If state law permits, there is another valid reason for transporting the carcass concealed inside the trunk or beneath a tarp in a pickup bed. You may be proud of your deer and want to display it, but many people will be turned off—and not just the anti-hunters, who are always looking for ways to reinforce their arguments, but the vast numbers of nonhunting Americans who don't care one way or the other about hunting and are perfectly willing to leave you alone as long as you don't wave dead game in their faces. Why antagonize people?

Many hunters simply carry their deer to a local processing plant where, for a nominal fee, they can have it skinned, butchered, and wrapped for the deepfreeze. But butchering a deer carcass yourself is fairly easy if you follow a routine.

First divide the carcass into equal halves by sawing through the center of the backbone. To quarter, cut each half in two by slicing between the last rib and the one forward. Most hunters make the wrong cut here, dividing the half behind the last rib.

Lay the hindquarter on a sturdy support, perhaps on an old bedsheet spread on the garage floor. Trim away meat on the leg bone and cut away the flank, placing this miscellaneous meat in a pan to be later ground into hamburger and chili meat. Position the ham so that the leg bone extends off to the right. Cut diagonally at the upper end of the ham to remove the triangular chunk which is the rump roast. Then slice round steaks to the thickness desired. The lower end of the ham, near the leg bone, can be cut into steaks or left intact as a heel roast.

Separate the shoulder from the loin section by cutting between the fifth and sixth ribs. Divide the tenderloin and ribs by cutting horizontally just three or four inches below the spine. The tenderloin then can be sliced into steaks, cutting vertically to desired thickness, by using knife and saw. The ribs can be divided into rib steaks or left intact for barbecuing, or the meat can be trimmed off for use in hamburger and chili meat. The rib section can be divided horizontally to make short or spare ribs.

Separate the neck from the shoulder just forward of the shoulder bone. The neck can be cut into pot roasts, chunked into stew meat, or used in hamburger and chili preparations. Cut the leg off and divide the shoulder in half, about halfway down, at the shoulder joint. The upper half of the shoulder makes a nice roast, while the lower half can be sliced into shoulder steaks, utilized as a roast, or ground.

HOW TO FIELD-DRESS YOUR DEER   Leonard Lee Rue III Method

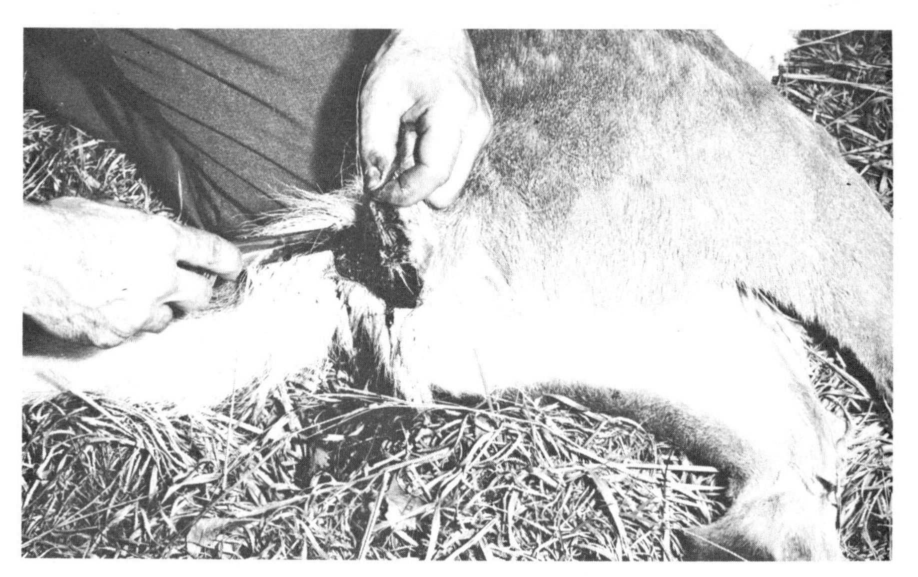

1. Start by cutting close circle around anus and connecting alimentary canal. Make cut as deep as knife will reach. 2. Open belly as shown, being careful not to cut intestines. Fork the incision to pass either side of sex organs.

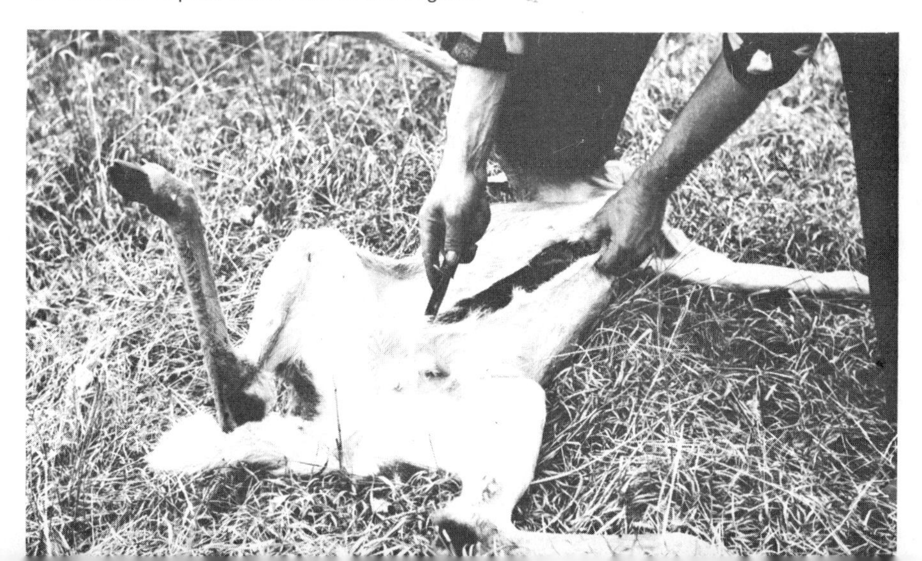

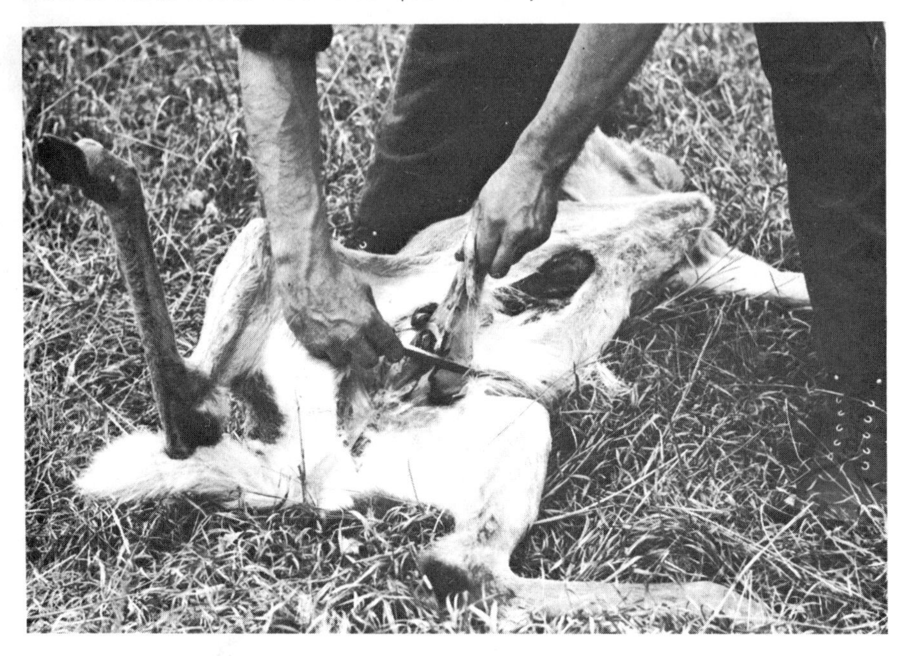

3. Make careful cuts to loosen scrotum and penis. Then pull detached anus and alimentary canal through pelvic arch.

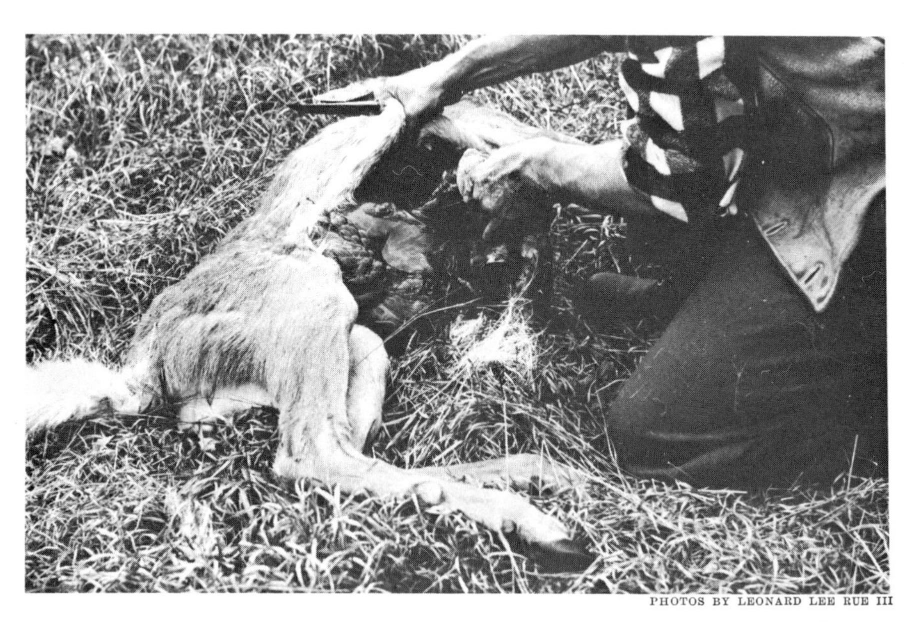

PHOTOS BY LEONARD LEE RUE III

4. Break membrane over chest cavity and reach far up to cut the windpipe loose. Pull out all the organs and entrails.

5. Put heart and liver in a bloodproof plastic bag to keep both meat and clothes clean.

6. Tip the carcass as shown and drain out blood collected inside. Wipe body cavity dry with cloth or dead grass.

7. Prop body cavity open with stick to let in cooling air. Hang carcass unless you plan to pack it out immediately.

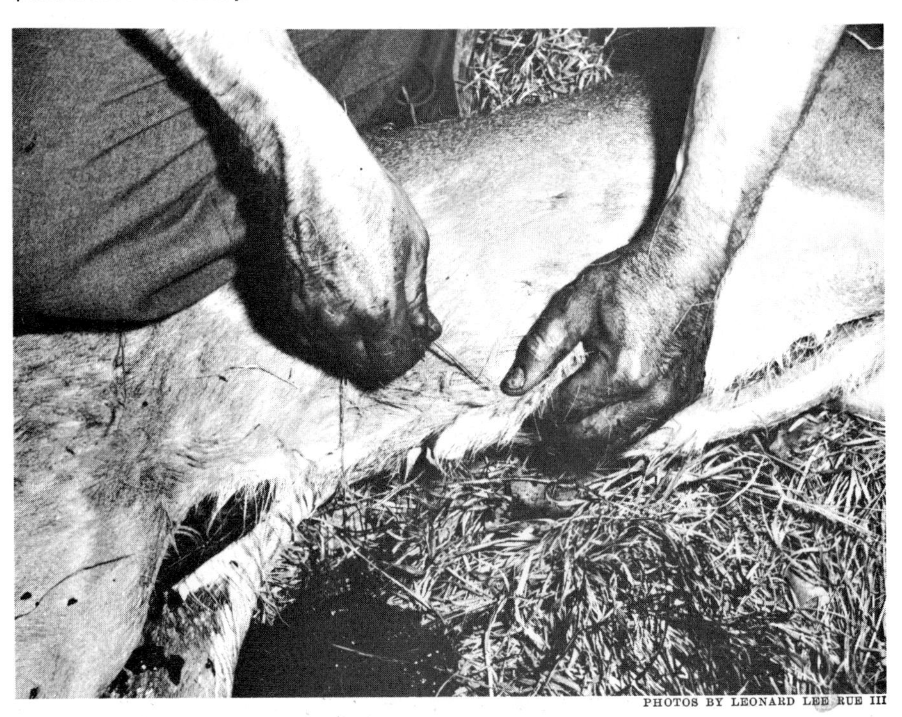

PHOTOS BY LEONARD LEE RUE III

8. If you have to pack your deer out of the woods, you should first sew up the body cavity to protect your clothes. Caution: If you carry your deer, drape it with blaze-orange fabric to avoid its picking up more bullet holes.

9. Some say the hair-tufted glands on hind legs taint meat. Avoid getting musk from the glands on your knife blade or your hands before you begin field-dressing.

10. At home or base camp, some hunters hang deer by neck or antlers for skinning. Author recommends hanging by hind legs.

How to Field-Dress Your Deer *(continued)*

11. Saw or knife off all four legs at center joints. Lower legs are waste.

12. Slit skin on inside of the four legs down to belly cut.

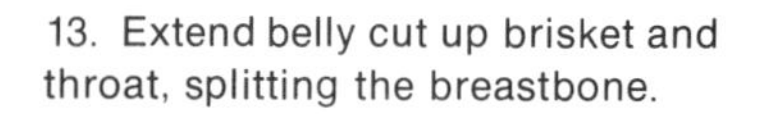

13. Extend belly cut up brisket and throat, splitting the breastbone.

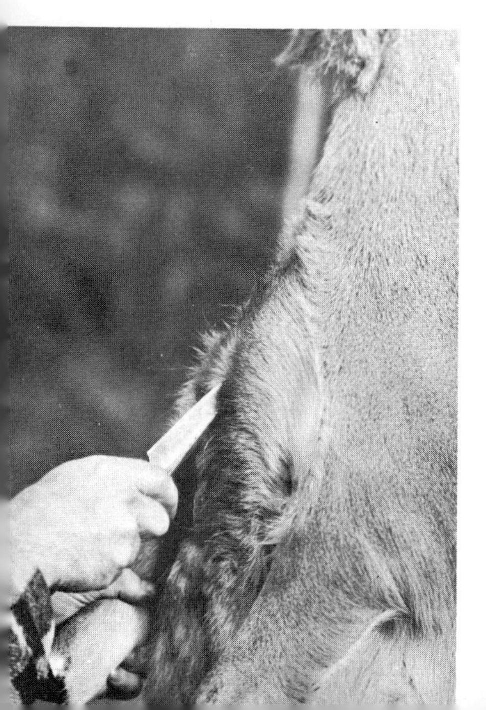

14. Cut around neck. If head is to be mounted, cut behind forelegs.

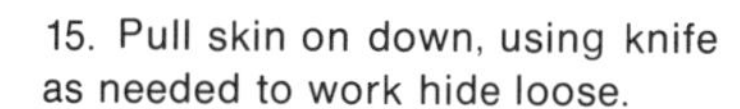
15. Pull skin on down, using knife as needed to work hide loose.

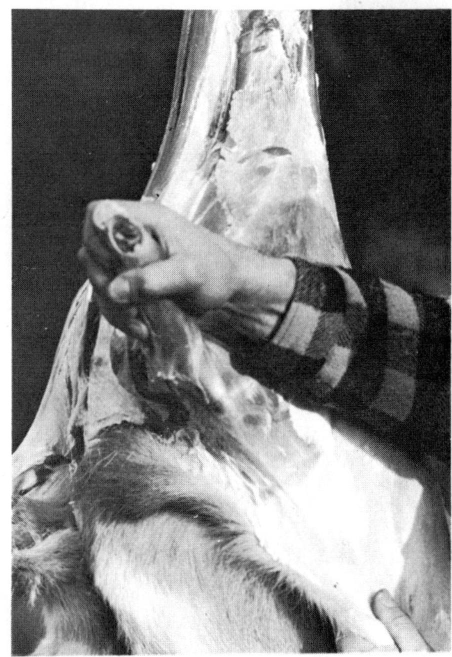

16. Hide will pull off like a stubborn banana peel. Knife is used only in the tight spots.

PHOTOS BY LEONARD LEE RUE III

HOW TO BUTCHER YOUR DEER
Sequence also by Leonard Lee Rue III

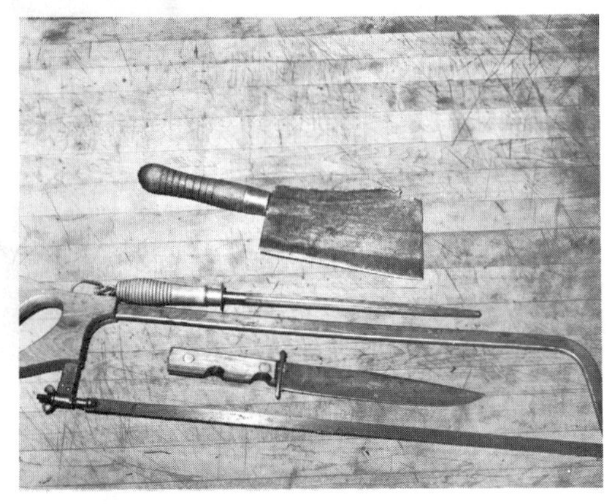

1. These are the tools needed to do quick and easy job of cutting up a skinned carcass: cleaver, sharpening steel, knife, and meat saw.

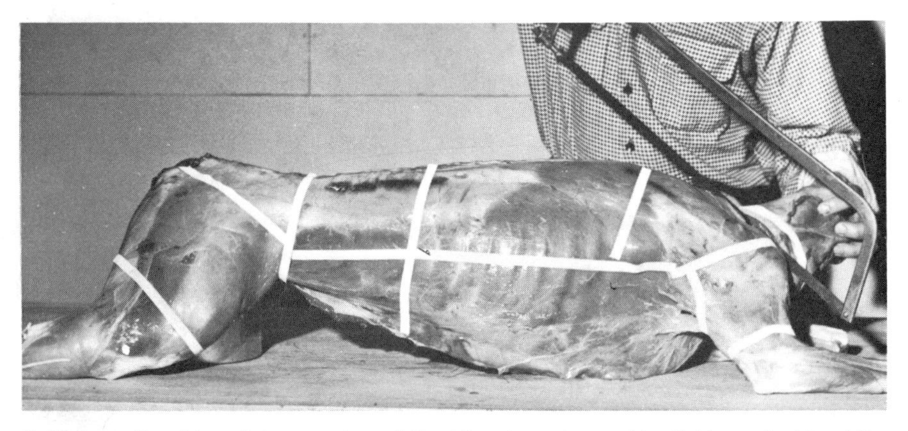

2. Tape on the skinned deer marks out the 11 major cuts used to divide each side of the carcass. Start with neck cut.

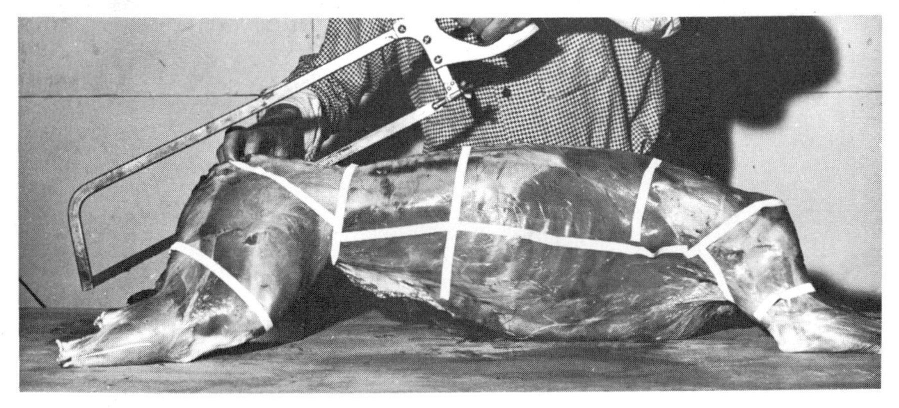

3. Toughest cut to make is long one down the backbone, shown above. It helps to have assistant to steady carcass at this point.

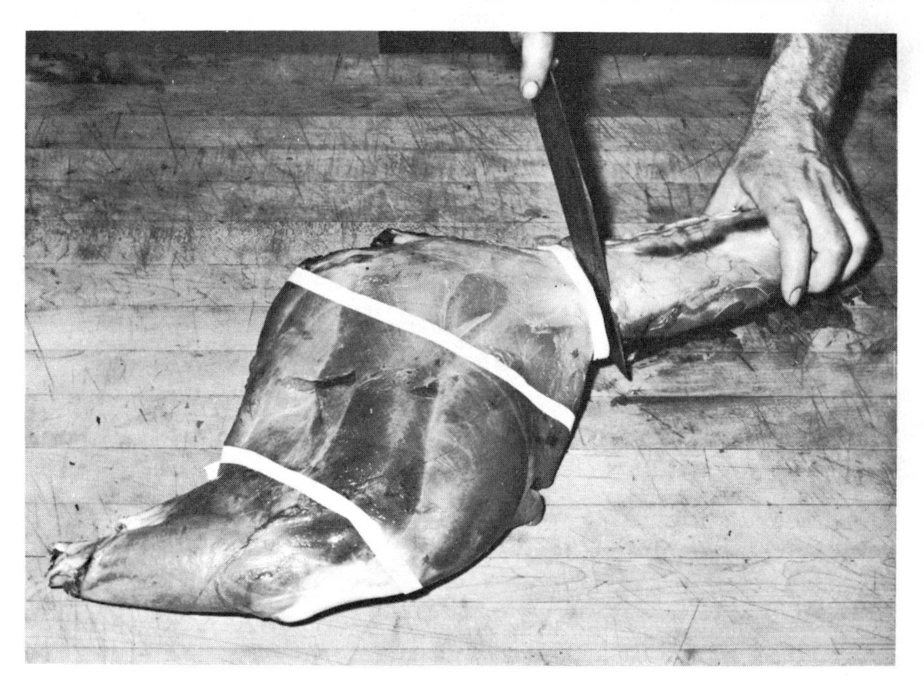

4. Flank has been cut off to be chopped up for deerburger. Knife cut being made here will lop off the loin portion.

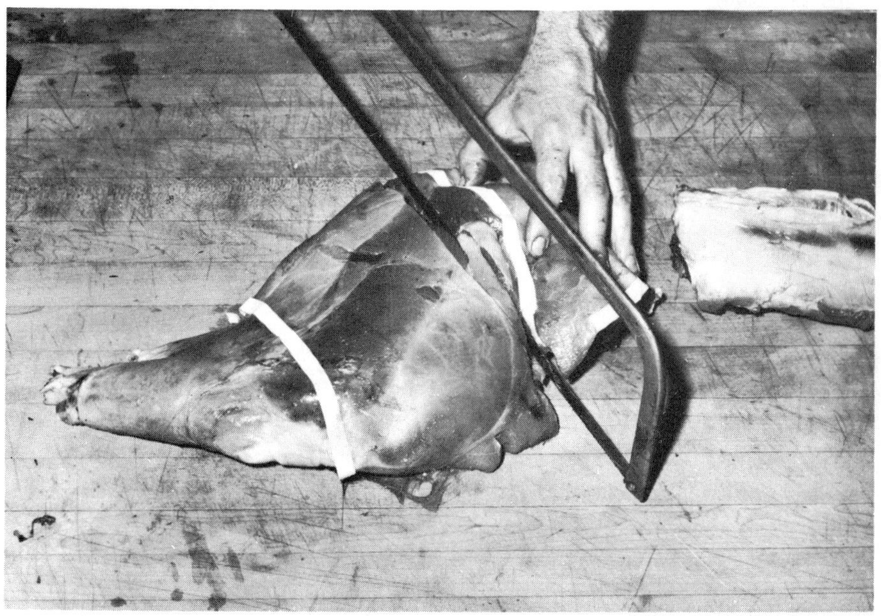

PHOTOS BY LEONARD LEE RUE III

5. Sharp knife makes cut to bone, which is severed with saw. Hand holds rump roast. Round steaks coming up.

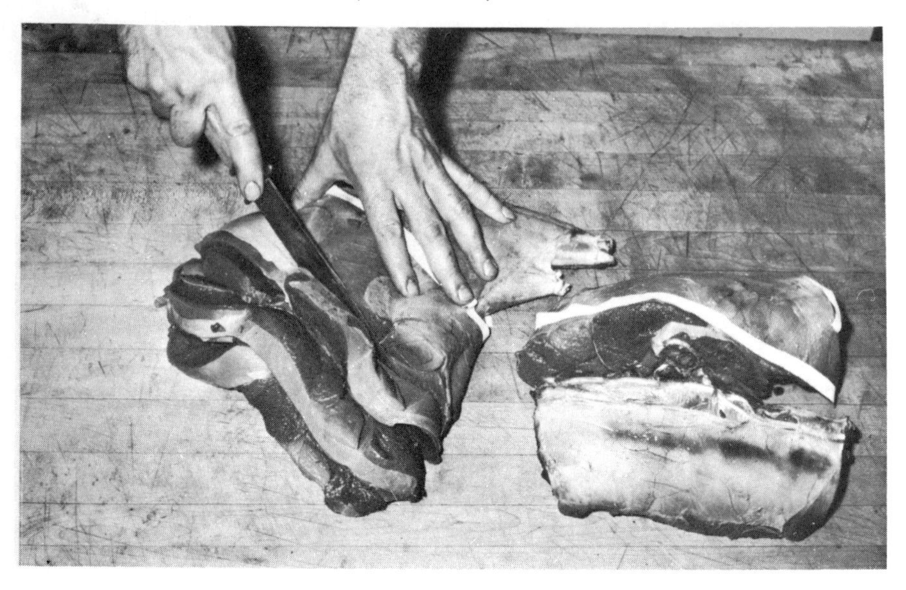

6. Round-steak portion should be divided into even slices about 1-inch thick with knife. Saw cuts center bone.

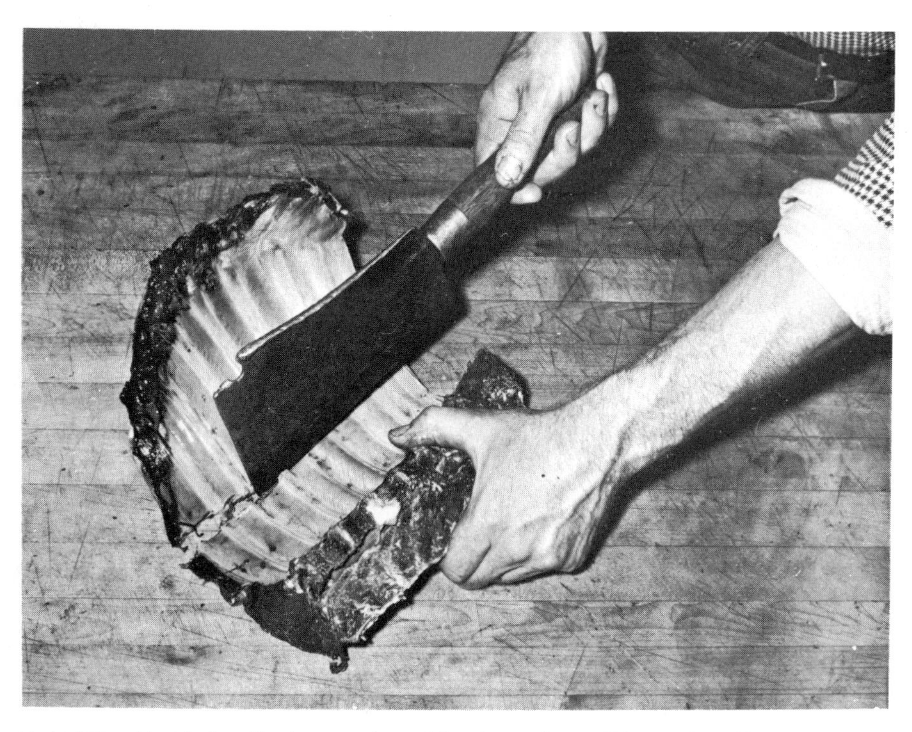

7. Left hand holds the rib-chop section while cleaver lops off lower ribs. Cleaver is faster than saw for this cut.

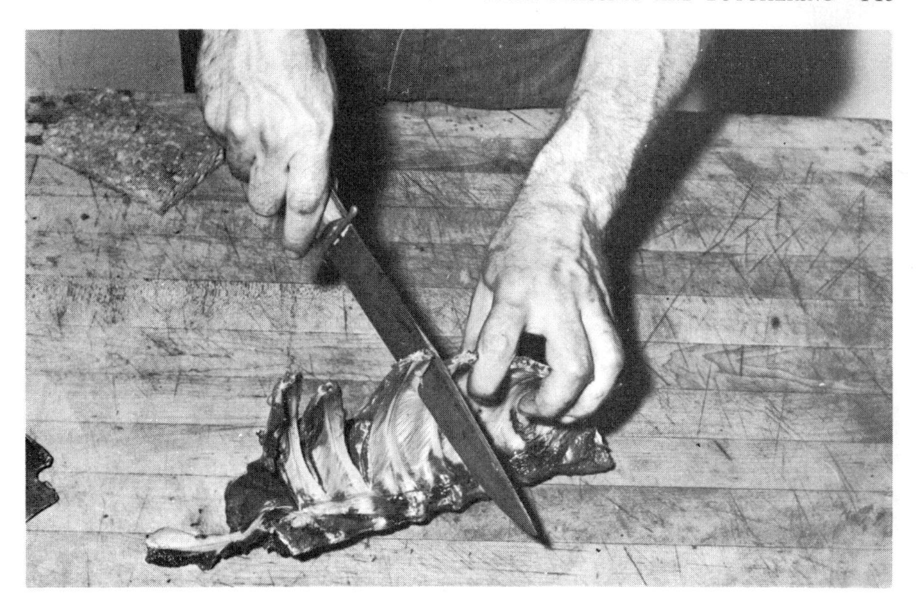

8. Knife cuts divide rib chops. Cleaver will clip the bone portion. Some leave this piece intact for rib roast.

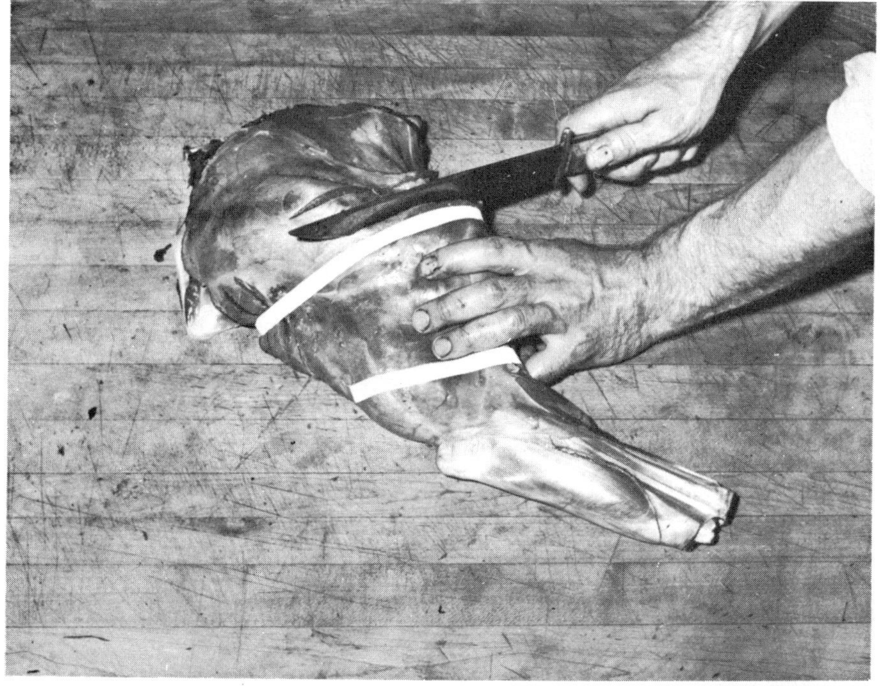

PHOTOS BY LEONARD LEE RUE III

9. Working up fore shoulder. The two tape-marked cuts at top make roasts. Shank is cut up for deerburger.

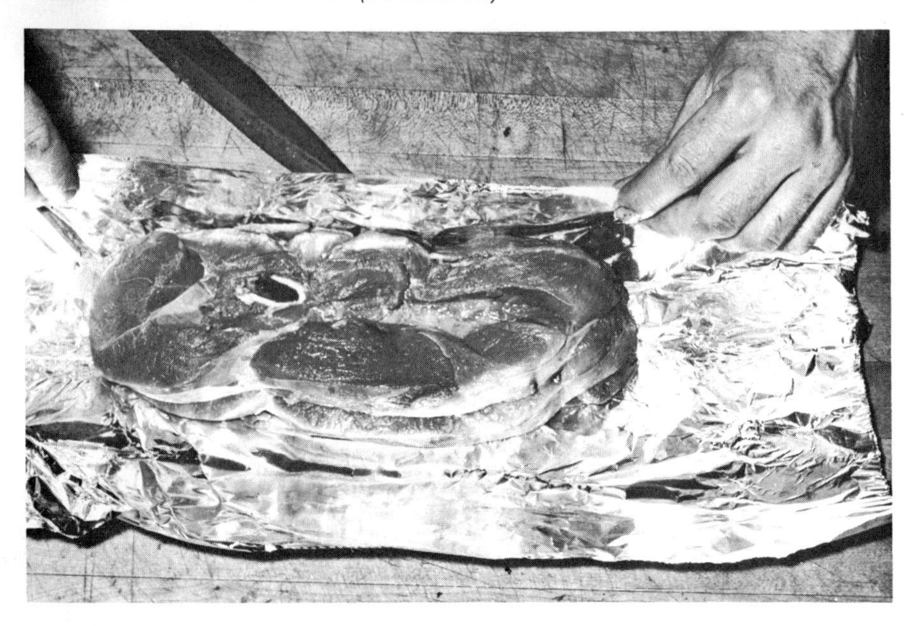

10. Round steaks are wrapped in aluminum foil for freezer storage. Use large sheets that cover meat completely.

PHOTOS BY LEONARD LEE RUE III

11. Cover foil-wrapped venison with airtight plastic bags tied securely. Frozen, the meat keeps indefinitely.

17

Preserving the Trophy

"IT'S HARD TO FIGURE," taxidermist Lem Rathbone told me. "A hunter gives loving care to his venison, yet he neglects or even abuses the head he intends to have mounted and hang on the wall for everyone to admire."

The quality of the finished head mount is determined to a large extent before the head reaches the taxidermist. In short, its your responsibility.

Rathbone, who collaborated with me on *Taxidermy Guide* (Stoeger), has been in business for some 40 years, and in that timespan he has seen some pretty weird things. Like the head of a buck chopped off just beneath the lower jaw. A deer not yet field-dressed that had been killed a couple days previously. Deer heads already spoiled with the hair falling out.

He passes along these suggestions as to what the hunter should and shouldn't do:

If you intend to have the head mounted, *do not* cut the animal's throat. This does absolutely no good whatsoever; the deer will be fully bled when it is field-dressed. A cut throat will be the most prominent spot on a mounted head, and damage is almost impossible to repair so that it isn't noticeable.

When field-dressing the animal, halt the belly incision before you reach the shoulders. Reach forward inside the body cavity and sever the windpipe, cut the lungs and heart free, and pull the whole mess out.

To skin, hang the deer by his hind legs and peel the hide down to the head before severing the neck. From the brisket to head, leave the skin tube-shaped with no cuts. It is wise to leave the entire hide attached to the head and take the complete package to the taxidermist, letting him judge how much of the hide he needs for a cape.

Rathbone personally prefers that the entire deer be brought in and he takes care of the skinning himself. This gives him total control. Your taxidermist might like it that way, too.

Once the animal is skinned, hang the head and skin in a shady spot with ample air circulation. Do not place it in any sealed container, such as a plastic bag. Trapped air soon warms and permits spoilage. Get it to the taxidermist immediately. If there is to be any delay, put in in a deepfreeze or a cold-storage facility.

Circumstances might dictate, however, that you skin the head yourself. If so, have your knife very sharp and work slowly and carefully. The job isn't that difficult, but it does take time. Trying to hurry will only result in damaging cuts that the taxidermist must later repair. I repeat, the quality of the cape will to a great extent determine the quality of the finished mount.

The head should be skinned so that everything—ears, eyelids, and part of the inner lips—comes off attached to the skin. When the cape is removed it should be reasonably clean, with very little flesh still attached.

Start by making a clean, straight cut across the top of the head from the base of one antler to the other. Use a blunt instrument such as a screwdriver to pry the skin away from the antler bases. If the skin does not separate easily, you might have to start it with your knife blade. Avoid cutting or tearing the skin or leaving any attached to the antler base.

Once the skin is freed from the antler bases, make another incision down the back of the neck. Start halfway in the cut between the antler bases and go down, making a perpendicular incision that should be straight and not zigzagged. Make this cut the full length of the cape, or past the shoulders down around the brisket. A common mistake is to leave the taxidermist too little neck skin to work with.

Commence separating this long cut as you skin the neck, turning the hide over the head as you approach the ears. Upon reaching the ear bases, cut the ears from the skull, leaving them attached to the skin.

Continue skinning the eyes. This is a crucial area. Go slowly and carefully. The skin is close to the skull here with virtually no flesh between. Remember as you cut around the eyes that the eyelids must be freed from the skull so they remain on the hide. Eyelids are difficult to patch; avoid cutting them if possible.

Rathbone offers this aid for making the job easier. Stick the index finger of your free hand (the left hand for a right-hander) into the eye socket and push back as far as you can. This serves a twofold purpose. By feeling around the end of your finger you can determine where the skin meets the socket. As you cut here you naturally progress carefully, since getting careless might result in cutting not only the skin, but also your fingertip.

Slightly below the eye is a tear gland. Gingerly separate the skin here with the end of your knife blade or the screwdriver.

Progress down to the mouth. Again, you can shove your index finger deep inside the mouth, in order to cut around the bulge created by the pressure of your fingertip against the skin. This is another crucial area

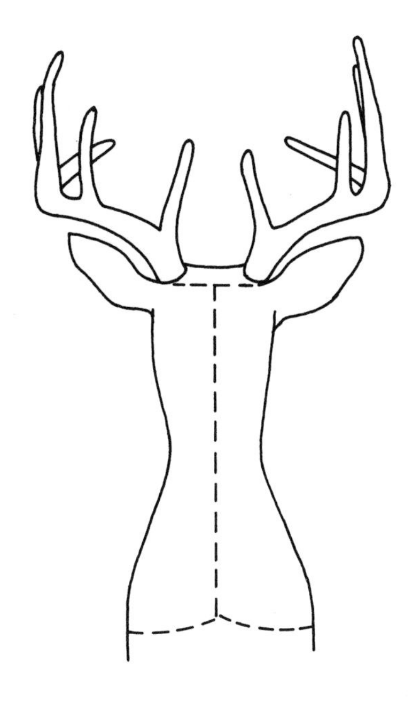

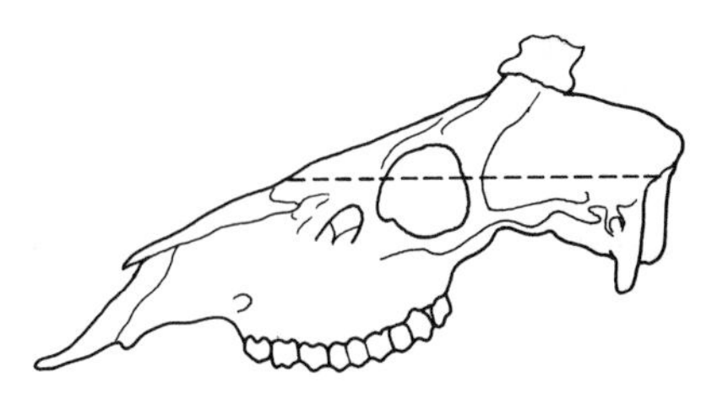

First make a straight, clean cut across the top of the head, from one antler base to the other as shown at left. Then make another cut down the back of the neck, to below the shoulders, on around the brisket area. As shown above, to remove the antlers from the skull, saw horizontally, beginning just behind the antlers and going straight through the eye sockets to emerge about halfway up the nose.

where you should work cautiously. As you skin out the mouth, save as much of the lips as possible, as they are needed in the mounting process.

Finish separating hide from skull by skinning the nose. Avoid leaving too much flesh around the nose and lips. It will spoil and cause the hair to come loose.

The cape should be turned inside out once it is freed from the skull. If any chunks of flesh remain, trim them off with your knife. Also skin the ears if it is going to be several days before you deliver the cape to a taxidermist. Otherwise they might spoil.

Begin this operation by skinning around the flesh that covers the cartilage where you separated the ear from the skull. Take care not to cut a hole in the bottom side of the ear where the opening comes down. Once you have skinned past the flesh, only cartilage and skin remain. Upon reaching the cartilage, push your thumb between cartilage and skin and, applying as much pressure as possible, separate the two to ear's end. As you progress, turn the ear inside out. You might have to use the screwdriver as you approach the end where the ear gets smaller. Be sure you get completely to the ear's end. Cut the cartilage where the ear ends, leaving the ear turned wrong side out so that it can later be salted. Follow the same procedure with the other ear.

Now liberally coat the flesh side of the hide with table salt. Use your hand to distribute the salt abundantly along every edge, in the ears, around lips and nose. You can't oversalt, but you can use too little. Any spots you miss will likely spoil. Roll the cape tightly, salted or flesh side in, and put it in a shady, cool, and dry spot. The importance of this salt application cannot be overemphasized. If the hide is salted and cured properly, there will be no spoilage and the taxidermist will have a quality cape to work with.

Finally, remove the antlers and skull plate from the head. With a meat saw, make a horizontal cut, beginning just behind the antlers, going straight through the eye sockets, and emerging about halfway up the nose. Clean the skull, removing all brains and flesh.

Get the cape and antlers to a taxidermist promptly. And start counting the days until you can hang your trophy on the wall.

Taxidermist Lem Rathbone shows what kind of finished mount you can expect if the trophy is handled properly.

18

Preparing and Cooking Venison

I ONCE HAD a business acquaintance who claimed he couldn't stomach the taste of wild meat, like venison. He said the gamy taste was repulsive. He didn't know it at the time, but he was to be the unsuspecting guinea pig in a scientific experiment of mine. The "laboratory" was a backyard barbecue grill. The ingredients were venison steaks, cut to a thickness of 1½ inches, a homemade barbecue sauce, some charcoal brickets, and hickory chips.

After an elaborate dinner, highlighted by reddish-colored venison cooked medium done, the man commented that he'd never tasted such delicious steaks. I didn't let him know differently, allowing him to go his merry way, still holding to his firm convictions, but I'd satisfied my own curiosity. Venison can, if prepared and cooked correctly, be a gourmet's delight.

Me, I like the wild taste of venison. If I prefer steak, I can get it at the corner supermarket cheaper and easier than I can get venison by deer hunting. One of the real bonuses of deer hunting, as far as I'm concerned, is the later treat on the dinner table.

But getting back to our venison hater. We fooled him, by concocting a preparation containing 1 quart of water, 2 tablespoons of vinegar, and a level teaspoon of household soda. The venison steaks were saturated in the liquid for 30 minutes, removed, and drained on paper towels. Then they were barbecued.

The vinegar tends to draw the wild taste out of venison, but you must watch and not oversoak, since the venison can acquire a vinegar flavor if left in the preparation too long. The soda acts as a tenderizer. Some people substitute a quart of sweet milk for the water-vinegar mixture, with the same effect.

My barbecue sauce is prepared by melting three sticks of margarine in a saucepan and adding 1/2 teaspoon of Worcestershire sauce, an 8-ounce can of tomato sauce or a cup of catsup, 1 teaspoon of black pepper, 1 teaspoon of salt, 1/2 cup of chopped onion, 1/2 cup of lemon juice, 1/2 teaspoon of oregano, 1/2 teaspoon of garlic salt, 1/2 teaspoon of rosemary, and 1/2 teaspoon of thyme.

Unlike steak, venison should be turned regularly, about every ten minutes, and basted liberally with the sauce. The margarine keeps the dry venison from becoming tough and juiceless, and the sauce forms a crisp crust on the meat. Or if you prefer, the venison can be marinated in the sauce for three to four hours before cooking.

Another way of improving venison for cooking, particularly roasts, is to trim away the tissue-thin membrane which covers the meat. Removal of this membrane allows juices to penetrate the meat more readily and makes it more tender.

Here are some other favorite venison dishes:

Broiled venison: Take venison steaks cut to desired thickness and rub with a split clove of garlic. Cook about 4 inches from heat, either on outdoor grill or indoor range, basting with melted margarine or butter. After the meat has seared, to hold the juices in, salt and pepper to taste. Don't overcook. Remove from fire when just a hint of red remains in the heart of the steak.

Venison stew: Cut 2 pounds of venison into 1-inch cubes. Brown the venison in frying pan containing 1 tablespoon of shortening. Place in pan with 4 cups of boiling water, 1 teaspoon of Worcestershire sauce, one medium cubed onion, one clove of garlic chopped, 1 tablespoon salt and 1/2 teaspoon black pepper. Allow to simmer until venison is tender. Add three medium potatoes cut into chunks, 1 cup of frozen peas and 1 cup frozen carrots. Continue cooking until vegetables are done and mixture thickens.

Venison cutlets: Take 2 pounds of cutlets. Roll in mixture containing 1 cup flour, 1/2 cup milk, 2 tablespoons water, 2 slightly beaten eggs, 6 tablespoons fat, dash of Worcestershire sauce, dash of celery salt, salt, and pepper. Fry over medium heat.

Venison steak 'n' sauce: Take steaks cut to desired thickness, place in pan, and sprinkle with salt and pepper, oregano, olive oil, and lemon juice. Turn steaks and repeat on other side. Place steaks in a covered pan and put in cool place and leave overnight, or at least 12 hours. Remove steaks, dredge in flour, and fry in hot skillet until done. Don't overcook. Drain excess oil after steaks are removed and pour cup of water into skillet. Add 1 level tablespoon of monosodium glutamate and a dash of Worcestershire sauce or wine. Pour sauce over steaks and serve.

Barbecued venison roast: Take 4-pound venison roast, 3 tablespoons fat, two cloves garlic, chopped, one stalk celery, 6 tablespoons vinegar, 3 tablespoons catsup, 3 tablespoons Worcestershire sauce, and salt and pepper. Season roast with salt and pepper. Melt fat in heavy pan. Add roast and brown slowly on all sides. Add garlic and celery. Combine vinegar, catsup, and Worcestershire sauce in a 1-cup measure. Add water to full cup. Pour over roast. Cover and cook slowly about three hours or until tender. Remove roast and add flour and water paste to liquid to make gravy.

Venison goulash: Take 3 pounds stewing venison, cubed, 2 pounds small white onions, sliced, 8 ounces lard or vegetable shortening, 1 tablespoon marjoram, 1½ tablespoons paprika, and two cans beef broth. Sauté onion slices in fat until soft. Add cubed venison and brown on all sides. Sprinkle in marjoram and paprika, cover with beef broth. Cover pot and simmer slowly for three hours or until meat is tender, stirring frequently and occasionally adding more beef broth. Gravy should be fairly thick.

Marinated venison: Take 3 pounds venison stew meat, two medium onions, sliced, one carrot, sliced, two stalks celery, chopped, one clove garlic, crushed, 1 teaspoon salt, ten peppercorns, five juniper berries, crushed, 1 tablespoon chopped parsley, one bay leaf, juice of one lemon, one 16-ounce bottle or can of beer, ½ cup salad oil. Cube meat. Combine with other ingredients in large earthenware bowl. Let stand in refrigerator one to two days, turning meat several times. Place meat and marinade in large kettle. Bring slowly to boil. Cover and cook over slow heat for 1½ to two hours, or until meat is tender. Remove meat and strain liquid, forcing vegetables through the strainer. If desired, thicken liquid with flour mixed with a little water.

Smothered venison steaks: Pound steaks thoroughly. Season with salt and pepper and roll in flour. Brown in pan to which 1 tablespoon of grease has been added. In another pan brown one medium diced onion, one-half medium green bell pepper, one sliced clove of garlic, and a pinch of bay leaf. Add mixture to pan in which steaks have been browned along with one cup of water. Simmer slowly until done, or about an hour. Add water as needed.

Hot venison chili: Brown lightly 2 pounds of coarse ground venison in tablespoon of shortening. Add 1 tablespoon cut red pepper, ½ teaspoon Louisiana hot sauce, ½ teaspoon Worcestershire sauce, two medium, finely chopped onions, three-fourths of a finely chopped green bell pepper, one-fourth bay leaf, two small cans tomato paste, one No. 1 can of whole tomatoes, 1 teaspoon garlic powder, and 2 tablespoons chili powder. Season to taste with salt and pepper. Allow to simmer for at least one-half day.

Deer fillets: Cut tenderloin in 2-inch squares, ½ inch thick. Wrap with bacon and secure with toothpicks. Season with pepper and salt, or garlic salt can be substituted. Lay in open pan in which a sauce concocted of one large, finely chopped onion, one small can mushrooms, and one small can mushroom gravy has been added. Cook in 325° oven, allowing meat to simmer in sauce, basting meat with sauce regularly. Allow from two to four fillets for each person served.

Deer sausage: Mix ratio of 40 percent venison and 60 percent pork. Season with salt and coarsely ground pepper. Stuff and smoke lightly.

Deerburgers: Add one part pork to every four parts of venison. One part fat beef also can be added, if desired. Mash into large patties and grill over charcoal fire with hickory chips added. Barbecue sauce can be used for basting, or meat can be basted with melted margarine to prevent dryness and shrinkage.

Venison finger steaks: Cut tenderloin into thinnest strips possible. Soak for two hours in salt brine to draw out excessive blood. Drain thoroughly on paper towels. Brown and drop in deep pan of sizzling hot grease. Cook for 30 seconds to one minute, or until golden brown. Don't overcook.

Fried venison liver: Slice in thin steaks, roll in cornmeal, salt, and pepper, and fry in hot grease.

Smothered venison liver: Slice in thin steaks, roll in flour, salt, and pepper, and brown in 1 tablespoon of shortening. Add enough water to cover meat along with two sliced medium onions. Simmer until tender, or about one hour.

Venison jerky: Use a flank cut or any cut of venison which has long grains of muscle. Remove all fat and gristle, which would turn rancid. Be sure to cut meat with the grain. Venison should be cut in strips about 5 inches long and 1/4 inch thick—even thinner if you can slice it. Place strips of venison in bowl or dish that can be covered. Put in a layer of meat, sprinkle liberally with hickory smoke salt, sprinkle lightly with black pepper, add a touch of garlic or onion salt for seasoning. Add another layer of venison and repeat, until all meat is in bowl. Cover dish and place in refrigerator for at least eight hours. This allows time for salt and seasonings to thoroughly permeate venison to give it a robust and hearty flavor. Next step is to blanch the meat, which destroys any bacteria on the surface. For each quart water add 1 tablespoon salt and bring water to a simmer. Dip each strip of meat into water and hold it there for about 15 seconds. Hot water will turn the red venison a whitish gray. After blanching, place strips of meat on a cookie sheet and put in an oven at the lowest possible heat for six to 16 hours, or until the meat is coal black on the outside and dark and dry throughout. Leave oven door ajar a little to allow moisture to escape. Slow heat dehydrates the venison and shrivels it. After it is cooled, jerky can be stored in a sealed jar.

19

The Camp

IT IS POSSIBLE that the person who first claimed that the only difference between men and boys is the size and cost of their toys might have gotten his inspiration in a hunting camp on the eve of the deer-season opener.

It's the night before Christmas and the excitement is contagious. These are the good times. Anticipation hangs heavy in smoke-filled cabins, tents, and assorted campers. Men, and perhaps women too, sit hunched over tables and only the shuffle of cards or the clink of dominoes violates the quiet concentration. In another room maybe, or outside beside a cheerful campfire where pungent tendrils of smoke rise to catch the air currents, others laugh and joke. Pessimism hasn't a chance here.

Stories are a year older and they seem to have grown since they were last told. Memories are the legacy of a deer camp. Time marches on, faces change, but tradition is difficult to shake.

The hunter who is by choice a loner because he has an almost fanatic desire to kill a deer is really missing much of what deer hunting is all about. It is the friendship, the camaraderie, the sharing of experiences, the good and the bittersweet.

A man dressed in a business suit and half-hidden behind a large and fancy desk can fool you, sort of like a photograph that is slightly out of focus. You see the whole picture but you can't make out the individual features. But get this same fellow in a deer camp and his personality and character, good or bad, soon surface. An old-timer once told me that if I wanted to judge a man, to learn his strength and weaknesses, I only had to take him hunting and share a camp with him for a few days.

Ah, yes, with age comes wisdom.

Gather a group—young and old, male and female—under the common denominator of deer hunting and those silly stratified rules of society are forgotten. The mechanic mingles with the bank president, the politician with the low-level government employee. There is a common bond which goes beyond finding a deer in a gunsight and pulling the trigger—a love of the outdoors, a strong sense of dedication, a concern for the environment.

You get this unique but pleasant mix in deer camps from Minnesota to Maine, Georgia to Oklahoma, across the land wherever the ubiquitous whitetail deer is found. It is a place to relax and to forget, if only briefly, those worries left behind at home. A deer camp is for deer hunters. And I can't think of a better compliment.

The right camp also will get you more deer. Perhaps your party pushes deep into the woods, away from the crowd, where there is less hunting pressure and consequently better opportunity. A camp also situates you closer to your hunting territory, which means you can spend more time hunting.

Make no mistake, all things else being equal, he who spends the most time pursuing his quarry stands the best chance of carrying home venison. This is one of the *secrets* of the successful, those who consistently get deer: hard, serious hunting, taking advantage of every minute of daylight. In short, spending more time in the woods and less time in camp or at home.

Describe a deer camp and I probably have visited something like it, everything from fancy lodges maintained by hunting clubs to a chilled two-man tent. Actually, it is impossible to portray the "typical" deer camp. It is simply the hunters' temporary home away from home. Perhaps it is nothing more than an abandoned farmhouse, or a crude frame building, maybe covered with tarpaper to keep out the wind, with a stove and rough bunks inside. Such camps are popular on private lands where an arrangement can be worked out with the landowner. Some Southern hunting clubs construct large and comfortable lodges. Such accommodations are common along the Mississippi River bottomlands, in southern Arkansas, Mississippi, and Louisiana. Some much less elaborate camps are even built in semi-wilderness areas where agreements can be made with state or federal agencies.

With the portable camp, such as a tent, it is wise to remember that in some areas such as national forests and timber-company lands there are designated spots for camping and camps must be erected in these plots and no other place. Also some areas require camping permits. Be sure of your campsite before setting up a home away from home.

Camp life is a relaxing existence. I remember a season in the Lincoln National Forest of New Mexico when Carlos Moore, Oscar Brown, and I couldn't seem to get a deer, no matter what we tried. But that was a memorable season for me if for no other reason than the enjoyable nights I spent in our camp. It was down in a canyon filled with towering pines and green spruce, near the village of Weed. There's something magic about lounging around a campfire, under a sky alive with stars, reliving the day's hunt, swapping stories about past hunts and simply taking life easy.

Some hunters are content to move into an area a day before the season opens and set up a makeshift camp. Or perhaps they'll come in two or three days early to scout out the area and get this home away from home in shipshape order. There are many little things to be done that will make a camp more livable.

For one thing, there's the matter of a shelter. If you're going to backpack into a remote area, perhaps you'll make a tarp lean-to suffice or one of those lightweight backpack tents. But if you're driving or going by horseback, I strongly recommend that you carry a shelter that is large enough to be comfortable. Spend a couple of days in a camp when the rain is pelting down, as I have, and you'll appreciate an adequate shelter.

Tents come in all sizes, shapes, and designs. The modern tent is functional, made of lightweight material and easy to erect. It is impossible to recommend any one type because needs can vary widely. Size of the hunting party is a primary consideration. Some camps have a larger "headquarters tent" for community gathering and cooking, smaller individual tents for sleeping. The big but bulky A-wall type is popular for larger hunting parties. Also the umbrella type with its frame of outside spring-loaded aluminum poles. Or the igloo-looking Pop Tent or a cottage tent or a wall tent.

Visit an outlet where camping supplies are sold and look at the various tent types. Analyze your own needs and try to select a shelter which best satisfies those needs. But whatever type you select, get a tent as large as you can, larger than you imagine necessary. You can't have too much room.

The site for your tent requires some thought. Select a spot that is well drained (if you're not in a designated campsite). Never, for instance, place your tent in the bottom of a draw where a sudden heavy rain will fill it with water. Put it near a good water supply. Even if you carry your own drinking water, you'll need water for other purposes, such as washing dishes and personal use. Try to put it where it is reasonably protected from wind, yet in a spot where it will be exposed to as much warming sunlight as possible during the day. This is important in the northern reaches of the country where the temperature is apt to plummet during the hunting season.

If you're not inclined to "rough it," one of the convenient, portable camp units is recommended: self-contained campers, fold-up tent trailers, pickup campers, and compact travel trailers. The major drawback to such a unit is the price. My personal selection for the best hunting rig is an 8½-foot camper on a half-ton ton pickup powered by four-wheel drive or at least compound (grandma) gear. You'll sacrifice room for maneuverability, but you can take this rig almost anywhere.

A fold-up camp trailer with its low profile and light weight can be carried over most backcountry roads. But with most self-contained units there are limits to where you can go. Use some common sense if you don't want to get marooned. Take any of these units over a logging road, for example, and get surprised by sudden rain or snow and your trip home might be delayed. A set of tire chains is insurance that no backwoods camper should be without.

While your shelter demands some forethought, perhaps equally important is your bed. Get a good night's rest and you can tolerate most anything else. Buying a sleeping bag and something to put beneath it is no capricious decision. You are after comfort, room, and warmth.

Like quilted insulated jackets, sleeping bags are made with a variety of fillers. A bag filled with 3 pounds of Dacron 88 polyester is sufficient for mild-weather Southern camping, but it isn't practical for the cold north country. Here the wise choice would be a down-filled bag rated for subzero weather. There is a sizable price difference between these two examples, but with sleeping bags you pay for quality.

The function of the sleeping bag is to retain whatever heat is generated by your body without allowing the accumulation of moisture. Down is best for this. But down bags are slow to dry, and a wet bag loses its insulating properties. Bags containing synthetic fillers—acrylic, polyester, and acetate—can be made as warm as down but the amount of filler must be increased, which adds to bulk. Yet when carried in a vehicle, the added weight and bulk are not that much of a disadvantage. Also some people are allergic to down.

Most bags are rated by weight of filler—as designated on the manufacturer's label—but when considering different bags, you must consider size as well. With any given amount of filler, the smaller the bag, the warmer it will be. But you don't want to feel as if you are sleeping in a straitjacket.

Keep in mind that a sleeping bag is an individual thing. Don't listen to others, because no two people will produce the same amount of heat or in the same pattern. I might shiver in a bag that you find comfortable.

As a rule of thumb it is smart to buy a bag which is rated for a lower temperature than you think you will need. You always can unzip the bag and let some of the heat escape if it becomes too hot. But there isn't much you can do if you become chilled. On a north-country hunting trip a couple years back I found that my bag wasn't adequate. My solution was to first climb inside a pair of insulated coveralls before getting into my bag. That made the difference. That works, or you can put one bag inside another.

I do like a bag, however, with inside tie tapes or tabs for securing a washable liner. It is easy to remove the liner periodically and launder it to keep the bag fresh and clean. But the problem with a flannel liner is that while it is warm against the skin, it tends to cling to clothing. You'll be warmer if you remove clothing damp with perspiration and sleep in the raw, or at least change to totally dry clothes.

For a comfortable night's sleep you also will need something under you, an air mattress or pad. In addition to providing insulation under the bag where body weight compresses the filler material, the mattress or pad also provides a cushion. Thick foam pads are lightweight and better insulators than air mattresses but are more bulky. Air mattresses also require inflation, either by mouth blowing or a pump, and they need some protection from sharp objects.

The matter of food also deserves some thought. It is said that a hunter with a full belly is an alert hunter. Hot meals give more pep and help to relax tired muscles. A tent stove is not necessary. For warmth, use a wall tent and build your fire near the entrance. For cooking, compact stoves fueled by gasoline, propane, or butane can't be beat. If there is no premium on weight and space, such as when traveling by vehicle, by all means have at least a two-burner stove. You'll need it when making coffee and frying at the same time. If you cook over an open campfire, a wire grate slung over a rock fireplace will make the task easier.

For lighting purposes, one or two gasoline, propane, or butane lanterns will suffice. Don't forget to carry extra fuel and extra mantles. Also have at least one flashlight for each hunter. This is an almost indispensable item.

One or two lightweight tarpaulins also serve many useful purposes around camp. Put one under your sleeping bag to keep out moisture. Toss one over the camp stove to protect it from rain and insects. Or extend it over your tent or rec-vehicle door for added rain protection.

It is best to plan your menus in advance so that you'll have enough food, but won't be burdened with excess supplies. For fresh meats, carry along one of the lightweight ice chests. Otherwise, the choice of groceries is pretty much a personal thing, depending on what you prefer. For light traveling, such as backpacking, the newer freeze-dry foods are lightweight, yet very tasty.

An ax is needed to supply firewood. If weight permits it, carry a full-sized ax. It is a rare convenience. You just can't do the same job with one of the smaller portable axes. And remember the hallmark of a good woodsman is a sharp ax and a sharp knife. A small honing stone is good insurance.

Also, if possible have a shovel along. Use it to dig drainage ditches around your shelter and to dig a latrine. Put the latrine at least 50 yards from camp. Also bury all your garbage and tin cans when you break camp, or, better yet, carry it with you.

You might also want to include a small bucksaw to be used in obtaining firewood. Maybe even a hatchet for doing smaller chores around camp. An oven which fits over the gasoline stove is another little luxury that makes camp life more enjoyable. A bucket is another item that will serve a lot of uses.

And finally, perhaps the most indispensable items for the deer camp are pencil and paper. Yep, you read that correctly. At home consider everything you will need and make a checklist. As you load, mark off each necessity as it goes aboard. It is dispiriting to get far from habitation and discover that you left something behind. Don't depend on your memory. It has a way of failing at the most crucial times.

20

Photographing Your Trophy

A PHOTOGRAPH of a deer hunter standing beside his "trophy" and grinning at the camera is a pretty unimaginative photograph. But it beats no photo at all.

Most hunters have no pictorial recollections of trips gone by, which is a shame. Shuffling through pictures of hunting camps and trophies taken can bring back a lot of memories.

My friend Alex Kibler has numerous color slides showing the good and the bad of his deer-hunting trips. He has succeeded where others have failed by adopting a very basic rule: "Wherever I go, my camera goes."

Some bucks are bigger than others, but for every hunter each one has a special meaning. Anyway, taxidermy is expensive and the hunter can display only so many heads. He might keep the antlers from others. But a set of antlers doesn't compare to a colorful photograph showing trophy, proud hunter, and the place where it was taken. It is a memento to treasure.

I add this brief chapter only as a postscript to the hunting know-how discussed previously because I have seen so many opportunities missed by fellow hunters. They haven't programmed themselves to think "picture," and consequently they return home without a record. A camera is of dubious value if it is unavailable when you need it. Maybe it is in the glove compartment of your vehicle or snuggled inside a foam-lined protective camera case. So you might see many photographic possibilities, but few if any are actually recorded on film.

Probably you own a camera. I guess everyone does. It will suffice if you realize its limitations. In photography, unless you do a lot of it, keep the procedure as simple as possible. Simplicity lessens the chance of error.

We won't go into a technical discussion of cameras and ancillary equip-

Here is a compact 35mm, center, with two conventional-size 35mm cameras.

ment here. Entire books have been written on the subject. Go to a camera shop and browse about and let a salesman show you what is available. Unless you've kept up with photographic trends over the years, you might be amazed at modern advancements.

The trend is to fully automatic cameras. Just point one and press the shutter release and it is almost impossible *not* to get an acceptable photo. The most sophisticated models are quite expensive, but there is no reason to invest that much in a camera unless you are a real photo bug. Many people buy more camera than they need, which usually adds to the complexity of its operation, automatic or not.

The automatic SLR (single-lens reflex) with interchangeable lenses is a company's top-of-the-line model, or the most expensive. The company also will have a wide range of "manual models" which you must adjust for everything: available light, shutter speed, distance, etc. As with an automobile, a SLR 35mm camera will be priced according to the number of features you desire.

The Kodak Instamatic or one of its many copycats is compact and light and can go anywhere with you in your coat pocket. This camera is adequate if you are satisfied with just snapshots. But the lenses are not of proper quality to permit sharp-focus blow-ups. And that's a factor because you might occasionally get a photo you would like to enlarge and hang on the wall. Most of these cameras have relatively slow shutter speeds, which increases the likelihood of fuzzy pictures, due to movement of the camera as the release button is pressed.

An instant-print camera like the Polaroid is all right if you are satisfied with a snapshot that doesn't come cheaply. With a conventional film-and-print camera you can get two or three shots for less than the cost of one instant-print photograph, and the quality will be better.

If you are thinking about buying a camera specifically to carry on your hunting trips (of course it can be used for other situations, too), I would recommend an automatic compact 35mm. Such a camera is small enough to be easily pocketable and weighs less than a pound. It is more rugged than the single-lens reflex with its delicate mirror mechanism, and a typical model costs about a third as much. This is a compact machine for the hunter who doesn't want to involve himself with setting anything except the focus. Among the models are the Rollei XF 35, Konica 35 Automatic, and Vivitar 35 CA. The one major drawback to these cameras is they do not have the lens-changing feature. But the fixed lens is of superior quality and you can get enlargements of virtually any size you wish.

Yet if you own a camera or are in the market for one, don't overlook the fact that is is a tool and nothing more. It "sees" what the person holding it sees. Automation is not synonymous with magic.

There are photos and there are photos, which is a polite way of saying a few are good, most are bad. Good photography is imagination. For one thing, unless you are taking scenics, move in on the subject and completely fill the viewing frame. In some photos I have seen it is difficult to distinguish the deer from the hunter, the images were so small. If you are taking a photo of your buddy with a deer, or vice-versa, try to visualize a different approach which will give the photo "life" or personality. Look at the animal rather than the camera. Maybe a shot of the hunter walking up on his deer. Or the action of hanging a deer in camp. Just a little bit of action, posed or otherwise, makes a whole lot of difference. And take photos in a natural setting with natural light for best results.

But most of all, *use* that camera. Instead of just one shot, take a half-dozen or more, varying the angle, the pose. Get a camp scene or two. Also maybe a scenic of the hunting territory. No matter what the situation, budget a few minutes to photography. You'll never regret the inconvenience. It is time well spent.

21

When the Fever Hits

THE DOE CAME easing deliberately down the trail. From where I lay bent over in a blind constructed of rotting stacked logs, I kept watching her intently. She was a full 75 yards away, traveling a course that would carry her within a dozen feet of my blind. Mentally, I had a point all picked out up the trail, perhaps 25 yards away. In my mind I had everything worked into a neat scheme. When the doe reached that fateful spot, I was going to ease up and drive a deadly razorhead-tipped arrow through her chest.

But sometimes the best-laid plans can go astray. . . .

Rancher Guy Clymer had directed me to this particular stand. On my Texas hunting license I was entitled to two buck deer and a "bonus" deer, which by law had to be a doe, a permit system designed to aid in reducing overpopulation in some areas. I'd been fortunate to fill my buck quota, and with almost half the season remaining I was going to try to collect my bonus deer with bow-and-arrow.

I contacted Clymer, who had many doe permits remaining on his ranch near the small community of Llano in central Texas. He invited me up. The following morning he drove me out a country lane in the predawn darkness and stopped where an electrical power line crossed the road.

"Remember that stand of stacked logs we hunted turkeys out of last year?" he asked softly.

I nodded.

"Well, follow this power line into the pasture, heading into the wind. Down there in the creek bottom you'll come to that stand. Climb in it, lie low, and wait. Chances are a deer will come down that trail and you ought to get a decent shot."

I eased into the blind just as the landscape around me started to brighten. As the new day dawned still and crisp, the live-oak trees scattered through the creek bottom literally came to life. Fox squirrels ran back and forth in the treetops, fussing and barking.

How the doe got into the picture so silently and quickly, I'll never know. One moment I looked up at the squirrels playing in the trees; the next, I glanced up the trail and there stood the sleek animal, so statuelike that she didn't appear real.

The doe was standing and staring right at my blind. Had the movement of my head given me away? I tried to stifle my breathing, to remain as still and quiet as was humanly possible. The doe looked fixedly at my stand for probably 30 seconds; it seemed like eternity. Then with a swish-swash of her tail she started toward me again. After 10 or 12 cautious steps she paused and looked once more.

The hand gripping my hunting bow became clammy. I wrapped the three fingers of my ring hand tightly around the bow string and squeezed the nocked arrow to keep it from falling out of place. The suspense was maddening.

Walk, look, walk, look. That's the way she came, deliberately, slowly, pausing every few feet to survey all that was going on around her. I dared not move, afraid the restless shifting would reveal my presence.

Time seemed to stand still. Finally, the deer approached my mentally laid-out execution point. I gripped the bow even more tightly and started drawing the arrow back as I raised up ever so slowly, to get above the stacked logs for a shot.

I couldn't have planned it any better. The unalarmed doe turned and looked directly at me, frozen in a classic three-quarter pose, not flicking a single hair. I pulled the string back the length of the arrow, and that's when it hit . . . the dread fever. My arms began shaking violently, making the arrow tip jump as if it had come alive. I lost my composure and let the arrow go before I had regained full control. It veered in front of the deer and clattered harmlessly in the brush. The doe wheeled and jumped out of sight. I could see occasional glimpses of her white tail bobbing through the creek bottom.

Now I was really shaking. I went all to pieces. It was as if all my muscles, tied up in knots and tensed for so long, finally relaxed.

I'd been stricken by that old hunting malady called "buck fever." It's a temporary, uncontrollable disease which strikes at the most inopportune times, usually when you are just drawing down on a deer, during that moment of truth when your finger tightens on the trigger or you start pulling back on the bow string.

When it happens you may as well laugh it off as just one of those things that can occur in hunting. Like Marvin Essex of Bardstown, Kentucky, did. This retired army officer came pulling a nice deer from the woods.

"Got him with one shot," he said.

"I thought I heard you shoot eleven times," said P. D. Johnson, his hunting companion.

"I did," Essex answered. "I shot once to attract the deer's attention, nine times to clear out the brush, and once to kill him."

At the climax of action, when the trigger tightens, is the time buck fever is most prevalent. But it can strike swiftly, unexpectedly, just about any time, when the hunter least expects it. At no time is the hunter really immune to it. And sometimes it can be drastic.

Like what happened to a hunter (no names, please) in northeastern Georgia. He was sitting up in the high fork of a treetop when this buck came wandering past. A well-placed, deliberate shot dropped the animal neatly. But then, as the deer fell, the fever hit. The hunter momentarily forgot he was in a tree. Jumping up, he ran toward the animal—right out into space. When searchers found him sometime later, he was clutching a broken leg, and not 50 feet away lay the dead deer.

The germs of buck fever penetrate the nervous system, and emotion overcomes reasoning. And no hunter, whatever his experience and age, is immune from the bugaboo. It can happen to the best of us.

Consider that deer my father missed several seasons back. He was sitting in a tree, on a board that had been hammered in a fork, overlooking a brushy draw while I worked around and tried to flush something in the open.

I was about halfway up the draw when I heard Dad shoot . . . once, twice. I ran ahead, confident he'd have a buck on the ground. But upon my arrival on the scene, he was still shaking his head in exasperation. The deer had slipped right up the draw as predicted, all right, but Dad had blown two easy chances. And the buck wasn't a trophy either, just an average six-pointer.

"I don't know what happened," Dad admitted. "I guess I just got a good case of buck fever."

It was quite a confession, coming from him. Dad has been hunting deer for more than 60 years. He's bagged some truly outstanding trophies, so just killing a deer is no banner-waving experience to him. But Dad is an addicted deer hunter; he gets wrapped up in the sport emotionally. And when those sensitive emotions are brought into play, the hunter is susceptible to buck fever. Anything can happen.

Curiously, the persons who have a reputation for being super-duper deer hunters are often those most susceptive to buck ague. In the presence of others, they must "prove" their reputation is earned, not blown into myth by talk. This pressure often makes them think, to try to reason out each shot, and when the hunter starts thinking he is throwing his defenses open to the fever.

When the sight settles on the deer's vital area and the trigger finger starts applying pressure, every move should be instinctive, made without any forethought or doubt. If there is a twinge of doubt in the hunter's mind as to his own ability, then, brother, he really is exposing his vulnerable side to this dread disease of hunting.

Most hunters have to work for their deer. Others just rely on luck. *George X Sand photo.*

A hunter does queer things when gripped by the fever. One incident happened a few seasons back in Potter County, Pennsylvania. A friend of mine took a neighbor of his, a novice at deer hunting, out to try and get him a buck. He sat the man down next to a big tree, told him to stay put and watch, and then started working around in an attempt to drive a deer within gunshot range. He jumped an exceptionally large buck and noticed the critter was heading directly toward the spot where the hunter lay in wait, on a course as straight and true as if an engineer had laid it out.

My friend, Ed Sparks, listened for the anticipated shot. The silence was overpowering. Surely, he thought to himself, the hunter had seen the buck. He couldn't have avoided it.

When Ed got back to the hunter, the latter appeared to be in momentary shock. His eyes were wild-looking and glassy. Ed asked if he'd seen the buck. The hunter nodded his head weakly.

"Yeah, but I missed him with every shot," he gasped dejectedly.

Missed with every shot? Ed hadn't heard him shoot, not once. He looked down to the ground and there, sparkling in the sunlight, were five live cartridges. In his excitement, the hunter had jacked them out of the rifle without once pulling the trigger.

Another time, a friend of mine, who will remain anonymous for obvious reasons, and I had just unloaded our rifles in preparation for getting into the auto and driving to another spot when, shockingly, a nice buck suddenly trotted out of the trees roughly 100 yards up from us and stopped in the middle of a large clearing.

My friend, his rifle still in his hands, fished frantically in his pocket for a cartridge. He came up with two, rammed them both into the magazine, and quickly pumped the rifle three times, throwing all three cartridges out, rested the rifle over the car door, and carefully squeezed off a shot. Naturally, the firing pin clicked harmlessly.

In that moment of nerve-racking excitement, when game is sighted, just about anything can happen. But a man is even more likely to catch buck fever when he has a chance to wait and think. Perhaps he sees a buck lurking off in the bordering underbrush, moving around where there isn't a chance for a shot. The hunter sits impatiently, hoping the deer will eventually show itself. All the while, he has time to think about the circumstance, the way he's going to handle the situation should it be legal game, where he's going to put the bullet.

As his nerves screw up tightly, the fever really goes to work on him.

Once my dad and I were stalking through some heavy timber when I chanced to see a deer slipping through the growth. I grabbed Dad's arm and pulled him down into a squatting position, pointing to the animal moving in the cover. All we could see were feet and legs.

Dad leaned over and whispered in my ear: "Acts like a buck." He pointed with his finger. "When he crosses through that clearing be ready to blast him if you see horns."

I raised the gun to half mast and positioned my finger on the safety catch, all the while watching the moving legs with concentrated attention. The closer they approached to the clearing, the more clammy my hands felt, the more my muscles started to tense and quiver.

The deer eased into the opening, stopped, and looked straight at us. It was a beautiful sight, the deer framed by the alley of trees, the antlers catching the sunlight. I couldn't have asked for an easier setup. The buck was less than 40 yards away.

The sights settled just behind the shoulder. That's when the fever grabbed hold unmercifully. The sight pattern started to waver. Instead of waiting for a split-second to try to calm down, I panicked, hurrying my shot before the deer ran. I jerked the trigger instead of squeezing properly. The boom of the big gun reverberated through the woods, and the deer vanished.

I turned and looked at Dad soberly. He was trying awfully hard to stifle a grin.

"You should have seen that rifle barrel of yours," he chuckled. "It was waving all over the place."

No one is totally safe; there is no immunization no cure for the fever. Many hunters believe they have outgrown the threat. But given the right circumstances—the sudden and unexpected sighting of a monster buck, perhaps—it can strike anyone. The symptoms might be many: temporary paralysis, uncontrollable shaking, glassy eyes, incoherent speech. But if and when you ever suffer a seizure, you won't need a doctor's diagnosis. Afterward you might feel a bit sheepish or even disgusted or furiously irritated. Different people react to the fever in different ways.

A friend was hunting with a business acquaintance named Terry, who was proudly showing the new outfit he'd bought, a .30/06 deluxe-grade bolt-action rifle fitted with a variable 2-7× scope sight. The gent was bragging, "I can drive tacks with it at 100 yards."

First day out, shortly after noon, Terry was hiking back to camp when ahead, in the cow-pasture road, he saw a doe cross followed by a big buck. Shortly, from the bordering brush, they came back in view, the buck in hot pursuit, only to disappear into the undergrowth again.

Hurriedly, Terry sneaked up the road, narrowing the distance, squatted down, and waited. As luck would have it, the deer reappeared, back again the way they'd just traveled, first the doe, then the buck. When the buck entered the road, Terry shouted. The sound momentarily confused the animal. He slammed to a halt, broad-sided, not 50 yards away.

Just hearing the story I felt a touch of sympathy for the hunter. He missed, of course. Not once but three times.

By the time he got to camp he was seething with rage. Only one other hunter was in camp when he returned.

Terry walked directly to the man, showed him the new rifle, and asked what he would pay for it.

The fellow, ignorant of the circumstances, hesitated a moment before replying, "At least 50 bucks."

"You've just bought yourself a rifle," Terry quickly answered.

Even later, after a period of calm, Terry was offered the expensive rifle back, but he stubbornly refused. Unfortunately, his blame was misguided. The culprit was not the rifle, it was the dreaded fever.

"The only real cure for buck fever is probably not giving a hoot whether you get a deer or not," observed noted outdoors writer John Madson. "Experience won't always cure it, for some ancient deerslayers habitually crack up at the sight of the first deer of the season. But what would deer hunting be without a case of the old buck ague now and then? Who has the most fun —the cold, clinical hunter, or the shook-up guy who bites through his pipestem when a deer jumps? We mourn for the man who's never had a flush of buck fever. He's never really been hunting."

To that I simply say, "Amen."

Appendix: Helpful Hints

- An alert deer might not become too alarmed at sounds which seem natural, like the snapping of a twig, but any unnatural noise such as cartridges jingling around in the hunter's pocket immediately signals danger to its sensitive ears. Eliminate this problem in several ways: carry spare ammo in store-bought cases, in a cartridge belt, in the finger of a spare pair of gloves, in one of those plastic cigarette packages, or bound together with a rubber band.

- Does cigarette smoke or a sweet-smell aftershave really spook deer? Probably not. Tests seem to prove that deer can smell human odor about as far as they can these artificial scents. So if you have the prevailing breeze in your favor, go on and smoke. But be extra careful when dousing a cigarette or knocking out a pipe. During the hunting season the woods often are dry and a serious fire could result.

- Never leave any litter in the woods or at your campsite. Let's treat the outdoors with some respect. It is the least all of us can do.

- If you carry an extra rifle as a spare, and the caliber is different from the gun you are accustomed to using, mark the ammunition boxes in a way to distinguish which cartridges go with which gun, maybe using plastic tape of different colors. I once went on a hunting trip and carried a 6mm and a .308 rifle. On opening morning, quite a distance from camp, I prepared to load my 6mm and, much to my dismay, discovered I'd brought with me a box of .308 ammo.

- That snap-top plastic container which 35mm film comes packaged in can be used for a variety of purposes by the deer hunter. As a watertight match box, maybe. Or fold a rag tightly and stuff it into the container and saturate it with machine oil. Put the top on and drop the container in your rifle's case. It is always there should you need the rag to run over your rifle after a day's hunt.

● The wise hunter prepares a checklist before he heads afield. As he is packing at home he marks each item off as it is loaded. This way you won't forget anything important.

● When doing any preseason scouting, don't spend too much time in the woods. Unnatural activity might make an old buck suspicious, and this could spook him out of his home territory or at least make him change his movement pattern. When scouting a big buck's movements, spend one day at it and do it right, then stay out of the area.

● A light rain might make you uncomfortable, but it provides good weather for hunting. Rain robs a crafty buck of his two main defenses: the ability to smell or hear the hunter. It also makes the underturf soggy and quiet underfoot so you can move quietly.

● If it is cold weather and a long hike is necessary to reach your stand, carry your heavy garments during the walk to avoid working up a sweat. A handwarmer will help you tolerate the low temperature, as will a Thermos of soup or hot beverage.

● If you get a shot at a deer, take it. Don't wait for a better chance. Hesitation is the hunter's worst enemy. Opportunity doesn't come calling often, and the successful hunter is the one who is prepared to take advantage when it does. Know your weapon, what it will and will not do. There is no excuse for not being prepared.

● Learn to use your ears as well as your eyes when hunting. When there is an abundance of dry leaves you often can hear an approaching deer before you actually see it.

● Respect no-hunting or posted signs. Always seek permission before hunting. Practice courtesy and you will be welcomed back; otherwise, you sour things for all of us.

● Plastic fletchings rather than feathers are preferred by many bow hunters when hunting in the rain. But be cautioned that plastic vanes will damage some arrow rests on bows.

● One way of keeping feather fletchings dry in a rain is to cover them with a plastic bag, such as Baggies sold in the supermarket. A sandwich-sized bag can be slipped over an arrow and twisted to stay in place, yet it is instantly removable for a shot.

● Always get in the habit of looking inside your shotgun or rifle barrel before loading the weapon, to be sure the barrel is free of obstructions. This is especially important if the weapon has been stored for any length of time. The adage that an ounce of prevention is worth a pound of cure is certainly applicable to deer hunting. Never take anything for granted.

- By your conduct and actions, support deer hunting and your state's game and fish department. Make no mistake, anti-hunting forces in this country are gaining strength and momentum.

- If you spray your gun with a rust preventive such as WD-40, regularly check the screws, especially in sight mounts, to be sure they are still tight. This fine liquid seeps around the screws and normal recoil of the firearm loosens them.

- That old saying that alcohol and gunpowder do not mix is still valid today. Drink at night if you must, but never consume any alcoholic beverage while hunting.

- If you wear prescription eyeglasses or contact lenses, carry a spare pair when you go hunting. Good eyesight is imperative when after whitetail deer.

- A modern firearm is a dependable and efficient piece of machinery, but occasionally something does happen to one. For this reason carry an "insurance" rifle on a hunting trip. One spare rifle generally will suffice for an entire party. The bow hunter also should have a spare bow. And another item not to forget is an extra bow string, already stretched and rigged and ready to go. Once I accidently hit my strung bow with a sharp broadhead and cut the string. I had no spare, but fortunately town—and another string—was close by.

- If you wear contact lenses, do not press the eyepiece of a binocular against your eyes. The pressure against the eyelid might pop a lens out. I've seen it happen.

- When entering your hunting territory, perhaps going to a stand, always approach into the prevailing breeze or have it quartering, never at your back. Should your scent forewarn the suspicious animals of your presence, your chances of seeing deer are much reduced. Telltale human odor carries for a long distance even with a light wind.

- Never climb a tree with a loaded firearm. Also never attempt to climb with razor-sharp broadheads. Pull your bow up later with a rope or have a buddy hand you the weapon once you get situated.

- If you wear yellow-tinted shooting glasses, you will find that you can see much better in the gloom of the underbrush early and late in the day, two prime deer-movement periods.

- Before going hunting, always read the game laws of the state where you are headed (even in your home state) and make sure you know what is legal and what is not. Ignorance of the law is no excuse.

● In an emergency the dip stick of your vehicle will provide enough lubrication to oil your rifle in camp. Another handy gadget is a lamb's-wool pad saturated with oil sewed to the flap of your gun case. The pad holds oil for a long time and is always there to use.

● If you should sight an unalarmed doe slipping across a clearing, wait and be patient. A buck may soon follow. The male habitually follows the female.

● A fast way of breaking in a pair of new hunting boots before the season is to soak them for 10 to 15 minutes in water. Now wear the boots until they are completely dry.

● When conducting a deer drive it is difficult to signal between hunters without making a lot of undue commotion and noise. One way is to carry an empty rifle cartridge. Blow into it for a shrill whistle. Makes a nifty signaling device, yet it won't alarm deer.

● Ever gone to deer camp, bagged your deer opening day, then had to wait around while your companions got theirs? Next time carry along a copy of your local game laws. Perhaps there is other game in season and you can spend your time hunting rather than waiting.

● If you buy a new rifle that's shorter than the old one and it won't fit snugly in the gun case, don't despair. Just stuff the barrel end of the case with old rags until you get a good fit.

● If you prefer a back or belt quiver to carry your hunting arrows, try wrapping the broadheads individually in newspaper before inserting the arrows into the quiver. The paper will prevent unnecessary noise and will keep the heads from rubbing together and becoming dull.

● One of the hardest parts of camp life is getting up in the cold of predawn and attempting to get a fire going with soggy wood. Eliminate this by laying out your fire the previous night, then covering it with a piece of tarp or plastic. The next morning the wood will be set up and dry, quickly lighted.

● Never bring a loaded weapon into camp. Always keep the safety on until you are ready to shoot. Always be doubly sure of your target before pulling the trigger. The careless hunter will soon find that he has no friends to hunt with.

● Waterproof matches are good insurance should you become lost. Make up some in a jiffy by dipping the heads in your wife's nail polish. If you have a waterproof match box, cut the stems in half. The box will hold twice as many matches this way.

● Ordinary furniture polish rubbed on rifle stocks will keep them shiny and new-looking.

● To eliminate glare from open iron sights, just run a lighted match over each sight. The carbon deposit eliminates the glare.

● When storing away your leather hunting boots, stuff them with newspaper. Paper helps the boots retain their shape, keeps wrinkles and creases out, and prolongs life of boots.

● When honing your hunting knife, do not use a dry stone. Special honing oil is recommended, but a fine machine oil will do. Oil floats the steel filings, preventing them from clogging the stone's pores, and allows the knife blade to move smoothly. An important factor in getting a sharp edge is to maintain a constant angle on both sides, about a 15° angle between the back of the blade and the stone. A handy item to carry on your hunting trip is a pocket sharpening steel. You can use it to restore the edge should the blade begin to dull.

● One of the keys to killing a trophy buck is the self-imposed restraint to pass up lesser bucks. You might go an entire season without getting a shot but that is the price you must pay to get a big 'un.

● Any broadhead hunting arrow, to be effective, must be razor-sharp. Rust quickly dulls sharpened edges. Keep them sharp by rubbing with wax. The protective coating eliminates rust.

● A handy rifle-cleaning rod for the deer camp can be improvised from a piece of rawhide. Slit one end to take a patch and draw it through the bore.

● Offhand shooting is the biggest gamble in deer hunting. Whenever possible, use a rest, even if you just drop to one knee and steady your elbow. A handy tree also affords a place to steady your rifle and makes bullet placement more of a sure thing.

● Rain or mist can fog up a scope sight and makes aiming difficult. Make a convenient lens cover by cutting a 2-inch-wide band from an old rubber inner tube. The band fits over the scope ends, keeping rain out, yet it can be removed in a jiffy for quick shooting.

● An ax with a naked blade laid carelessly around camp is inviting disaster. Cut a piece of old garden hose the width of the ax blade, slit one side, and slip it over the edge. Two rubber bands will hold the protector tight over the blade.

Index